20.VII
1920

Sixty works by Joseph Southall, 1861–1944 from the Fortunoff Collection

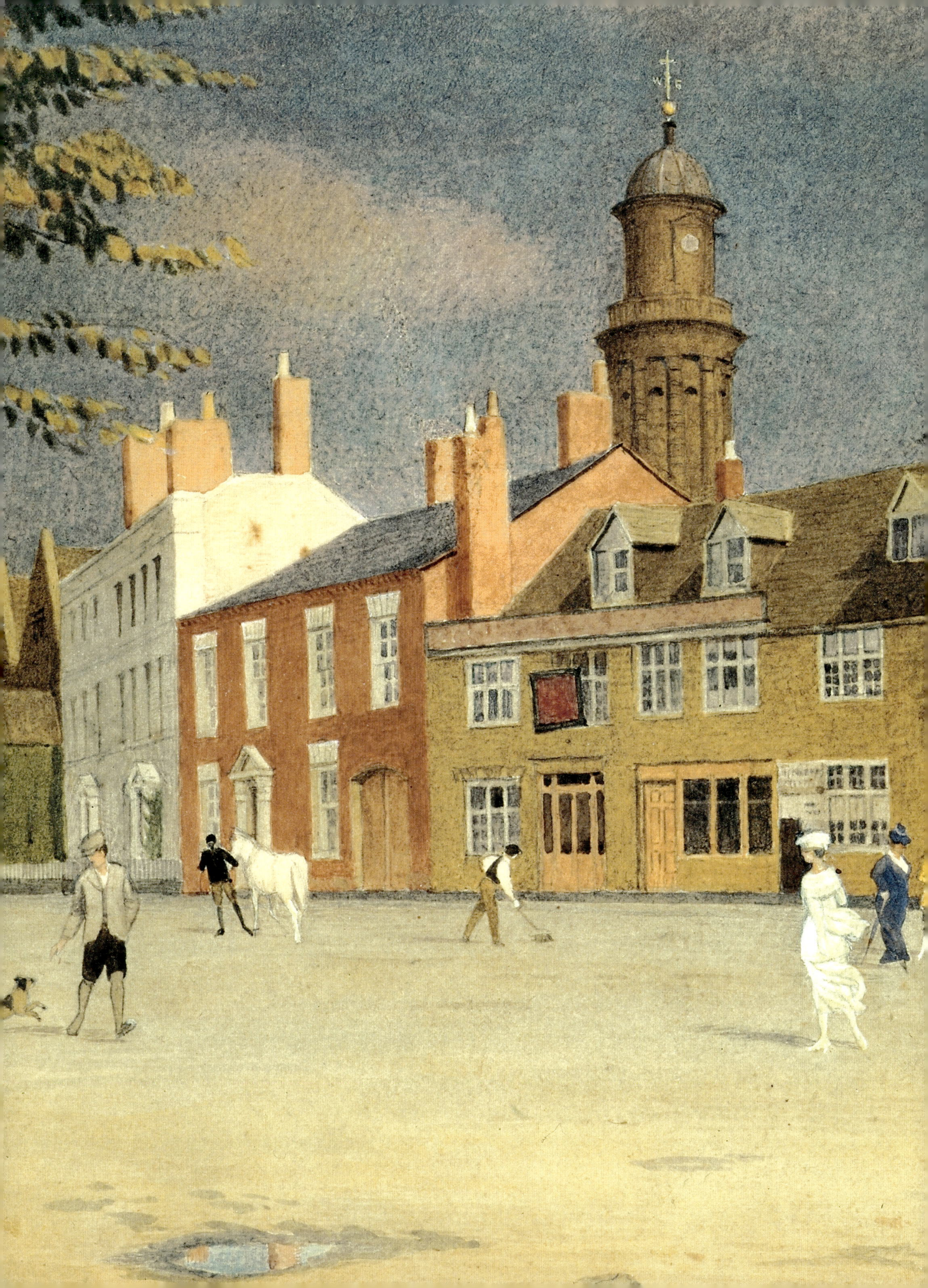

Sixty works by Joseph Southall, 1861–1944 from the Fortunoff Collection

With essays by George Breeze, Peyton Skipwith and Abbie N. Sprague

'All forms, and ornaments, and images, have a moral meaning as a natural one.'
John Ruskin, *St Mark's Rest*

The Fine Art Society
148 New Bond Street, London W1S 2JT
15 March – 16 April 2005

Cheltenham Art Gallery and Museum
Clarence Street, Cheltenham, Gloucestershire, GL50 3JT
23 April – 4 June 2005

The Fine Art Society
148 New Bond Street, London W1S 2JT
telephone + 44 (0)20 7629 5116 facsimile +44 (0)20 7491 9454
email art@faslondon.com
www.faslondon.com

6 Dundas Street, Edinburgh EH3 6HZ
telephone +44 (0)131 557 4050 facsimile +44 (0)131 557 8382
email bourne@fasedinburgh.com
www.bournefineart.com

Cheltenham Art Gallery & Museum
Clarence Street, Cheltenham, Glos. GL50 3JT
telephone +44 (0)1242 237431 facsimile +44 (0)1242 262334
email ArtGallery@cheltenham.gov.uk
www.cheltenham.artgallery.museum

Sixty works by Joseph Southall from the Fortunoff Collection
Edited by Peyton Skipwith, copyright George Breeze, Peyton Skipwith & Abbie N. Sprague
Published by The Fine Art Society PLC
148 New Bond Street, London W1S 2JT

ISBN 0–905062–17–5

Design Webb & Webb Design Limited
Printed in England by Empress Litho
Endpapers: cat.nos. 33, 35, 47 and 56 (details)
Frontispiece: cat.no.17. *The Green at Banbury*, 1920 (detail)

Acknowledgments

Exhibitions are collaborative affairs and, in addition to my colleagues at The Fine Art Society, many people have had an input, either through discussions or by direct participation. The exhibition would not exist at all without the support of Helene Fortunoff, who, despite having sold us her late husband's collection of works by Joseph Southall, has continued to take an active interest in the whole project. The catalogue would not exist in its present form without the unstinting co-operation of George Breeze; having worked with him on the earlier exhibitions of Joseph Southall and Arthur & Georgie Gaskin, it has been a pleasure to work with him again and to share his enthusiasm and scholarship. I would also like to thank his wife, Rachel for her support. Mary Greensted of Cheltenham Art Gallery & Museum responded enthusiastically to the idea of sharing the exhibition; their acquisition of *Beauty Seeing the Image of her Home in the Fountain* and *Hortus Inclusus* is particularly appropriate as Southall is not only the Arts and Crafts painter *par excellence*, but, prior to its purchase by Alan Fortunoff, *Hortus Inclusus* belonged to Southall's niece, Elizabeth Baker, a long-time resident of Cheltenham. Abbie N. Sprague's researches into the Tempera Revival, both in this country and the United States, have added considerably to our knowledge of an otherwise rather neglected chapter of twentieth-century art history. My thanks also to Charlotte Gere; it is now thirty-six years since we collaborated on *The Earthly Paradise* exhibition, based on the impressive collection of works by Southall, Cayley Robinson and members of the Birmingham Group formed by Lord Blanesburgh (1861–1946) and bequeathed by him to the Royal Caledonian Schools at Bushey, of which he had been chairman. Andrew Patrick had been consulted by the late James Fitton, RA, concerning the disposal of the collection, the Royal Caledonian Schools having been advised by Christie's that they had 'no records' of any of these artists; Andrew's response on seeing the works was electric, and the resulting exhibition was a revelation. Others who I would like especially to thank include Mrs Alexander Ballard, Julia Baron and the Barrow family, copyright holders to the Estates of Maxwell Armfield, Harry Morley and Joseph Southall respectively; Susan Grinols, Fine Arts Museums of San Francisco; Haydn Hansell, Picture Librarian, Birminham Museums & Art Gallery; Rupert Maas; Alison Miles, Tate Picture Library and Ursula Oldenburg, Bridgeman Art Library. As always, it has been a pleasure to work with Brian Webb and his assistants, Dan Smith and Chris Gloster, on the design of this catalogue; Brian's natural enthusiasm for the work has been stimulated to an even greater extent by a shared love of Southwold, the setting of so many of Southall's seaside scenes and all the beach-studies in this exhibition. Finally, I would like to thank my wife, Anne, who has had to put up with jobs put aside or neglected in the interest of the realisation of both the catalogue and the exhibition.

Peyton Skipwith, 4 January 2005

Contents

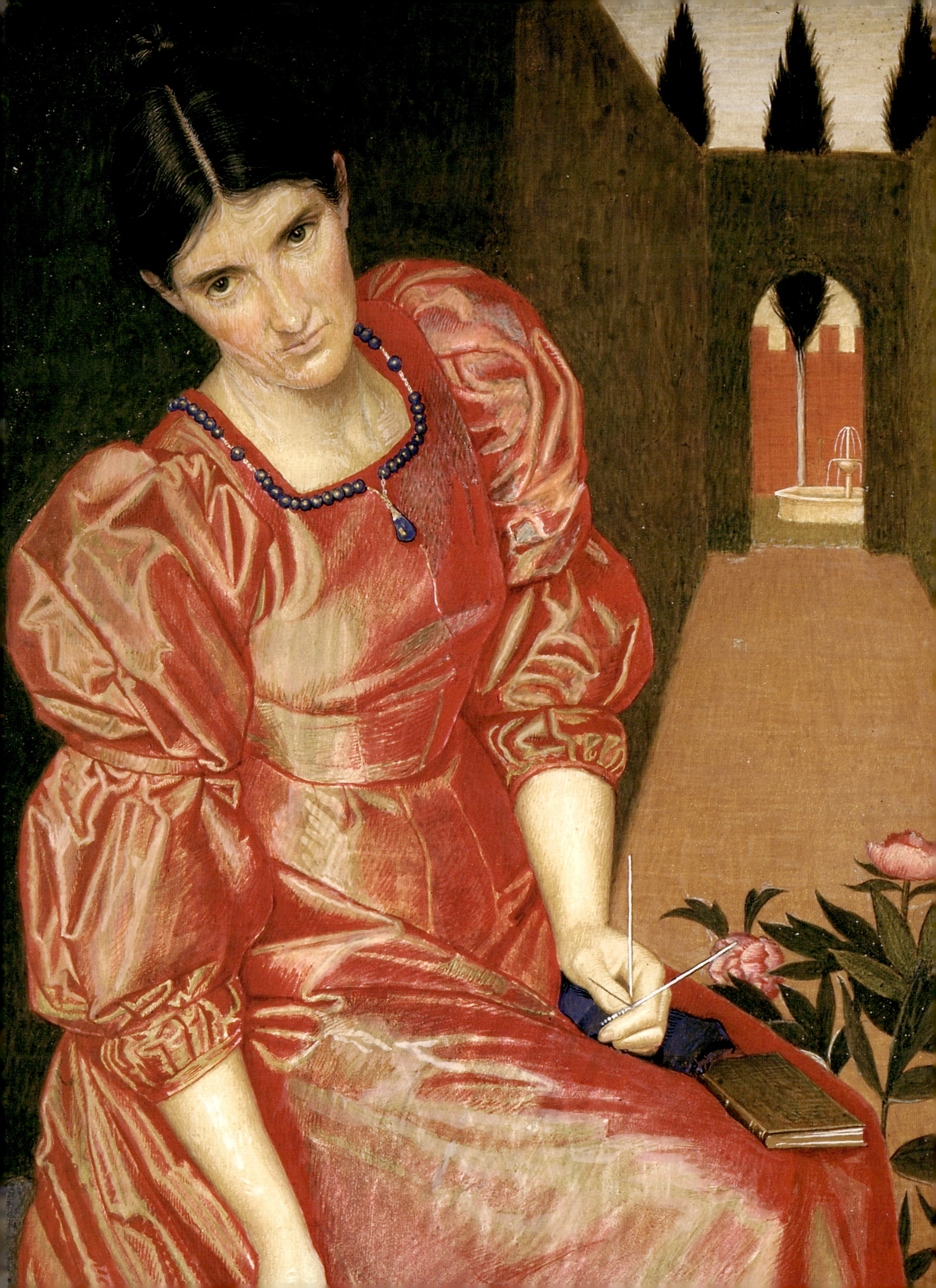

Foreword
Mary Greensted, Cheltenham Art Gallery & Museum

The acquisition of two important paintings by Joseph Southall, *Beauty Seeing the Image of her Home in the Fountain* and *Hortus Inclusus* (detail opposite), is a tremendous coup for Cheltenham Art Gallery and Museum. Cheltenham's Arts and Crafts Movement collections are acknowledged as being nationally significant by the award of Designated Status since 1998. The main strength of the collection is its furniture but it does include work by the Birmingham School most notably by Charles March Gere whose painting, *The Tennis Party* 1900, portrays Margaret Gere and Edith and Henry Payne among others. There are also examples of the distinctive jewellery produced by Southall's closest associates, Arthur and Georgie Gaskin, as well as paintings by William Rothenstein and other Arts and Crafts artists.

Cheltenham's lack of a significant example of Southall's work was recognised as a major omission because, of all the painters of the period, he epitomizes Arts and Crafts approach in his work. His strength and his interests were in the decorative – both in terms of composition and in the minutiae of the settings, costume and accessories. Influenced by John Ruskin he produced designs for Greek lacework which were made by his mother and featured in Arts and Crafts exhibitions. Some examples were given to Cheltenham in the 1980s including a design that is almost identical to the bodice lace worn by the model in *Beauty*. Southall saw the painting and its frame as a whole and regularly designed and carved his own frames. Above all his self-taught passion for the tempera technique was typical of the Arts and Crafts approach.

The acquisition of these two Southall paintings will ensure that the fine art of the Arts and Crafts period is well represented at Cheltenham. It will also be a fitting memorial to the late Margaret Bellwood of Chipping Norton, Oxfordshire who all her life derived great pleasure from looking at art and whose generous legacy, made through the Friends of Cheltenham Art Gallery and Museum, initiated this double acquisition. Additional funding came from the National Art Collections Fund and the MLA/V&A Purchase Grant Fund and we are very grateful to all these bodies, to the individuals involved, and to George Breeze and Peyton Skipwith for their support and assistance.

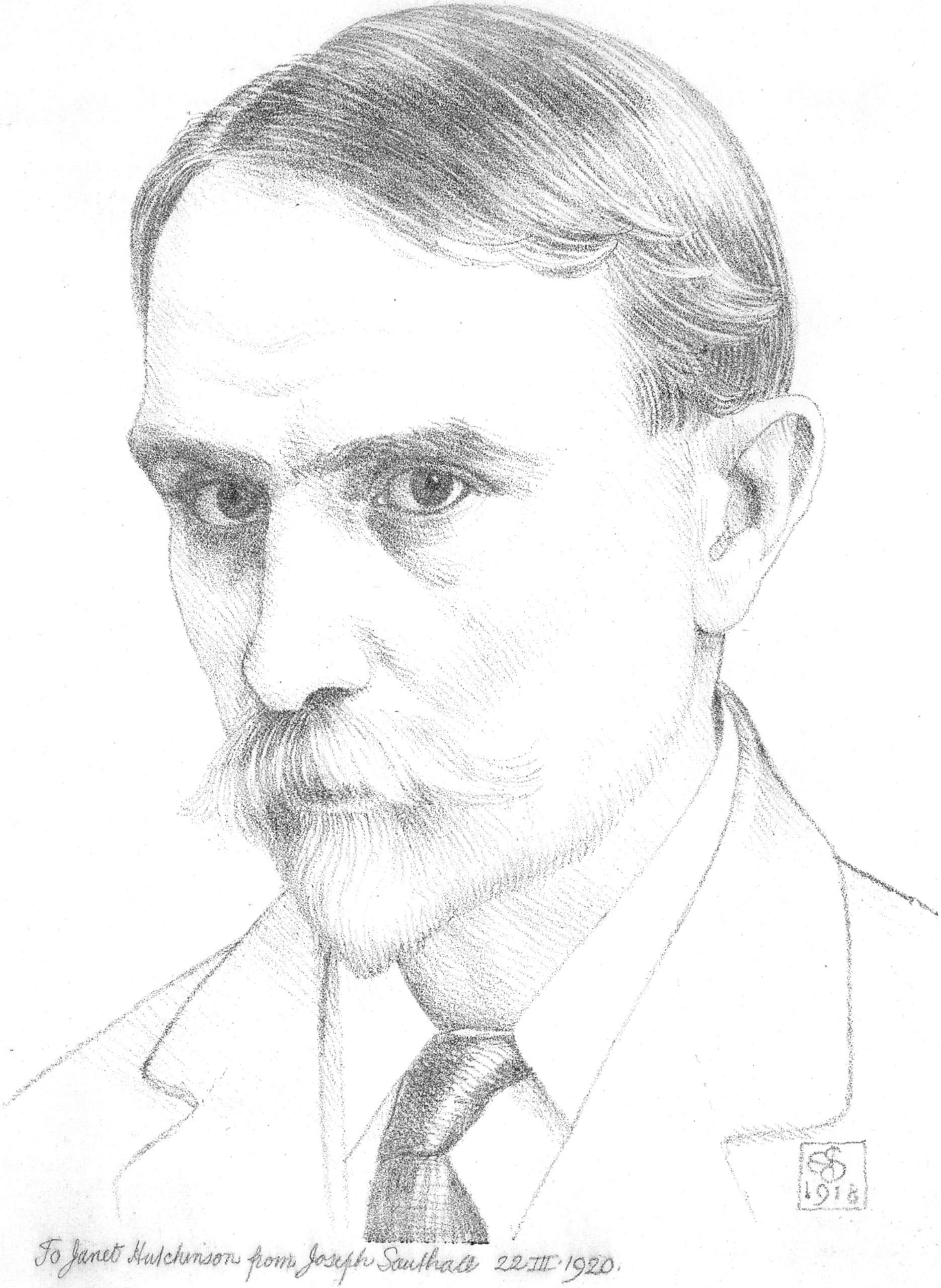

To Janet Hutchinson from Joseph Southall 22·III·1920.

Joseph Southall, 1861–1944
Peyton Skipwith

Joseph Edward Southall was born in Nottingham on 23rd August 1861, the son of a grocer, Joseph Sturge Southall, and his wife Elizabeth Maria Baker, both scions of distinguished Quaker families. The elder Joseph died the following year aged only twenty-seven and his widow and baby removed to her mother's house in Edgbaston, Birmingham. The young Joseph's childhood and schooling followed the traditional pattern for a family of his class and background; he attended the Friends' School at Ackworth and later, in 1872, the Friends' School at Bootham, York, where he was taught watercolour painting by Edwin Moore, a brother of the marine painter Henry Moore and the even better known artist, Albert Moore, whose stylish arrangements of classically-draped young women came to epitomise the Aesthetic Movement of the 1870s. After Bootham he went to a school at Scarborough, whilst continuing to take lessons with Edwin Moore; then, on 1st September 1878, a few days after his seventeenth birthday, he entered the offices of the distinguished Birmingham architectural partnership of Martin and Chamberlain, where he was to work for the next four years. During these years he pursued his art studies at evening classes and also immersed himself in the writings of Ruskin and William Morris, which were to remain central to his concerns for the rest of his life.

A few months before leaving Martin and Chamberlain Southall made his first trip to Northern France; inspired by his reading of Ruskin and Morris he visited Bayeux, Rouen and Amiens, where he was deeply impressed by the ancient cities and their Gothic cathedrals. Martin and Chamberlain's main work was in the Gothic Revival style popularised by Pugin, Scott and Street, and it was the young architects from Street's office – Morris, Webb and Sedding – who were to evolve and develop the tenets of the Arts and Crafts Movement. Amongst these was a profound belief that architecture was in urgent need of reinvigoration from a craft-base upwards, and it was with this very much in mind that Southall left the architectural practice to pursue his studies in painting and carving. Early the following year, in the company of his mother, he visited Italy for the first time and took with him, as a guide to Venice, a copy of Ruskin's *St Mark's Rest*, which had been appearing in parts since 1877. The two of them visited Pisa, Florence, Siena,

Orvieto, Rome, Bologna, Padua, Venice and Milan, before returning through Switzerland. Southall came back from this trip with a profound admiration for the Italian Primitives and a desire to study and practise the art of painting in tempera. Over forty years later he recalled that he could never forget 'the thrill of joy which I experienced when, without any knowledge of what I was about to see, I stepped inside the enchanting cloisters of the great Campo Santo of Pisa. There I found myself at 21 years of age face to face with a vast series of frescoes, so quiet and yet so gay, so reticent in manner and so lively in essence that words must ever fail to convey even the faintest expression of what I felt.'[1] On his return, inspired by the impact of Benozzo Gozzoli's frescoes, he made his earliest experiments in tempera painting at the Birmingham School of Art, and it was here that he met Arthur Gaskin (1862–1928), who was to become his closest friend and confidant. Under the inspired headmastership of Edward R. Taylor Birmingham had become one of the leading schools of art in Britain, and the foremost for the study of the crafts. Taylor believed that students should be encouraged to increase their 'art power' by acquiring various skills in addition to painting and drawing, and that they should learn to express themselves in a variety of techniques.[2]

By this time Southall was installed at 13 Charlotte Road, Edgbaston, a house which belonged to his uncle, George Baker, which was to be his home for the rest of his life. George Baker was a friend of Ruskin's as well as being Master of the Guild of St George, to which he had given a substantial amount of land in Worcestershire adjacent to his own home near Bewdley. Baker was to play an important role in his nephew's life, both by showing some of his 1883 Italian drawings to Ruskin, and also, probably, in stimulating his interest in radical politics. The Bakers had been radicals since the seventeenth century, and the earliest evidence of Southall's political interest is a sketch of John Bright addressing the Borough Meeting in January 1885 (private collection).[3] The septuagenarian Quaker MP, described as the 'most effective radical speaker of the Victorian years',[4] had, like the young artist, been educated at Ackworth and Bootham. Ruskin's interest in his drawings, and his appreciation of Southall's grasp of architecture, had a more immediate result with a summons to Brantwood and a commission to design a museum to be built on the property his Uncle Baker had so generously given. However, nothing came of this in the end as Ruskin resolved a long-running dispute with Sheffield Town Council and reverted to his original intention of establishing the museum there rather than at Bewdley, but not before Southall had made a second trip to Italy during the spring of 1886 partly with a view of seeking inspiration for the museum building. This visit took him to Pisa, Florence, Siena and Assisi. The next few years were hard for Southall; he was not only deprived of the chance of becoming an architect and realising Ruskin's vision, but progress with tempera was slow and frustrating, leading him to abandon it for a time in favour of oil.

After a third visit to Italy in 1890, and a brief infatuation with the works of Titian and Veronese, he fell once again under the influence of the Italian primitives and gradually resumed his experiments with tempera. Over the next few years he was given considerable encouragement by Sir Edward Burne-Jones, a fellow Birmingham artist, who he had probably originally met as a visitor to the School of Art. Burne-Jones was personally responsible in 1897 for sending Southall's tempera self-portrait, *Man with a Sable Brush,* to the New Gallery, along with his own work, and he expressed particular admiration for *Beauty Seeing the Image of her Home in the Fountain* (cat.no.4). These works, among others, established Southall as one of the foremost tempera painters in the country and led to his participation in the exhibitions of the Arts and Crafts Exhibition Society and the exhibition of Modern Paintings in Tempera at Leighton House, which immediately preceded the foundation of the Tempera Society, of which he became one of the leading members.

In June 1903 Southall married his cousin, and long-time fiancée, Anna Elizabeth Baker. She was forty-four and he nearly forty-two; they had been intimate friends and companions for many years and had always intended to marry, but because of their close kinship had consciously waited until she was passed child-bearing age. The earliest image of his future wife in the present exhibition is *The Coral Necklace* (cat.no.2) of 1895, but many earlier portraits exist, whilst the meticulous recording of hours spent by Miss Baker on the gessoing and gilding of the 'frame for Joe for portrait of myself and Colin' – *Hortus Inclusus* (cat.no.5) – show both the intimacy and professionalism of their relationship.[5] The years between 1897 and the outbreak of the Great War saw Southall at the height of his powers and, after many struggles, finally receiving the recognition he deserved. His work was widely exhibited in Britain, France, Italy, Belgium and the United States and he was elected a member of the RBSA, the Art Workers Guild and the Union Internationale des Beaux-Arts et des Lettres. The two most significant exhibitions of his work were probably the Birmingham Group show at The Fine Art Society in 1907 and his highly successful one-man exhibition at the Galeries Georges Petit in Paris in 1910, from which he sold over eight-hundred pounds worth of pictures as well as receiving a number of commissions. All this was brought to an abrupt end in 1914.

Southall's active involvement in politics is usually attributed to his opposition to the jingoistic reaction to the Jameson Raid of 1895, although we have already seen him drawing John Bright some ten years earlier at the Borough Meeting.[6] His allegiance was first of all to the Liberal Party, but later he transferred this to the Independent Labour Party, whose Pacifism coincided more closely with his own beliefs. Many years later the *Birmingham Post* recorded that he had always been 'an enthusiastic supporter of that Socialism or Communism which William Morris expressed in his *News from Nowhere*.'[7] His propagandist activities and assiduous attendance at tribunals and public meetings during the war years, as discussed by George Breeze in a separate essay, mitigated against painting, though he still managed to find time to paint one of the huge murals for the great Arts and Crafts Exhibition at the Royal Academy in 1916. This exhibition, orchestrated by Henry Wilson, was not only the largest Arts and Crafts Exhibition ever held, it also became the focus for a national patriotic celebration. Henry Payne and Charles Gere, fellow members of the Birmingham Group, also painted murals for the Hall of Heroes.

The interwar years were calmer with a regular pattern of spring or autumn travels to France and Italy, interspersed with sojourns at Southwold in Suffolk, where they went every July, and on the Fowey Estuary in Cornwall. These travels invariably produced a body of work, mostly in watercolour these days, which was regularly shown in exhibitions at the Alpine or Leicester Galleries in London and the Ruskin Galleries in Birmingham, as well as at the RBSA, the RA and the Paris Salon. A great sadness at this time was the death in 1928 of Arthur Gaskin, who had not only been a friend, but had given practical encouragement and support at a period when it was most needed. A highlight, though, was provided by the 1930 Winter Exhibition at the Royal Academy[8] devoted to Italian Painting, which stimulated a renewed interest in tempera painting, with the result that at the ensuing Summer Exhibition an entire room was set aside for works in tempera, this was in stark contrast to previous years when the Hanging Committee were ambivalent as to whether tempera should be classed with oil painting or watercolour.

Joe and Bessie Southall made their last trip to Venice in the Spring of 1937; later that year he was taken ill and had to undergo major surgery from which he never fully recovered. His illness, although never accurately diagnosed, necessitated frequent spells in hospital for the remainder of his life, but he still doggedly carried on painting, revisiting old themes such as *The White Barque at Fowey,* (cat.no.27), painted the year before he died, and resurrecting earlier studies such as *The Dish of Fruit* (cat.no.26), and working them up into finished watercolours. *The Dish of Fruit,* a striking, almost art-deco, image bears the date 1941, but on the reverse of the sheet is a 1922 annotation concerning the Whatman board. Equally, although his energy was much reduced, he never ceased to work in the cause of peace. The last painting in tempera on which he was working was a memorial portrait of the Bradford MP, Frederick William Jowett[9] (1864–1944), a founder member of the Independent Labour Party; on the table in front of him is a copy of the ILP newspaper with a headline 'IS THIS WHAT YOUR MEN FIGHT FOR?' Jowett had died early in 1944 and the painting was still not quite finished when Southall died ten months later; it was subsequently completed by Maxwell Armfield, before being presented to the City of Bradford. Southall died on the 6th November and was buried four days later in the Friends' section of Witton Cemetery. The Birmingham Post records that at his funeral his cousin, Evelyn Sturge, spoke of his courage and 'great love of truth, and of his willingness to be unpopular in the cause of truth, and of his care for the downtrodden and for justice'. Perhaps an even more fitting epitaph is provided by George Breeze in the *Dictionary of National Biography* where he states: 'In his life Southall brought together the gathered stillness of a Quaker meeting, the jewelled calm of tempera painting, and the peace sought by pacifism.'[10]

Notes

1. J. E Southall "The Graphic Arts in Education" in *The Friends' Quarterly Examiner*, No.234, Fourth Month, 1925, p.142.
2. For a fuller description of Taylor's beliefs and teaching methods see Charlotte Gere's Introduction to *The Earthly Paradise*, The Fine Art Society, June–July 1969.
3. Peyton Skipwith 'Peace, Politics and Painting', *Country Life*, January 30, 1992, p. 65
4. Miles Taylor, *Dictionary of National Biography*, 2004
5. See *Joseph Southall 1861–1944: Artist Craftsman* , Birmingham 1980, cat.no.E10 for full details.
6. Peyton Skipwith op.cit
7. Obituary, 7 November 1944
8. The Chairman of the British Executive Committee for the Exhibition was Lady Chamberlain and her husband, Sir Austen, was one of the Honorary Vice-Presidents. Southall had been expelled from the Labour Party in 1927 for supporting a Communist candidate against Austen Chamberlain. The fact that the exhibition assembled in London many of Southall's favourite works of art was rather ironic since, as Abbie N. Sprague points out, under Lady Chamberlain's chairmanship the exhibition became a forum for proclaiming the glories of Mussolini's Italy. Mussolini, himself, headed the list of members of the Italian Honorary Committee for the exhibition.
9. Jowett was the first commissioner of works with a seat in the first Labour Cabinet; he is probably best remembered for his authorisation of the erection of Epstein's *Rima* – the W.H. Hudson Memorial – in London's Hyde Park in 1924.
10. George Breeze, entry for Joseph Southall, *Dictionary of National Biography*, 2004

Page 8 cat.no.14. Self Portrait, 1918
Opposite cat.no.20. Pleasures of the Seaside, 1925

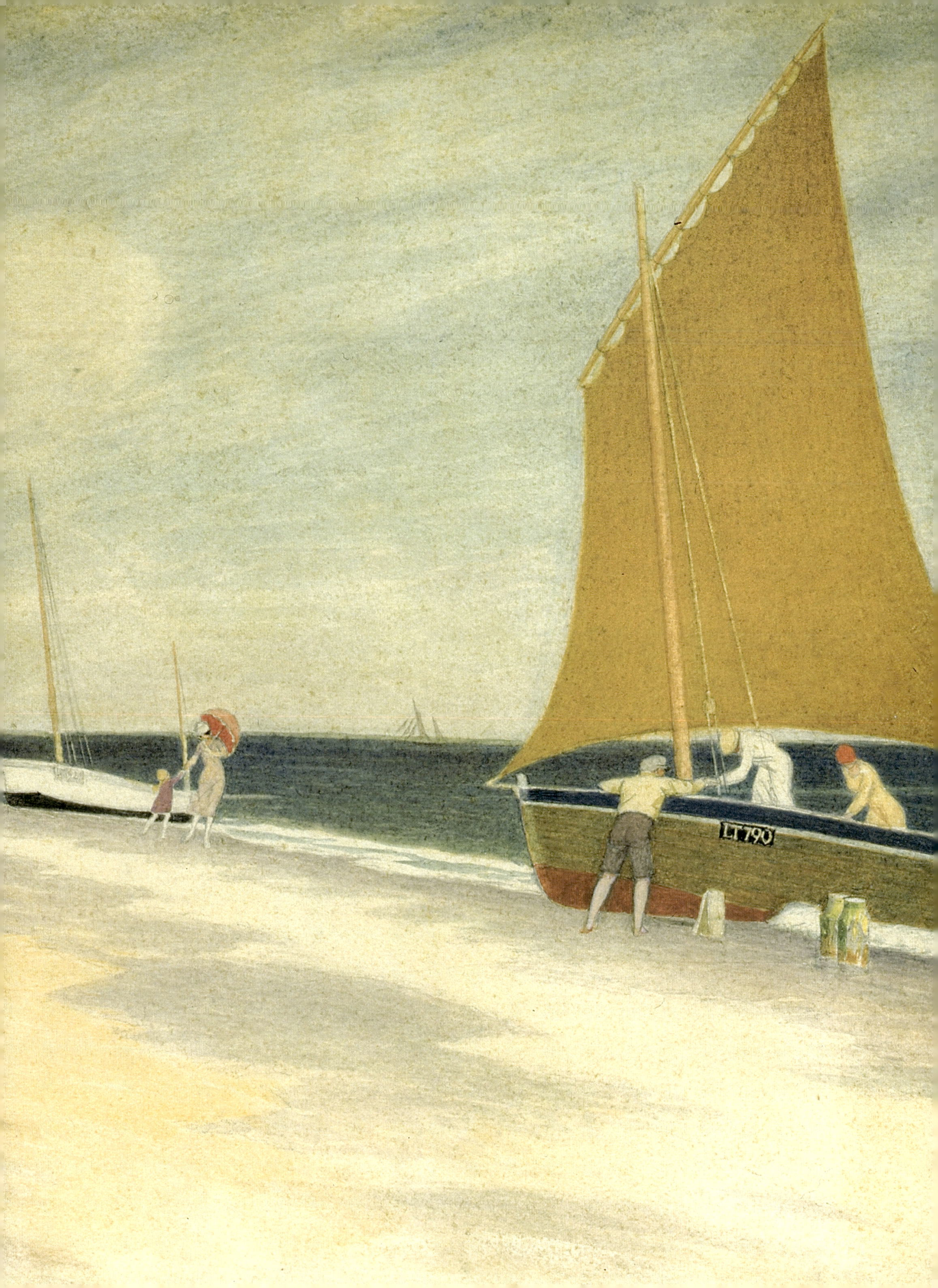
LT790

Chronology

1861	23 August. Born Nottingham
1862	Father died. Moves with mother to grandmother's home in Edgbaston, Birmingham
1872	Attends Friends' School at Ackworth.
1874	Attends Friends' School at Bootham, York (January). Instructed in watercolour by Edwin Moore. September, moves to a school at Scarborough.
1878	Leaves school. 1 September articled to the Birmingham architectural firm of Martin and Chamberlain.
1879–80	Attends evening art classes first at the Osler Street Board School and then at the Central School of Art, Birmingham.
1882	May. Visits Bayeux, Caen, Lisieux, Rouen and Amiens. August, leaves Martin & Chamberlain to study painting and carving.
1883	February–April. Visits Italy and develops deep admiration for the Italian Primitives; on his return makes first experiments with tempera. Attends Birmingham School of Art and meets Arthur Gaskin.
1884	Awarded a drawing prize for *A Study of a Head* . JES's uncle, George Baker, shows drawings made in Italy the previous year to Ruskin.
1885	December. Summoned to Brantwood by Ruskin and commissioned to design a museum at Bewdley for the Guild of St George.
1886	Spring, second visit to Italy – Pisa, Florence, Siena and Assisi.
1887	First exhibit at the RBSA
1888/9	Renounces tempera for oil.
1890	Spends three weeks in Venice and also visits Verona. Fascinated by the work of Veronese, Titian and Tintoretto.
1893	17 February. First interview with Edward Burne-Jones. Visits Burford with Arthur Gaskin and stays the night at Kelmscott with William Morris.
1894	8 February. Second visit to Burne-Jones.
1895	First exhibit at the Royal Academy, a watercolour *Cinderella* (Tate Gallery). Takes up tempera again.

1896 Trip to France, visits Paris and Chartres.

1897 Receives much encouragement from Burne-Jones, who sent Southall's self-portrait, *Man with a Sable Brush*, (Private Collection) to the New Gallery, London. Visits Pisa, Lucca, Florence, Prato, Milan and Lucerne together with Arthur Gaskin.

1898 Elected an Associate of the RBSA.

1899 First exhibit with the Arts and Crafts Exhibition Society.

1901 Participated in the exhibition of Modern Paintings in Tempera at Leighton House. November. The Society of Painters in Tempera founded.

1902 Elected full member of the RBSA.

1903 May. Elected a member of the Arts and Crafts Exhibition Society. 23 June, married Anna Elizabeth Baker.

1904 JES and AES visit Italy returning via Switzerland. Exhibited at the St Louis International Exhibition.

1905 JES and AES visit Paris and Chartres. While in Paris visited Maxwell Armfield, Norman Wilkinson (of Four Oaks) and Keith Henderson in their studio. Exhibited for the first time at the New Salon (Société Nationale des Beaux-Arts), Paris.

1906 Autumn. JES and AES visit Italy, joined by Charles and Margaret Gere.

1907 November. First exhibition devoted specifically to the Birmingham Group held at The Fine Art Society.

1908 Death of AES's father

1909 May. JES and AES to France – Paris and Rouen. Autumn to Italy – Orta, Padua, where they met Charles and Margaret Gere, and Venice.

1910 January. Death of JES's uncle, George Baker. March. Very successful one-man show at the Galeries Georges Petit, Paris. May. Invited to join L'Union Internationale des Beaux-Arts et des Lettres, Paris. Elected a member of the Art Workers Guild.

1911 Exhibited at the Rome International Exhibition.

1913 May. Visited Florence and San Gimignano with AES. Exhibited at the Ghent International Exhibition.

1914 May. To Paris with AES. Exhibited at the British Arts and Crafts Exhibition, Paris.

1914–31 Chairman of the Birmingham City Branch of the Independent Labour Party.

1915–16 Painted *Corporation Street, Birmingham, in March 1914* for Birmingham Art Gallery in *buon fresco.*

1915–18 Active in politics as a Pacifist. Drew political cartoons and wrote fables about the evils of war.

1916 Major Arts and Crafts Exhibition at the RA organised by Henry Wilson as a national celebration. JES, Henry Payne and Charles Gere painted three of the huge murals for the Hall of Heroes.

1917 March. Lectures to the Art Workers Guild on 'Craft and Media in Painting.' Also lectures at the Royal College of Art.

1919 Exhibition of the Birmingham Group at the RBSA.

1921 Lectures to the Civic Society, Birmingham on 'The Value of Colour in City Life.' One man Show at the Little Art Rooms, Adelphi, London, where he meets Lord Blanesburgh, who becomes an important patron. Visits Venice and Ravenna with AES.

1922 March–April. One Man Show at the Alpine Club Gallery, London; the largest showing of his work since 1910. July. One Man Show at Manchester. 7 November death of JES's Mother.

1923 Visited Paris and Chartres with a cousin, Olaf Baker, who later bequeathed his collection of JES's work to the Victoria Art Gallery, Bath. Ethelbert White spent a week studying tempera whilst JES worked on *Five Fishermen Pushing a Boat* [*Fishermen and Boat* cat.no.19].

1924 Visited Paris, Limoges and Cahors with AES.

1925 January. Gave a paper on 'Art in School Life' to Friends' Guild of Teachers, Saffron Walden. May. Elected Associé (a la section de Peinture) of the Société Nationale des Beaux-Arts, Paris. Elected an Associate Member of the RWS and a Member of the NEAC. Visited Venice, Verona and Desenzano with AES.

1926 March. One Man Show at the Leicester Galleries. April. Visits Genoa, Pisa, Assisi, Florence and Paris with AES.

1927 February. One Man Show at the Ruskin Galleries, Birmingham. May. To Venice with AES.

1929 September–October. Visits Paris, Lille, Cahors, Albi, Cordes, etc. with AES.

1930 Exhibits in Canada. Major Winter Exhibition at the RA devoted to Italian Painting, stimulating renewed interest in tempera. Summer Exhibition at the RA, an entire room devoted to tempera painting.

1931 March–April. Second One Man Show at the Leicester Galleries. September–October. Visits the South of France with AES. November. Elected a full member of the RWS.

1932 April–May. Visits Venice with AES.

1933 April–May. Visits Paris, Laval, La Rochelle and Angers with AES. September–October. One Man Show at the RBSA, Birmingham. Appointed Professor of Painting at the RBSA. October. Lectured on 'Mural Decoration' at the RBSA.

1934 February–March. One-man show at Dudley. April–May. Visits Venice and Paris with AES. Elected Vice-President of the RBSA.

1935 June. Visits Paris, Verona and Venice with AES.

1936 May–June Visits Paris, Chartres, Cahors, Limoges, Poitiers, Amboise, etc. with AES.

1937 April–May. Final visit to Venice with AES. Began mural decoration in the Council House, Birmingham. August. Became very ill and underwent a major operation; never fully recovered.

1939 January. One Man Show at the Ruskin Galleries, Birmingham. Elected President of the RBSA, a post held until his death.

1944 6 November. Died at Birmingham. 10 November. Interred in the Friends' part of Witton Cemetery, Birmingham. Estate left in its entirety to AES.

1945 Memorial Exhibition at Birmingham, London (RWS) and Bournemouth.

1947 29 October. AES died.

1948 23 March and 6 April. The majority of AES's possessions sold by auction in Birmingham. Bequests of important paintings by JES to Birmingham, Bournemouth, Nottingham and Oldham Art Galleries.

The British Tempera Revival

Abbie N. Sprague

A small exhibition of tempera paintings opened at Leighton House in the spring of 1901. John Roddam Spencer Stanhope (1829–1908), Christiana Herringham (1852–1929), and Joseph E. Southall (1861–1944) were among the contributors. With seventeen artists represented and forty works on display, including Southall's *Beauty Seeing the Image of Her Home in the Fountain* of 1897–8, (cat.no.4) this ground-breaking exhibition was the first solely devoted to contemporary works in egg tempera. Demonstrating that tempera painting was no longer a lost art, the exhibition heralded the resurrection of this ancient technique. The movement became the British Tempera Revival.

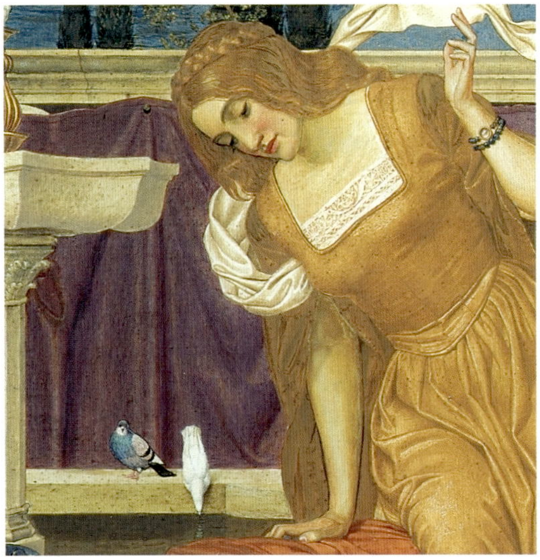

Cat.no.4. Joseph E. Southall (1861–1944)
Beauty Seeing the Image of Her Home in the Fountain (1897–8) (detail)

Egg tempera reached its zenith during the fifteenth century; however, as the *quattrocento* came to a close, oils were introduced from the North. With its ease of manipulation and preparation, this new medium quickly became the preferred technique. The labour-intensive craft of tempera painting slowly fell into disuse. Over three hundred years later, developing out of a fascination with ancient styles and techniques, tempera emerged out of obscurity. William Blake (1757–1827) was first among British artists to experiment with egg yolk as a binder for pigments. In a desire to find an alternative medium, Blake's experiments lead him to *Il Libro dell'Arte*, Cennino Cennini's treatise on renaissance techniques.[1] Augmenting

Cennino's recipes with other materials, some of Blake's works have not had the lasting effect he desired. Nonetheless, he was instrumental in introducing alternative painting media and techniques to early nineteenth century British artists, including Samuel Palmer (1805–81) and George Richmond (1809–96). Oils no longer had the monopoly.

The project to decorate the Houses of Parliament in frescoes revived an interest in ancient techniques in the mid-nineteenth century. Providing the artists with a technical manual, Mary Philadelphia Merrifield (1804–89) published the first English translation of Cennino's treatise in 1844. Including recipes and instructions for gilding, fresco, and tempera, Cennino's *Il Libro dell'Arte* is regarded as the authority on early renaissance techniques. Though not her intent, Merrifield's translation provided the early revivalists with their first practical manual for working in tempera. Such is the significance of Cennino's treatise that through the next hundred years, additional translations were completed and published. Herringham's more complete version, with chapters based on her own experiences, was published in 1899; later in 1933, Daniel V. Thompson, Jr. (1902–80) published the most comprehensive and accurate translation to date. With each updated and improved version another generation of artists discovered the technique, creating a framework for the revival of egg tempera.

The tempera revivalists are often categorised as Pre-Raphaelite followers; understandably since they shared a common emphasis on religious and allegorical themes. However, the tempera artists took their work one step further as they mastered the medium and technique of early renaissance artists. Cognisant of ancient techniques, the Pre-Raphaelites reintroduced the white ground that was essential to their brilliant colours. By the time the British Tempera Revival gained momentum, most of the Pre-Raphaelites were nearing the end of their careers. William Holman Hunt (1827–1910) expressed his regret for not having discovered the medium sooner to a gathering of tempera artists, 'If I had my time over again I should be in the thick of it – one of you!'[2] Nonetheless, the Pre-Raphaelites had a profound influence on the tempera revivalists and their encouragement spurred on this next generation of artists. Spencer Stanhope, a friend and pupil of the Pre-Raphaelite Brotherhood, was the first British artist to work solely in tempera. His admiration of Botticelli led him to study the medium on a trip to Florence. Learning the technique in the early 1870s, he abandoned oils by the later part of the decade.[3] His tempera masterpiece, *Love and the Maiden*, was shown at the opening exhibition of the Grosvenor Gallery in 1877 alongside works by Edward Burne-Jones (1833–98) and Dante Gabriel Rossetti (1828–82) (fig. 1).[4] The next wave of interest, and thus the real beginnings of the British Tempera Revival, developed out of a movement to return craftsmanship to the fine arts.

Emerging in the 1890s, a group of artists working in tempera found a home with the Arts and Crafts Movement. Characteristic of the movement, these

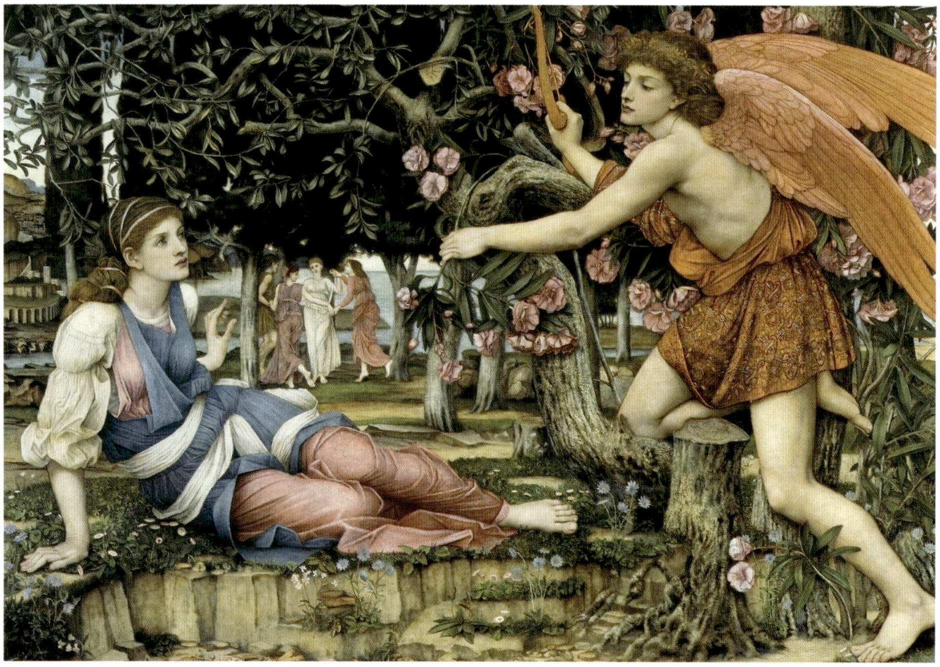

Fig. 1. John Roddam Spencer Stanhope (1829–1908)
Love and the Maiden, (exhibited 1877)
Tempera, gold paint and gold leaf on canvas; 54 x 79 (137.2 x 200.7)
Fine Arts Museum of San Francisco, Museum Purchase, European Art Trust Fund, Grover A. Magnin Bequest Fund and Dorothy Spreckels Munn Bequest Fund, 2002.172

artists took a traditional and neglected technique and learned its secrets through trial and error. What precisely were these artists reviving? True egg tempera consists of fine powdered pigment mixed with egg yolk. Some water is added to keep the medium more manageable. After the careful preparation of materials, using small brushstrokes numerous thin layers of paint are applied to a gesso ground. Like fresco, tempera sets rapidly, leaving little margin for error. Though it does not completely harden for some time, once thoroughly dried tempera is incredibly durable, attaining a considerable degree of resistance to damp and dirt. In addition to durability, richness of colour was a key quality attracting artists to the medium. The effect of under-painting produces intensity of colour similar to that of stained glass – colour glowing through superimposed layers. By the mid 1800s, artists were far removed from the actual preparation of materials. Tubes of paint were bought from the local art supply shop, along with pre-stretched canvases and gesso panels. Determined to lead fine art back to the craftsman, the pioneering tempera artists went to considerable lengths to be involved in all aspects of the artistic process – from applying numerous layers of gesso to their panels, to mixing the egg yolk and pigment together. The artists completed the process by designing and gilding frames for their works. Kate Bunce's (1856–1927) *The Keepsake*, painted between 1898 and 1901, exemplifies these craftsmanship ideals, with its beaten copper frame and meticulously applied brushstrokes (fig. 2).[5]

Due to the success of the Leighton House exhibition and a growing interest in the medium, in November of 1901 the Society of Painters in Tempera was established, providing an organisation where tempera artists could devote their efforts to 'improving the Art of Tempera Painting by interchange of knowledge and experiences.'[6] Armed with Herringham's translation of Cennino and emphasising craftsmanship in their work, the artists had set the British Tempera Revival in motion. Through the years the members met at one another's studios to discuss techniques and share their work. Papers read at these meetings were collected and circulated throughout the membership. Selected lectures and articles were eventually published, enabling their experiences to reach a wider audience. In 1908 the Society published the first volume of *The Papers of the Society of Painters in Tempera*. In all, four volumes were published covering the years from 1901 to 1954.

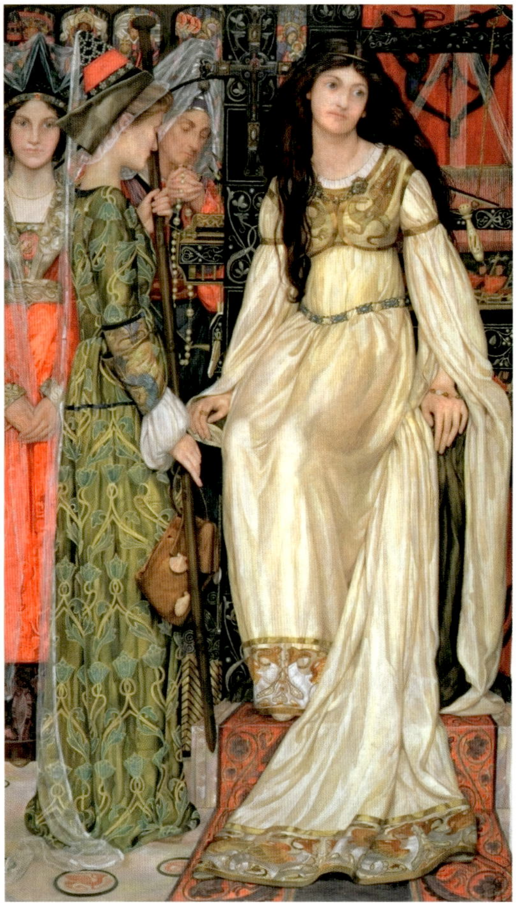

Fig. 2. Kate Bunce (1856–1927)
The Keepsake (1898–1901)
Tempera on canvas; 32 x 19 1/2 (81.3 x 49.5)
Birmingham Museums and Art Gallery / The Bridgeman Art Library

The artists continued to exhibit their works. A few months after the Leighton House exhibition, several of the tempera revivalists submitted works to the New Gallery's Fourteenth Summer Exhibition. Charles Gere (1869–1957) and Walter Crane (1845–1915) were among the new artists represented. Over the next few years, the tempera artists continued to exhibit works at the New Gallery. By 1905, four years after its establishment, the Society of Painters in Tempera held its first official exhibition. Their numbers had grown. Over forty artists were represented at the Carfax Gallery in London, including the recently deceased George Frederic Watts (1817–1904). His unfinished work *The Utmost for the Highest* (now lost) was exhibited in his honour. Southall contributed *New Lamps for Old* of 1900–1901, which included portraits of his friends Gaskin, Gere, and future wife, Anna Elizabeth Baker (1859–1947) (fig. 3). Two years later in 1907,

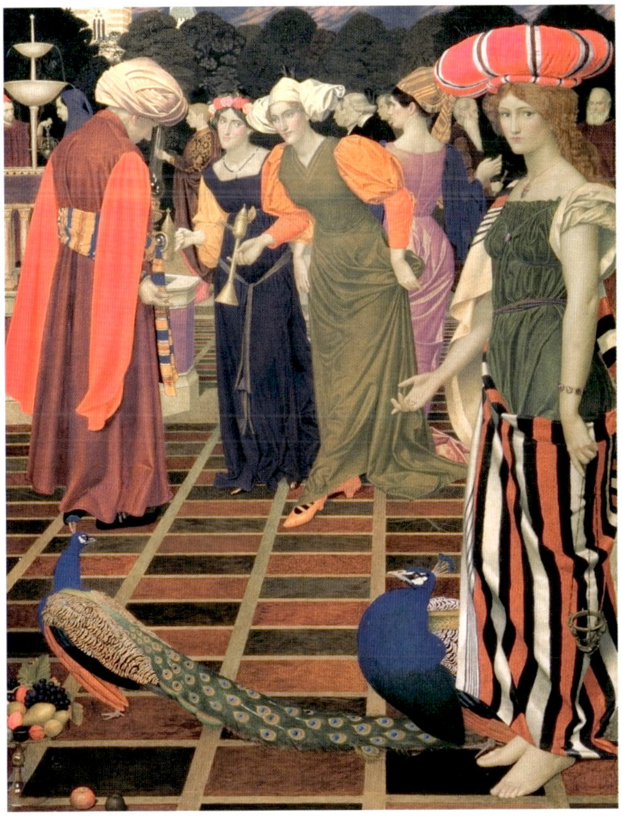

Fig. 3. Joseph E. Southall (1861–1944)
New Lamps for Old (1900–01)
Tempera on canvas;
38 x 29 1/2 (96.5 x 74.7)
Birmingham Museums and Art Gallery / The Bridgeman Art Library

The Fine Art Society mounted an exhibition of Birmingham painters and craftsmen; several works were by members of the Society. This marked the beginning of a long relationship between the tempera artists and the Fine Art Society.

Under the leadership of Herringham and Southall, London and Birmingham became centres for the practise and instruction of tempera painting. London, in its prominence, was the focal point for exhibitions. The city was also home to several of the leading tempera artists, including Marianne Stokes (1855–1927) and John D. Batten (1860–1932). Birmingham, already a centre of the Arts and Crafts Movement, rivalled London in its cultivation of tempera artists. A group of students from the Birmingham School of Art, who became known as the Birmingham Group, embraced the technique, applying it to both the fine and decorative arts. Southall, through his work and informal lessons given at his studio, led the revival in

Birmingham. Among his converts were his close friends Arthur Gaskin (1862–1928) and Maxwell Armfield (1881–1972). Armfield, a staunch supporter of the craftsmanship tradition, continued the work of Southall and taught tempera painting to fellow artists.

The British Tempera Revival was not a male dominated movement; all artists had equal standing regardless of gender. Prior to the establishment of the Society, the Art Workers' Guild provided a forum for tempera artists. The Guild offered a place where they could meet and converse with fellow craftsmen.[7] The exclusively male membership of the Guild was a disadvantage; women were not allowed to attend the meetings until 1920.[8] The Society of Painters in Tempera had no such restrictions. With Herringham championing the revival, women were encouraged to become active. Many were wives or sisters of tempera artists which may have been their introduction to the medium; however, they soon found their own niche and contributed to the movement through paintings or designing frames. A copy of *The Triumph of the Duke of Urbino* by Piero della Francesca , of about 1905, exemplifies a collaborative female effort. Painted by Margaret Gere (1878–1965), the frame was designed and gilded by her sister Edith Payne (1875–1959) (fig. 4).

Through the changing art scene and two world wars, the Society continued well into the twentieth century. In 1912, the Society of Painters in Tempera joined together with the newly formed Society of Mural Decorators. Fresco and tempera being close cousins and with many artists practising in both media, the organisation became the Society of Mural Decorators and Painters in Tempera.[9] They expanded their realm and began to show works outside London, with exhibitions in Birmingham and Brighton. The organisation remained as such until 1957 when the Society reverted to its original name. That same year, the Society began to reach its membership on a yearly basis through their publication *The Yearbook of the Society of Painters in Tempera.*

Tempera's intricacies had been mastered by the 1920s. In the decades to follow, artists began to apply tempera to modern themes. This transition from revival to modern medium is most evident in 1930. The year began with a political showcase of Italian masterpieces, opening on New Year's

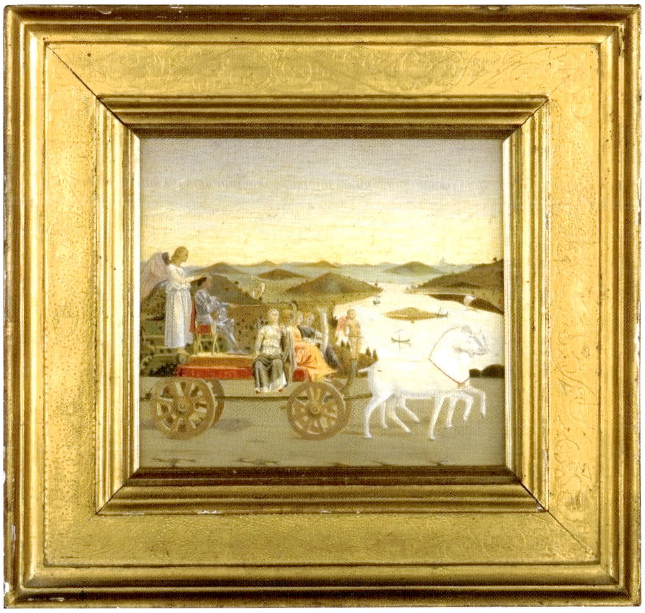

Fig. 4. Margaret Gere (1878–1965) and Edith Payne (1875–1959)
A copy of *The Triumph of the Duke of Urbino* by Piero della Francesca (c. 1905)
Tempera on panel; 6 x 6 3/4 (15.3 x 17.2)
Private Collection

Day at the Royal Academy. Spearheaded by Lady Chamberlain, the exhibition became Mussolini's forum for expounding the glories of Italy. Over half a million people flocked to see the exhibition, which included paintings, illuminated manuscripts, decorative art, drawings, and sculpture.[10] Botticelli's *Birth of Venus*, the most famous of tempera paintings, was the star of the show. A few months later, the Royal Academy accepted thirty-six tempera paintings by contemporary artists for the Summer Exhibition. Included was *The Young Bacchus* by Harry Morley (1881–1943) (fig. 5). Approaching the classical subject with simplified modern lines, Morley exemplified this new generation of artists working in tempera. The Royal Academy increased its support of tempera artists throughout the thirties, first incorporating their works into the watercolour section and eventually giving tempera paintings a room of their own.

In July of 1930, the Society of Mural Decorators and Painters in Tempera organised an exhibition at the Whitechapel Art Gallery. With over a hundred and twenty works displayed, the exhibition was a mixture of works by tempera revivalists and contemporary artists. Advertised as *An Exhibition of Modern English Tempera Paintings*, the title distinguishes the exhibition from the *quattrocento* paintings displayed earlier that year at the

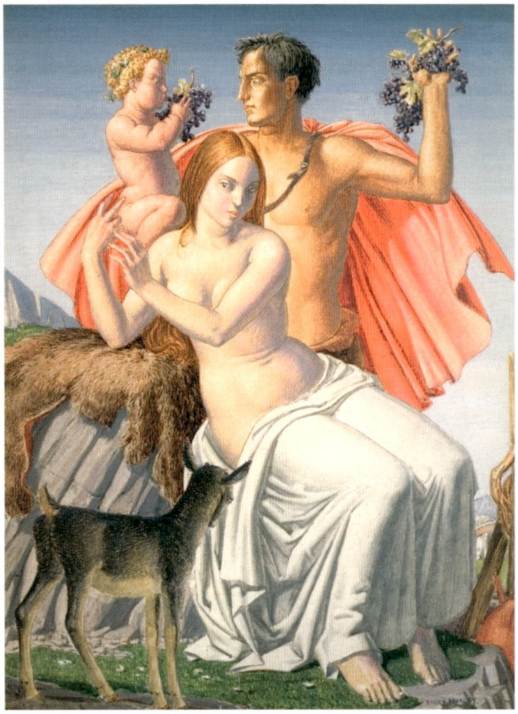

Fig. 5. Harry Morley (1881–1943)
The Young Bacchus (1930)
Tempera on board; 18 x 14 (46 x 36)
Private Collection

Royal Academy. Abstract paintings by Edward Wadsworth (1889–1949) were hung with works in memory of Herringham and Spencer Stanhope. The exhibition celebrated an innovative younger generation of artists while giving homage to the revivalists who came before them.

Cut short by war and the rationing of materials, the thirties ended for the tempera artists in 1938 with an exhibition in Birmingham. Similar to the Whitechapel exhibition, paintings with both modern and traditional subjects were shown. This time, however, the movement towards establishing tempera as a modern medium was more evident. Not only were younger artists deviating from the traditional technique as detailed in Cennino's treatise, they were absorbing the modernist influences from Europe. Surreal and abstract works by Wadsworth, John Armstrong (1893–1973), and Augustus Lunn (1905–86) were a stark contrast to the medieval tales and religious stories depicted in works by Southall, Gaskin and Batten. Wadsworth's *The Beached Margin* of 1937, an example of the dream-like marine paintings he created during this period, illustrates this departure from traditional subjects (fig. 6). As one critic described the works, 'paintings which jerk us clean out of the allegoric and the subject picture rut… …a picture that shouts in the company of its mild-mannered companions, but it is a good and heartening shout of genuine twentieth century origins.'[11] As British artists recreated tempera for the twentieth century, American artists began to discover the medium.

Edward Waldo Forbes (1873–1969), later director of the Fogg Art Museum at Harvard University, developed a passion for early renaissance art during his travels in Italy.[12] Beginning in 1909, he taught courses on Florentine painting to the Harvard community; by 1924, Forbes's courses were devoted solely to techniques, with special emphasis on tempera and fresco.[13] As his students graduated, many took significant posts as scholars, museum directors, artists and conservators, dispersing the tempera technique throughout the United States.

The American translation of Cennino's treatise was published by Daniel Thompson, one of Forbes's devoted pupils. Though versions by Merrifield and Herringham found their way to the United States, Thompson's 1933

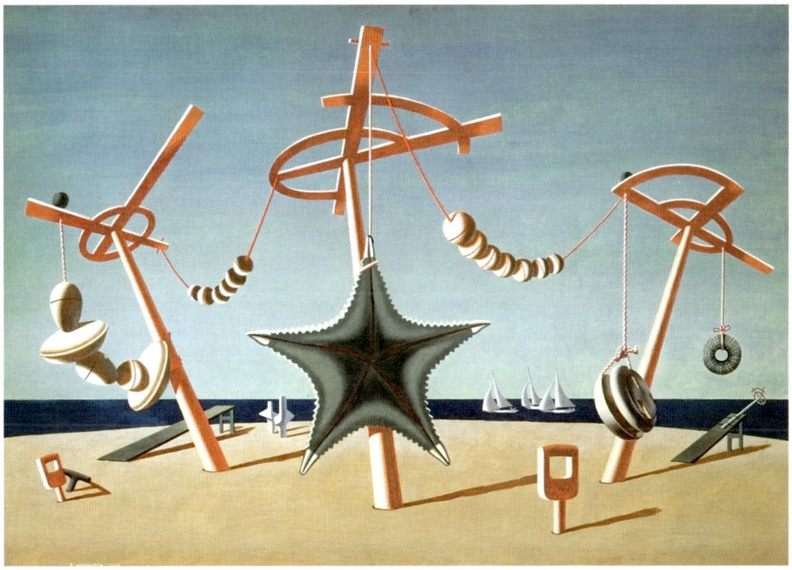

Fig. 6. Edward Wadsworth (1889–1949)
The Beached Margin (1937)
Tempera on linen on wood; 28 1/4 x 40 (71.1 x 101.6)
Copyright Tate, London 2005

translation had the widest distribution and greatest impact on the American revivalists. Eventually republished by Dover Publications, seventy years later Thompson's work continues to be the most accurate and popular translation on both sides of the Atlantic.

Unlike the British artists who were centred in Birmingham and London, the American Tempera Revival was geographically, as well as stylistically, diverse. As the movement developed throughout the middle of the twentieth century, several areas of concentration emerged. In New Haven, Connecticut, Thompson and Lewis York (1904–88) encouraged students to experiment in the medium at the Yale School of Fine Arts. In New York City, Kenneth Hayes Miller (1876–1952), a tempera artist in his own right and teacher at the Art Students League, taught the tempera technique to Isabel Bishop (1902–88) and Reginald Marsh (1898–1954). In Chadds Ford, Pennsylvania, after being introduced to tempera by their in-law Peter Hurd (1904–84), both N.C. Wyeth (1882–1945) and Andrew Wyeth (1917–) began to work in the medium. Thomas Hart Benton (1889–1975), though not an exclusive tempera artist, influenced a generation of American painters in the Midwest at the Kansas City Art Institute in Missouri. In addition to these notable instructors, Paul Cadmus (1904–99) and George Tooker (1920–) chose to devote their artistic careers to tempera. With these and other artists working in the medium, the American Tempera Revival thrived through the 1930–50s.[14]

By the mid-twentieth century Victorian and Edwardian art had become unfashionable. The tempera revivalist might have been forgotten had it not been for a series of exhibitions starting in the late 1960s. The first of these was *The Earthly Paradise* at The Fine Art Society in 1969. Emphasising artists from the Birmingham School of Art, the exhibition reintroduced the public to Southall, Gaskin, the Geres and Armfield. The success of the exhibition brought about a second Earthly Paradise exhibition in 1975. With Victorian paintings rising in market value, more dealers began to take notice of the tempera revival. In the 1980s, the tempera revivalists found a home outside commercial galleries. Owing to exhibitions curated by George Breeze, the tempera revivalists experienced a rebirth in popularity. The first of these exhibitions was *Joseph Southall (1861–1944): Artist-Craftsman*, at Birmingham City Museum and Art Gallery and The Fine Art Society in

1980. The success of this exhibition led to *Arthur and Georgie Gaskin* (1982), also held in Birmingham and London, and two years later, *Margaret Gere (1878–1965)* in Cheltenham.

Tempera's popularity waned in the second half of the twentieth century as revolutionary materials were introduced in contemporary art. By the end of the 1970s the Society of Painters in Tempera faded away; however, twenty years later, a group of American artists resurrected the old Society. Under the leadership of Michael Bergt (1956–) and Lora Arbrador (1949–), the renamed Society of Tempera Painters was established on 1 July, 1997. A year later, a British branch was organised. Through its quarterly newsletter and the internet, the Society is able reach a broad audience. With a current membership of over a hundred and fifty artists in the United States, Canada, and Britain, the Society of Tempera Painters continues to instruct and promote tempera artists. Like their predecessors, the contemporary artists continue to exhibit their works. Exactly one hundred years after the original Society's exhibition at Leighton House, the revival of tempera came full circle. On 14 May, *Tempera 2001* opened, exhibiting a hundred and twenty-two works. As a tribute to the pioneering revivalists and to showcase new British and American tempera artists, Leighton House was once again chosen as the venue.

Tempera was mastered in the early renaissance, forgotten, and then rediscovered in the nineteenth century. The inherent strengths of the medium, durability and brilliance of colour, drew artists back to the technique. With Cennino's guidance, the pioneers of the British Tempera Revival struggled with tempera's intricacies. Once the medium was conquered, the artists created luminescent paintings that combined the stylistic influence of the Pre-Raphaelites with the ideals of the Arts and Crafts Movement. Through their dedication to all aspects of the artistic process, they succeeded in returning craftsmanship to the fine arts. The establishment of the Society of Painters in Tempera created a community that cultivated artists and supported their works through exhibitions and publications. This structure provided younger artists with the means to discover the medium. Undeterred by technical challenges, the tempera revivalists resurrected this forgotten technique and transformed tempera into a modern medium for future generations.

Notes

1. Robin Hamlyn, "William Blake at Work: 'Every thing which is in Harmony'" in *William Blake: The Painter at Work*, edited by Joyce H. Townsend (London: Tate Publishing, 2003), 37.
2. Viola Borradaile and Rosamund Borradaile, *The Student's Cennini: A Handbook for Tempera Painters*, (Brighton: The Dolphin Press, 1942), 5.
3. Roddam Spencer Stanhope, "Yolk of Egg Tempera," *Papers of the Society of Painters in Tempera 1901–1907*, vol. 1 (1908): 38–39.
4. With his aversion to turpentine (required for removing oil paint from brushes), Burne-Jones seems a likely candidate for tempera. Current research by Colette Crossman (doctoral candidate at the University of Maryland) on Burne-Jones demonstrates that he was aware of the intricacies of the technique, but the extent he worked in the medium is yet to be determined.
5. Exhibited at the New Gallery Summer exhibition in 1901, her work was selected as 'Picture of the Year' by the *Pall Mall Gazette*. Jan Marsh and Pamela Gerrish Nunn, *Pre-Raphaelite Women Artists*, 3d ed., exhibition catalogue (New York: Thames and Hudson, 1999) 147.
6. Mary Sargant-Florence, "A Survey of the Society's History," *Papers of the Society of Mural Decorators and Painters in Tempera, 1925–1935*, vol. 3 (1936): 137–138.
7. H.J.L.J. Massé, *The Art-Workers' Guild 1884–1934* (Oxford: The Shakespeare Head Press, 1935), 104 and 180. Over the years various topics were covered including 'Tempera and Size Painting' and 'Grounds and Mediums in Painting.'
8. Ibid., 180.
9. Sargant-Florence, 139.
10. Francis Haskell, *The Ephemeral Museum: Old Master Paintings and the Rise of the Art Exhibition* (New Haven: Yale University Press, 2000) 123.
11. "Tempera Painting: Symphony in Colour," *The Birmingham Mail* (Monday January 17, 1938): 11.
12. Trusted assistant to Ruskin and Rossetti, Charles Fairfax Murray (1849–1919) taught Forbes how to work in egg tempera.
13. *Edward Waldo Forbes: Yankee Visionary*, exhibition catalogue, (Cambridge, Massachusetts: Fogg Art Museum, 1971) 9 and 144. Jan Marsh and Pamela Gerrish Nunn, *Pre-Raphaelite Women Artists*, 3d ed., exhibition catalogue (New York: Thames and Hudson, 1999) 147.
14. For an in depth look at the American Tempera Revival, see Richard J. Boyle, Hilton Brown and Richard Newman, *Milk and Eggs: The American Revival of Tempera Painting 1930–1950* (Chadds Ford, Pennsylvania: Brandywine Museum, 2002)

I would like to acknowledge the support of the Robert H. Smith Fellowship and the National Gallery of Art, Washington, DC, which made this research possible.

Opposite cat.no.7. The Old Fisherman, 1903

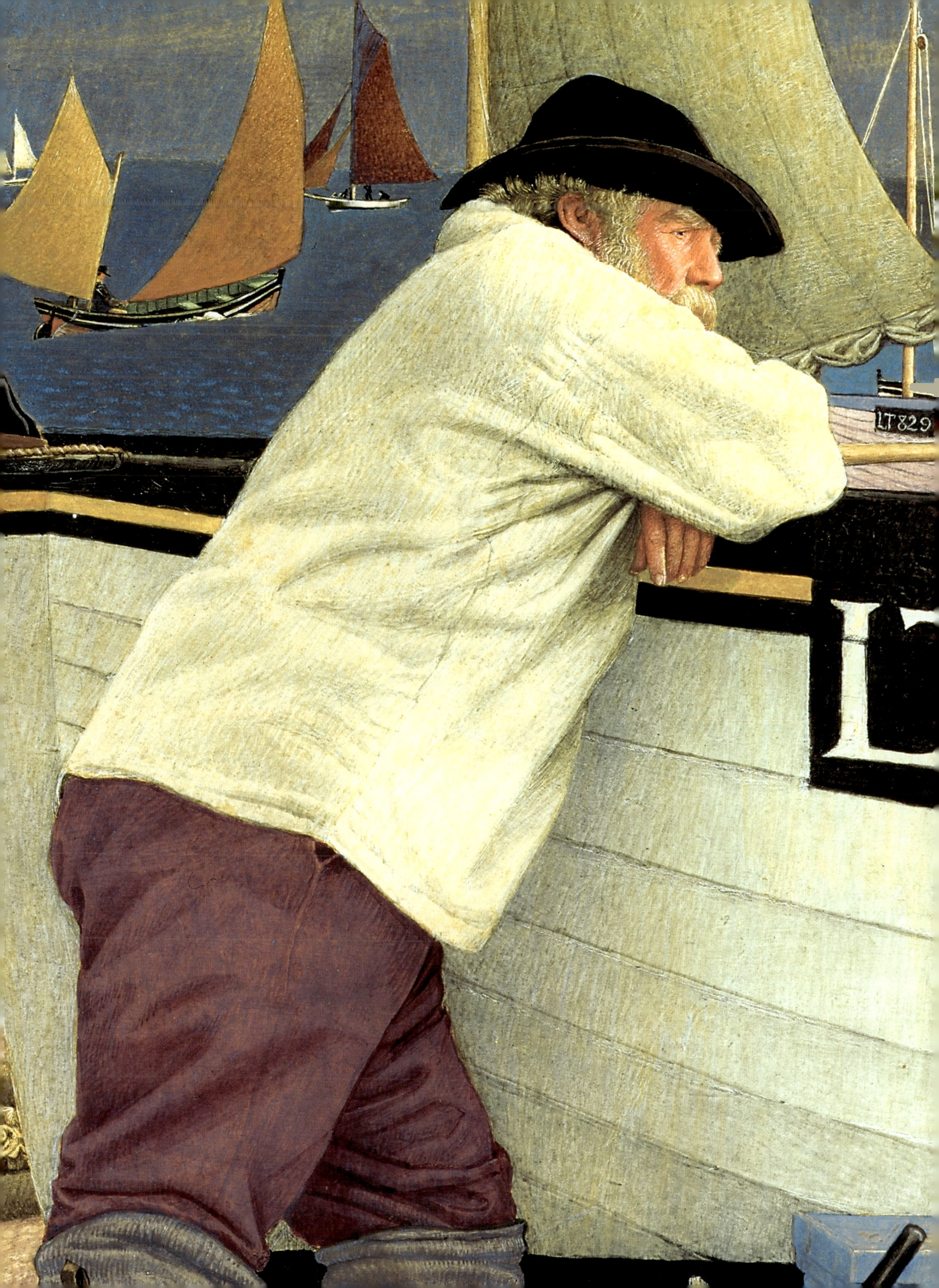
LT829

John's Tune

NOW GOD BE PRAISED WHO GIVES US LIGHT,
AND HILLS ON WHICH THE LIGHT MAY FALL,
AND A SONG TO SING AT THE END OF THE NIGHT
WHEN OVER THE PADDOCKS THE STARLINGS CALL.

THE SUN IS WAITING IN THE SKY
AND SURELY HAS BUT KIND TO SAY,
AND WITH NEVER A CLOUD FOR COMPANY,
SO COME, AND WE'LL TRAVEL AWAY TO-DAY.

A ROAD FOR YOU, A HILL FOR ME,
A RIVER JOE MAY SHINE UPON,
NEVER HAS BEEN SUCH LUCK OF THREE
SINCE FIRST WENT WALKING ANY JOHN.

SHAKE OUT YOUR STARS FROM POCKETS LINED
WITH PENCE ENOUGH FOR PILGRIMAGE,
NOT ONE OF US ALL BUT HAS A MIND
FIT TO CHALLENGE THE EARTH'S OLD AGE.

John Drinkwater

Joseph Southall and the Fortunoff Collection

George Breeze

This poem, *John's Tune,* was published by John Drinkwater in 1916 and dedicated to two of his close friends, the artist-craftsmen Arthur Gaskin and Joseph Southall.[1] Gaskin and Southall were, in their turn, the very closest of friends, referring to each other as Artie and Joe. The poem well sums up many of the first impressions made on the viewer by Southall's work. The closeness of Gaskin and Southall is well shown in their extensive correspondence and is evidenced in the Fortunoff collection by the illustrated letter from Joe to Artie, *Balloons to Sell!,* (cat.no.9) and perhaps especially by the letter attached to the reverse of *The Old Fisherman,* 1903, (cat.no.7) (below).

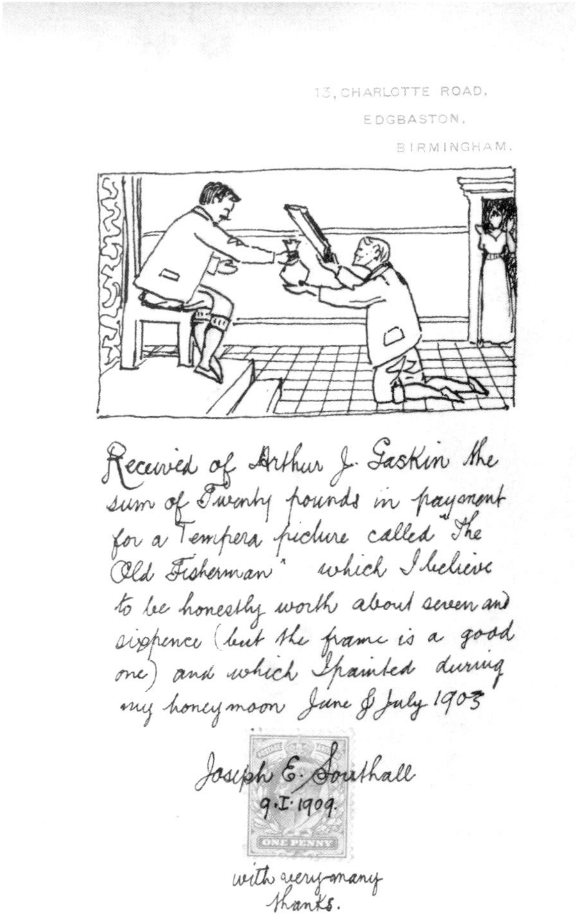
13, CHARLOTTE ROAD,
EDGBASTON,
BIRMINGHAM.

Received of Arthur J. Gaskin the sum of Twenty pounds in payment for a Tempera picture called "The Old Fisherman" which I believe to be honestly worth about seven and sixpence (but the frame is a good one) and which I painted during my honeymoon June & July 1903

Joseph E. Southall
9.I.1909.

ONE PENNY

with very many thanks.

The other great friendship in Southall's life was that with his first cousin, Anna Elizabeth Baker, whom he married in 1903. Because of their close relationship they consciously had no children. There are no less than five portraits of her in the Fortunoff collection, which are discussed below. She was a mistress of the art of applying gesso, gilding and burnishing the frames which he designed, leaving records of the extensive preparation required (as well as the charges she made to him for her time).[2] These frames are an important characteristic of many of Southall's paintings – and The Fine Art Society has commissioned a number from latter-day crafts-people where there was none previously.

Within those frames, Southall's tempera paintings and, indeed, his watercolours – so often difficult to distinguish from those in tempera[3] – are suffused with a jewelled calm. The combination of the bright flat colours, the carefully delineated subject matter, and the gleaming gilt frames gave Southall's work a particular appeal.[4] Egg tempera, the form most used by the artist, is at the heart of this distinctiveness. It is not a medium like oils where change of mind can easily be made: it requires the colours to be built up carefully in thin layers one upon another.[5] This meant that there needed to be careful preparatory studies. Southall's sketchbooks – the Fortunoff collection is rich in pages from these – contain a number of such studies for realised and unrealised paintings (see, for instance, cat.nos. 32 – 35, 36 and 58).

The earliest work by Southall owned by the Fortunoffs was his *Portrait of Isabella Harlock*, (cat.no.1), executed in 1888, from a period – pre 1895 – of scarce output, or certainly of scarce surviving output, and executed predictably in watercolour and bodycolour, since this was a period when he had abandoned attempts at tempera painting due to the great difficulties he was having in handling the medium. The first tempera painting in the collection, *The Coral Necklace*, (cat.no.2), dates from 1895, the year he took up tempera again. This is a key work from the point of view of the medium since it has so many technical notes inscribed on the reverse. The *Study For 'The Mystic Burial'*, (cat.no.29), a strange subject for which there is no known painting, comes from this same period where the rich glowing colours of the early Italians, that so influenced the artist, are apparent.

These three carefully chosen works admirably set the scene in a private collection for the mythological and romantic subjects on which Southall said his reputation rested.[6] The Fortunoffs owned one of the most spectacular of these, *Beauty at the Fountain*, (cat.no.4), important for a variety of reasons: its clear homage to Italian *quattrocento* painting in its setting and colouring; the recorded endorsement of Edward Burne-Jones for it (see the catalogue entry); and its distinguished provenance, having belonged to Laurence Hodson, a discerning Wolverhampton brewer and High Churchman (at first sight an unlikely collector for the work of a Quaker teetotaller) who pursued the Anglo-Catholic line of bringing people closer to God by declaring His glory through visual splendour.[7] And what visual splendour is here!

On the other hand, *Music*, (cat.no.12), is a strange addition to the collection. Executed in 1912 after Southall had ceased painting the major mythological and romantic subjects which established his reputation, and never exhibited in his lifetime anyway, it remains a curious work, of which possibly the best part is the rabbit in the bottom right corner, entirely depicted in pencil with a thin washing-over of medium. Another curious composition that fits in this category is the *Study for "Bacchus and Ariadne'*, (cat.no.13), probably created in the same year as *Music*.

Portraits, of the artist himself, of Anna Elizabeth Baker, both before and after her marriage to him, of fellow Quakers and friends, were a vital part of Southall's output, but his work in this area was limited to these subjects: he did not undertake general portraiture. By the end of the nineteenth century it had become acceptable for Quakers to have their portraits painted, the traditional aversion to such vanity having been overcome. The Fortunoffs only owned a lithographic portrait of the artist himself, (cat.no.14), but what they lacked here they more than made up for in portraits of Anna Elizabeth. We have already discussed *The Coral Necklace*, (cat.no.2), from 1895. There is also a *Study* from 1901, (cat.no.30), and *Contentment*, from 1928, (cat.no.23), the latter with the favourite cat of the time, Toddie. But without doubt, the finest of all portraits of Anna Elizabeth is *Hortus Inclusus*, (cat.no.5). Executed in 1898 in watercolour and enclosed in a frame designed by the artist and gessoed, gilded and burnished by the sitter, Anna Elizabeth is shown engaging the viewer with a direct gaze, while she tends the cat Colin. In her manuscript note (private collection) on the gilding process for the frame, the sitter describes it as being 'for Joe for portrait of myself & Colin'. This was an intensely personal and private portrait by the artist of his future wife, staring longingly at him, the *hortus inclusus* or "garden enclosed" being their own private world, 'a quiet resting place called the pleasaunce; ... No shadow ever falls between the two dear friends who walk together hand in hand along its pleasant paths. So may they walk in peace...'[8]

Portraits, *per se*, of others, to be found in the Fortunoff collection, are limited to those of the collector and friend, Janet Hutchinson, 1918, (cat.no.41), his friend the social activist Henry Nevinson, 1941 (cat.no.59) and the artist's nephew Ned Allen, the subject of the delightful *Balloons to Sell!*, 1909, (cat.no.10). There are other portraits but these are studies for his shore scenes (e.g. cat.nos.7, 19, 42 and 54) and a late study of the head of an unidentified boy (1934), (cat.no.57).

Landscapes constituted Southall's greatest output, the variety of their subject matter fuelled by regular travelling, particularly to Fowey (Cornwall) or Southwold (Suffolk) in this country, and to north and central Italy abroad. Examples of these not unnaturally constitute the major part of the Fortunoff collection. The most engaging are shore scenes set at Southwold (cat.nos.6, 7, 19–20, and most of the studies included in this exhibition) and the harbour scenes from Fowey (cat.nos.15, 25, 27). The most outstanding are: *Cleaning the Lines*, (cat.no.6), one of the earliest shore scenes, dating from 1900, which had belonged to Southall's fellow tempera painter, Maxwell Armfield, and was submitted to more exhibitions than any of Southall's other landscapes; and *Fishermen and Boat*, (cat.no.19), from 1923, which is essentially a larger version of *Up From The Sea*, painted three years earlier and now in the Castle Museum, Nottingham. It is to be regretted, however, that the Fortunoffs sold *On the Beach*, 1911, one of the most charming and lively of Southall's scenes of those other than fisherfolk enjoying the shore, although studies for it remain in the collection (cat.nos.32–35). It is interesting to compare such scenes with those of other artists who were capturing the Suffolk shore at a similar time. For instance, Philip Wilson Steer's *Walberswick, Children Paddling* (Fitzwilliam Museum, Cambridge) is the antithesis of Southall's approach, but effectively evokes the heat and sense of Summer. There is more of a sense of an on-shore breeze in Southall's depictions.

Turning inland, one finds a small collection of scenes in the Fortunoff collection from quite a narrow chronological band, 1915–1921. Such views were evidently prized in Southall's day, measured by the number of times they may be found in exhibition catalogues, but they are not as well known nor as widely seen today as his shore scenes or Italian views. *The Meadow*, (cat.no.16), and *The Green at Banbury*, (cat.no.17), both watercolours from 1920, are characteristic of his rural and urban views. *Dinham Bridge, Ludlow*, (cat.no.18), a tempera painting from a year later, does not appear to have ever been exhibited: it had possibly been in the possession of Miss Allen, a relative, from the start.[9]

Looking across the English Channel, the Fortunoff collection includes four Italian scenes (cat.nos.8, 21, 22, 24). The most prized of these must be *In Tuscany*, (cat.no.8), from 1906, which appeared in most of the one-man shows devoted to Southall during his lifetime including the most important, the 1910 exhibition at the Galeries Georges Petit in Paris. Orta, in the Italian Lakes (cat.no.27), was often a stop *en route* to more southerly climes, the *environs* of the quay being a favourite location.

While in Italy, Southall made studies of frescoes. The Italians decorated their churches and public buildings with frescoes, why did the British not do the same thing, at one and the same time providing aesthetic delight on otherwise blank walls and social improvement through the subject matter depicted? This was of course something that had been espoused by others such as GF Watts and, in a more specific area, the Select Committees of the 1830s and '40s for the decoration of the new Palace of Westminster. It was the Campo Santo in Pisa which had first inspired Southall's interest in the subject during a visit in 1883 and the Fortunoffs owned a watercolour copy of his of a Benozzo Gozzoli fresco from there (1897) (see entry for cat.no.3). Impressively, the Fortunoffs owned one of the artist's few transportable true frescoes (or *buonfresco*), *In the Rue de Rivoli*, (cat.no.11), though where it was originally displayed is not known. No attempt at representing Southall's *oeuvre* would be complete without an example in *buonfresco*, and this piece has survived better than the other known smaller examples.

The Fortunoff collection lacks representation of several of the subject areas or media that Southall espoused but which are mainly on the periphery of his output. Excluding the fresco study (cat.no.4), there are no religious subjects, there are no pendants or cameos, there is no decorated furniture (but then only two pieces are known to exist), no book illustrations or engravings, and no designs for Greek lace or *reticella*, a form of cut work in linen (though, unbeknown to the Fortunoffs, Beauty's bodice in *Beauty at the Fountain*, (cat.no.4), is actually a direct copy of one of Southall's Greek lace designs). Most significantly, there are no subjects depicting the evils of war and pursuit of peace, an area of the artist's work covered in a separate essay: one suspects that the Fortunoffs were looking for something more placid, less politically charged than Southall's strongly emotive representations of political and pacifist themes.

It is an excellent collection and a pity in some ways that it is to be broken up, but then many collectors like to see their collections dispersed, giving to others the thrill of building their own. It is doubtful if anyone could now reassemble a collection of Southall's *oeuvre* that could rival the Fortunoffs' in range and quality, especially as two of his finest acquisitions are now entering the portals of a public art gallery.

Notes

1. From John Drinkwater's collection of poems called *Olton Pools* (London, 1916, p. 28).
2. See, for instance, the catalogue entry to *Hortus Inclusus* (cat.no.5).
3. For example *Contentment* (cat.no.23) exhibits the short hatched brushstrokes which are characteristic of his works in tempera, but an inscription on the reverse states 'watercolour on vellum.' The nature of the supports which Southall used and the use of transparent glazing over white grounds to avoid difficulties he found with white pigments are other reasons why his tempera paintings and watercolours can be confused.
4. Charlotte Gere, in her introduction to the catalogue of The Fine Art Society's exhibition *The Earthly Paradise*, 1969, p.2, suggests that it was Joseph Southall to whom Picasso was referring on a visit to Violet Gordon Woodhouse in the late 1920s: the artist in whom Picasso 'doubtless perceived some original vein that had not yet been exploited, some vision he had not yet essayed.' See Osbert Sitwell's *Noble Essences* (London, Macmillan & Co., 1950, p.261): Picasso kept going into a room to admire a group of pictures 'bought from an "old gentleman", who devoted that part of his time left to him from the study of the Gothic ages to a portrayal, in pure, bright, almost encaustic tones of paint, of sailing ships in full rig against a flat sea.'
5. For a full and clear exposition of the tempera medium see Jill Dunkerton's essay *Joseph Southall's Tempera Paintings* in my 1980 catalogue, pp.18–24. I remain most grateful to her for her research on the subject.
6. The importance of these pictures is demonstrated by the fact that they constituted a major element of the 1910 exhibition at the Galeries Georges Petit, where they are all listed first. In 1922 Southall wrote to his fellow tempera artist and friend, Maxwell Armfield: 'the main thing is reputation and money follows in the long run – at least I think so. It is hopeless to suppose that mere quality of work *alone* will make a living for a painter, isn't it!' (letter of 20.III.1922 formerly in the collection of Alexander Ballard).
7. The Non-Conformists and Anglo-Catholics were two key constituents of the market for the work of the Arts and Crafts Movement in Birmingham, combining integrity in creation with visual splendour. Donald Hope is an example of a radical Non-Conformist Birmingham manufacturer who collected in this field: he was a former owner of Southall's *The Three-Masted Schooner* (1919), (cat.no.15).
8. Quote from the introduction by Albert Flemming (p. xiii) to John Ruskin's collection of letters published under the title *Hortus Inclusus*, (Orpington, 1887). Flemming was here speaking of Bacon's Royal Order of Gardens.
9. Another view of Ludlow, that of Ludford Bridge, not in the Fortunoff collection, was regularly exhibited.

I would like to acknowledge the help of my wife, Rachel, and Peyton Skipwith

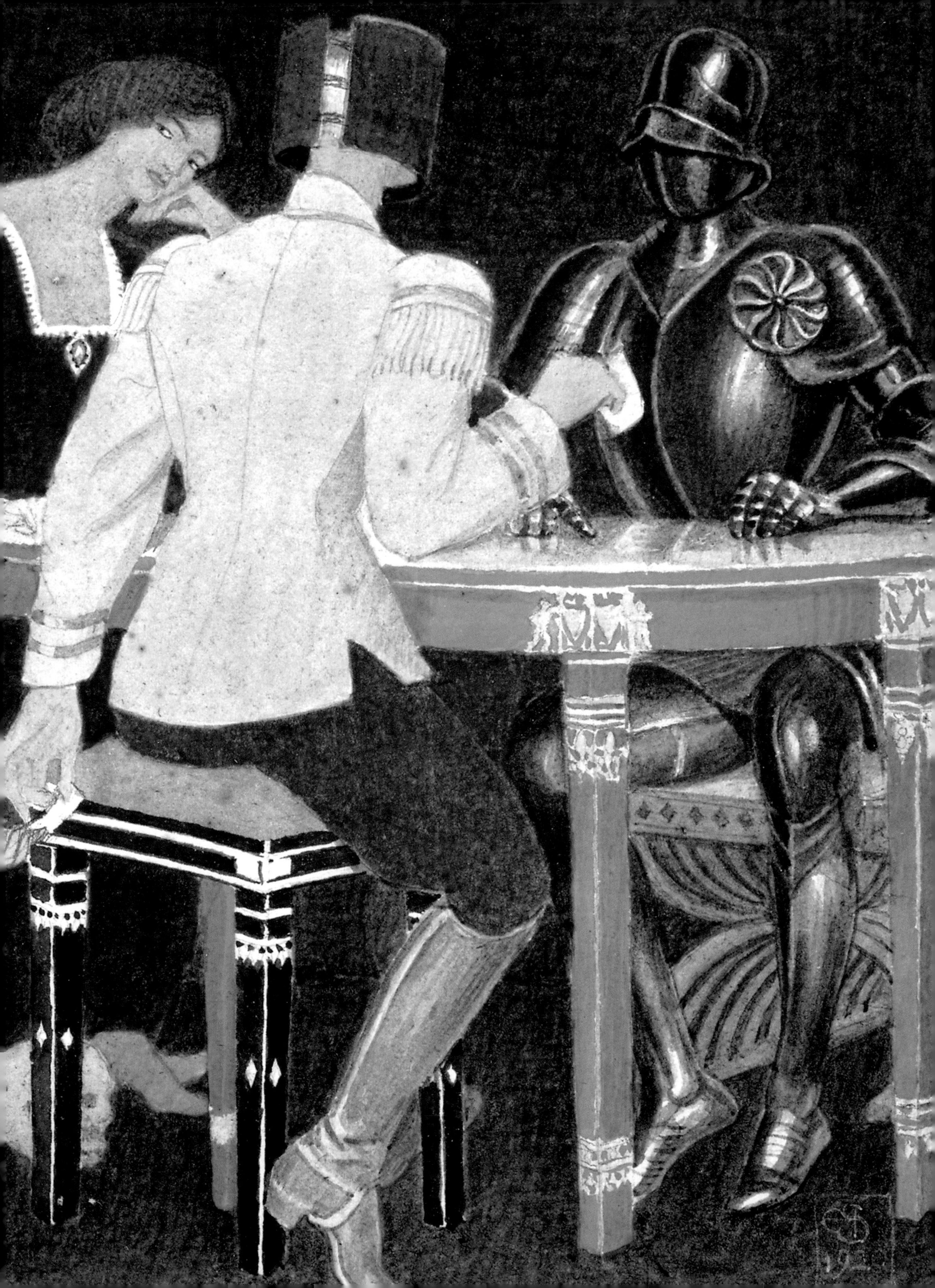

Joseph Southall and the Pursuit of Peace

George Breeze

Joseph Southall's best known creative output in tempera and watercolour may possess the hall-mark of a jewelled calm, but his creative output which rages against the futility of war and for the pursuit of peace is marked by acerbic wit and a distinct sense of unease.

Southall was a prominent peace campaigner throughout the Great War and beyond, writing many speeches, as well as letters to the press, on the issue. A pacifist subject in the Fortunoff collection would certainly have rounded out the comprehensive nature of a two-dimensional collection of Joseph Southall's work and one particularly might have expected such an inclusion bearing in mind that Alan Fortunoff was a pacifist too. The watercolour, *The Gamblers*, 1920,[1] (opposite) where lives are being played with as though they were playing cards, belonged to The Fine Art Society at the time of the 1980 Southall exhibition and could have been bought by the Fortunoffs. Little of Southall's pacifist art, however, is in tempera or watercolour, most being published in pamphlets and booklets whereby it could more readily reach a mass market. Also the quality of these illustrations, in artistic terms, is of a differing standard to his main work, but then its purpose was propaganda rather than aesthetic delight.

Southall's interest in politics was first stirred by the jingoist reception in London, in 1895, to the Jameson Raid on Boer land in South Africa. He was ashamed of his country's stance. Political activism was in his blood. On his father's side, his grandmother was the sister of the pacifist and Chartist Joseph Sturge, while on his mother's – and wife's – side the Bakers had been Quakers with strong radical sympathies since the seventeenth century. His activity was such during the years of the Great War from 1915 to 1918 that his mainstream work in tempera and watercolour was considerably reduced. Illness from 1937 until his death in 1944 much reduced his output in any event during the Second World War, but he managed to continue campaigning against the evils of war and in 1939 helped found a Birmingham branch of the No-Conscription League. Aged 53 in 1914, he would have been too old to be subject to conscription, but had he been young enough he would doubtless have made a strong case as a conscientious objector. He was too opposed to war to be considered as an official war artist and therefore never personally experienced the battle front.

In its obituary of the artist on 7 November 1944, *The Birmingham Mail* described Southall's "political radicalism" as blossoming "into very pale pink aesthetic Communism". Southall himself said he was a socialist in the William Morris tradition (like many involved in the Arts and Crafts Movement), but he was expelled in 1927 from the Birmingham Borough Labour Party, where he was a vice-president, for supporting a communist candidate, Dr Dunstan, against Sir Austen Chamberlain in the West Birmingham constituency. He continued, however, as a member of the Independent Labour Party (ILP), an organisation that shared his views on war and pacifism, and it was here that he felt most at home politically[2]. He had joined the ILP in 1914 on the outbreak of war and he soon became chairman of its Birmingham City branch, a post he held until 1931. In 1914 he was also chairman of the Birmingham Auxiliary of the Peace Society and a vice-president of the Birmingham and District Passive Resistance League.

The range of Southall's political views are summed up in an unpublished note, dated 20.VII.1913, which he wrote in one of his sketchbooks:

> 'As I lay on my bed in the inn at Domodossola [in the Italian Alps] very early in the morning..., looking up at the frescoed ceiling (how cleverly frescoed it was but in such decadent taste) there came before my mind with great clearness a vision of the 3 great evils which mark the life of the people of Europe viz. The military system, the factory system and the clerical system.
>
> 'The Military System with its false cry of patriotism divides the poor heedless workers into hostile camps furiously attacking each other with fratricidal strife, but oblivious of their common *foci.*
>
> 'The Factory System turns the free workman into a pitiable slave, and by depriving him of his joy in his work, ruins his life, breaks his spirit and prepares him for further degradation and oppression. Oh the squalor, the material & still more the spiritual poverty of this grinding blinding process – oh the meanness, littleness, numbness that it begets. All are impoverished by it – the rich as well as the poor.

> For God gives to Dives the desire of his breast but sends leanness to his soul.
>
> 'These two great evils straddle over the earth & grow fearfully – They are both the instruments of oppression of robbery & death yet there is a worse evil and it is Clericalism or the making a trade out of preaching religion.
>
> 'Clericalism covers the other two evils with the cloak of religion, shields the oppressor & beguiles the oppressed. Clericalism explains away both the teaching and the example of Christ. It blesses war in the name of the Prince of Peace – it blesses Dives in the name of Him who had no where to lay his head. What shall we say of the false shepherd who dines daily with the wolf?'

Southall was clearly infuriated that the Church should support the warring factions even though Christianity espoused peace. This, of course, goes back to Augustine of Hippo's and Thomas Aquinas' theories of *jus ad bellum* or the Just War. Quakers are opposed to war regardless and Quakerism was fundamental to Southall's life.[3] He called himself "an absolute pacifist".[4]

It is interesting that while the well-dressed gentleman and lady are often portrayed in Southall's paintings, sketchbooks and photographs with an eye for the fine figure, they are not depicted as the oppressors of society, which they are in his political illustrations. An image of 1915 by Southall in *Ghosts of the Slain*,[5] a pamphlet by the ILP Member of Parliament R L Outhwaite, makes the latter point.[6] (fig. 2) The caption reads 'Those who sit in the high places cast the people into the pit.' A copy of this pamphlet was sent to the *Morning Post* for review. Published on 27 July 1915 under the heading 'Treason in Disguise' the reviewer said that 'it preached the most pestilential doctrine – doctrine which in some of its terms is hardly to be distinguished from treason…' He went on: 'Mr. Southall whose work is a *reductio ad absurdum* of the Walter Crane style of decorative design, has scored a surreptitious point by making his blind-folded Generals, and Bishops, and Secretaries of State resemble actual personages in a sly, slick fashion. And what he lacks in art he tries to make up for in venom, as when he pictures the representatives of Church and State pushing a

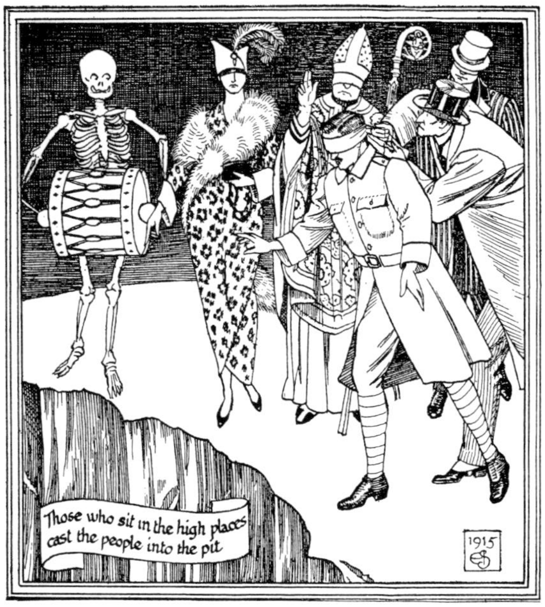

Fig. 2. "Those who sit in the high places cast the people into the pit", 1915, from RL Outhwaite: *The Ghosts of the Slain: A Vision of the Future*, 1915, first page.

blindfolded Tommy over a precipice. From the artistic point of view, the whole thing is contemptible.' [7]

Such reviews just made Southall and his colleagues try harder to persuade others of the peace-not-war cause.

In the same month of the same year Southall gave a paper on *Art and Peace* to a London conference on the Pacifist Philosophy of Life.[8] Very much Ruskinian in tone, Southall speaks of the tedious toil of the workman, no longer able to express himself in his work: joy in creativity needs to be given back to him. There can be no peace while there is this exploitation. The link with war is that 'our commercial and industrial system has been animated largely by the same spirit as that of the military system.... Those who have never been taught to see the joy of construction are ready to enter into the orgies of destruction'. 'The contempt for beauty and indifference to art pervade all classes in this country', he goes on, politicians, for instance, talk of re-building Belgium but they 'cannot bring back to life the dead hands that made Ypres and Arras, Bruges and Antwerp'. With a resonance that reverberates down to our own day, Southall speaks of the 'bloodshot eyes [with which] we watch one another through the Periscope of Fear'. There can be no peace while there is fear. He believes his main duty is 'to use any little power I might have towards the immediate quenching of those fires of passion and revenge that bid fair to destroy all that makes life worth living'. He continues, again with Ruskinian overtones: 'We who are here today must desire above all, that Nations should learn to see and to know one another – to see that they are not enemies but brethren, and that all this madness of destruction was caused by blindness and the fear that blindness makes possible.... In the future Art must again become one of our chief concerns. It is the special function of the Artist to see, and to help others to see.... And Art has this immeasurable advantage, that it is an international language'.[9] He concluded his speech with these words: 'Then may we see to it that Art shall no longer be a sauce to tempt the worn-out appetite of the Epicurean, but a wholesome ingredient in the daily fare of the people'. Southall saw his role not simply as one that would help to bring about peace (as he saw it) but, when that peace came, help others to see again.

Southall did not completely neglect his art during this difficult period, giving a substantial talk to the Art Workers' Guild on "Craft and Media in Painting" on 2nd March 1917 and in the previous year participating in the Arts and Crafts Exhibition Society's (A&CES) annual show, at the Royal Academy. This was the first temporary exhibition in Britain in which a major part was given to mural decoration, the idea of the Society's President, Henry Wilson. Southall was one of eight artists chosen to decorate the main space, titled the "Hall of Heroes". Southall's mural, some 6.25 metres high, was called *The Return of Peace* and depicted a winged figure of Peace, standing on a pedestal with a family at its foot looking up to her, and his beloved Fowey estuary, with a brig in full sail on it, in the background.[10]

While chiefly putting his point of view over by speeches, and letter writing to newspapers, Southall also wrote fables (as he called them) with an anti-war moral and often illustrated them.[11] In 1918 he collected a group of these together and published them under the title *Fables and Illustrations*.[12] The preface says that it was produced in a limited edition of 47,000 but as it is all written in a manner full of irony, the fact may be argued. But the author does wish 'to acknowledge his indebtedness to the ruling classes of Europe, whose unfailing courtesy has provided him with all the material necessary

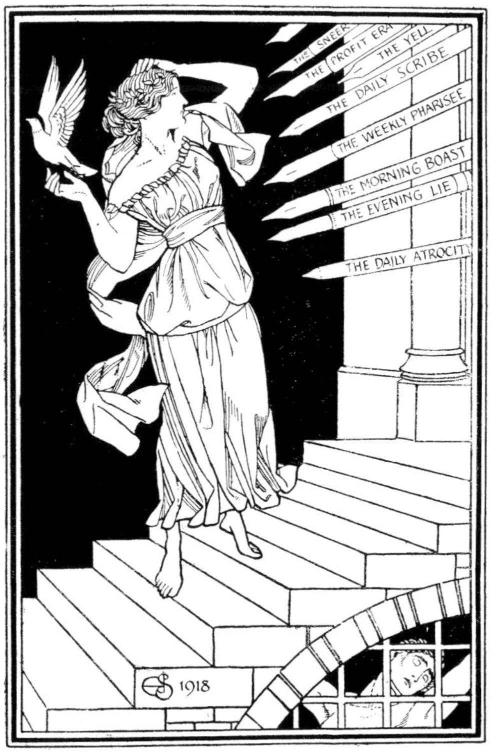

Fig. 3. The Enemies of Peace, 1918

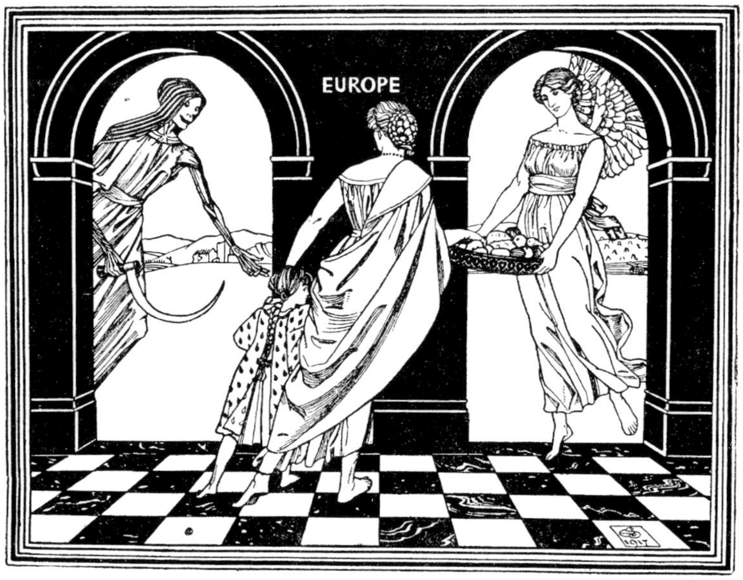

Fig. 4. Peace or Famine – Which?, 1917

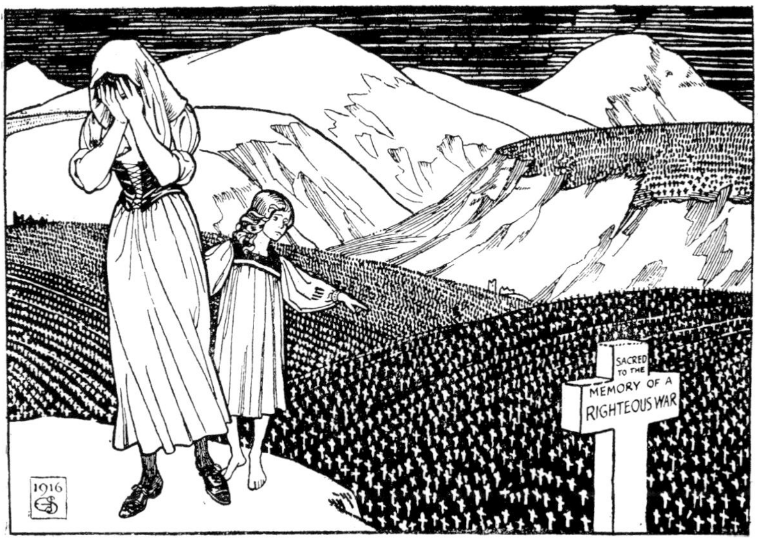

Fig. 5. A Permanent Peace, 1916

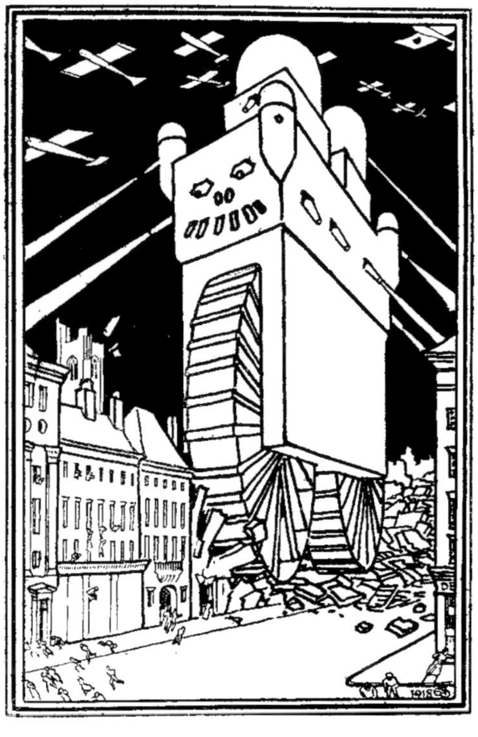

Fig. 6. The Obliterator, 1918

for the compilation of his work.' The sordid lies told by the press, as Southall saw it, were one of his regular targets, illustrated by *The Enemies of Peace* (1918)[13] (fig.3). *Peace or Famine – Which?* (1917)[14] (fig.4) has his familiar winged figure of Peace, similar to that in the A&CES mural *The Return of Peace*, with her basket of fruit – 'the fruits of peace'. *A Permanent Peace* (1916)[15] (fig.5) echoes his persistent refrain about the unrighteous nature of the Great War. But the most original is *The Obliterator* (1918)[16] (fig.6) which has the following accompanying text:

> "Obliterator" Ltd., 1925
> The "Obliterator" is supplied impartially to all civilised Governments and has given entire satisfaction. It is guaranteed to leave nothing standing and nothing breathing.
> It is made in three sizes, small, medium, and large.
> The illustration given represents the Medium size, suitable for country towns.
> For complete list of cities, towns, and villages already destroyed, see our 64 page illustrated pamphlet.
> It is estimated that "The Obliterator" has already shortened the war by at least nine years and is making a clean sweep of civilisation, thus preparing the way for a clean peace.
> ————————
> Unsolicited testimonial (one of thousands). "I returned last Thursday to N——————, my native city, containing a cathedral and many historic monuments. The day before I arrived it had been "obliterated", and I could discover nothing bigger than half a brick."
> Yours. A K....k O.t B..w.

The "Obliterator" anticipated the terrible obliteration of whole cities, such as Dresden, that was to come in the next World War. From as early as 1919 Southall foresaw another war coming, disbelieving the League of Nations could ever prevent it.[17] He was consistent, deeply believing in his mission to proselytise the cause of peace and thereby help bring about a better world for all. As Vera Massey put it in *A Testimony to the Life of Joseph Edward Southall*, following his death: 'Towards any form of pretence, hypocrisy, shallow or muddled thinking, he was merciless ... many were the sharp encounters which reminded us of simple but vital principles in danger of being smothered by more material concern. And then, the battle over, who has not seen him shaking hands with his late adversary over a cup of tea, beaming through his half-moon spectacles with the world's most celestial twinkle in his eyes, the clear parchment pallor of his face broken into what would have been the smile of a benevolent old gentleman had it not somehow been pointed with the wit of a Joseph Southall.'[18]

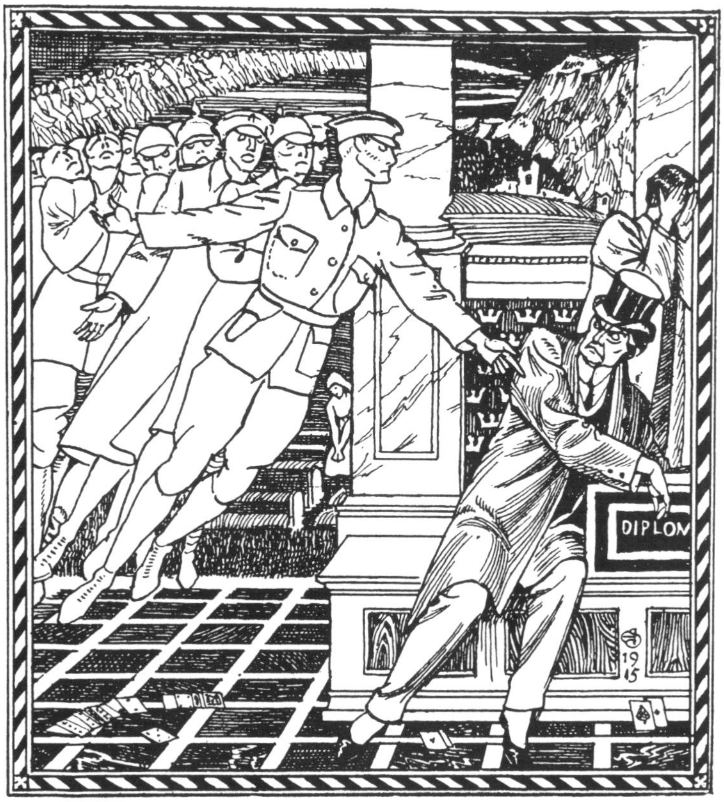

Fig. 7. The Ghosts of the Slain, 1915, 5 1/8 x 4 3/4 (13 x 12.1) from RL Outhwaite: *The Ghosts of the Slain: A Vision of the Future*

Notes

1. *The Gamblers,* watercolour, 6 1/2 x 4 3/4ins. (16.3 x 12.2 cms). Signed in monogram and dated *1920* (br). (see *Joseph Southall, 1861–1944: Artist-Craftsman,* Birmingham, 1980, p. 105, for details).
2. The ILP was founded in 1893 and was a hugely influential British socialist movement in the first thirty years of the twentieth century, whereafter it went into decline.
3. The Quaker Peace Testimony goes right back to the roots of Quakerism in the seventeenth century. Quakers 'recognised the realities of evil and conflict, but it was contrary to the spirit of Christ to use war and violence as means to deal with them.' George Fox, the founder of

Quakerism, wrote in 1651, 'I told [the Commonwealth Commissioners] I lived in the virtue of that life and power that took away the occasion of all wars... I told them I was come into the covenant of peace which was before wars and strife were'. See *Quaker Faith & Practice* (the book of Christian discipline of the Yearly Meeting of the Religious Society of Friends (Quakers) in Britain), 2nd edition, London, 1999, particularly chapter 24 "Our peace testimony" (no pagination).

4. Southall called himself an "absolute pacifist" in a letter published in the *Daily Herald*, 10 June 1927.

5. R L Outhwaite: *The Ghosts of the Slain: A Vision of the Future*, with drawings by Joseph Southall, published by The National Labour Press (the press of the ILP), Manchester, 1915 (small 4to) (no pagination). Sketchbook studies (private collection) suggest the original title was to be *The Ghosts of Armageddon*.

6. First page of story. Actual image is 5 x 4 3/4 ins. (12.8x 12.0 cms)

7. Walter Crane, sixteen years Southall's senior, had a well established reputation for producing socialist campaigning images. He died in 1915.

8. Caxton Hall, London, 8.VII.1915, the text of the speech he probably actually gave used here (in a private collection). The conference papers were subsequently published by the League of Peace and Freedom, London, 1917, this one as *Peace and Freedom Pamphlet no.4*. Most of Southall's speeches left to us are in the form of headline notes. This is unusual in being written out in full, probably because it was to be subsequently published.

9. More accomplished at bridging boundaries than Esperanto, Southall adds.

10. 11th Arts and Crafts Exhibition Society exhibition, 1916, catalogue no.622. The work was in tempera on canvas. The artist was assisted by his wife and decorative borders were executed by members of Birmingham School of Art. Only a design for the mural survives in a private collection and photographs (see *Joseph Southall, 1861–1944: Artist-Craftsman*, Birmingham, 1980, pp. 92–93, for details).

11. Some doubtless never made it to publication because of official censorship, though there appears to be little evidence of tussles with censors in his surviving correspondence. When Southall presented a copy of Outhwaite's *The Ghosts of the Slain* to the Library of the Society of Friends at Friends House, London, he enclosed a note, including the line '[it] is one of the things that the police have spared in repeated raids on the Labour Press.'

12. Published by the National Labour Press, London, priced 2 shillings (10p.) (4to).

13. Page 19. Image 6 1/2 x 4 1/2 ins. (16 x 11 cms)

14. Page 31. Image 4 1/2 x 6 ins. (11 x 15 cms). Originally published in *The Woman's Dreadnought*, 16 June 1917. The figure of Peace, albeit wingless, seated and mellower, re-appears in his *buon fresco* of Peace (1939), in the decoration of the lunette at the east end of the banqueting suite of the Council House, Birmingham.

15. Page 27. Image 4 1/2 x 6 1/2 ins. (16 x 11 cms). Originally published in *Labour Leader*, 30 November 1916, supplement, p.8 with the caption *"They Made a Desolation and Called It Peace"*. It reappeared on the eve of the Second World War in *Peace News*, 19 May 1939.

16. Page 21. Image 6 1/2 x 4 1/2 ins. (16 x 11 cms). Text is on p. 20.

17. The League of Nations came into being in 1920. Southall opposed it right through the 1920s and 1930s, expressing his opposition in such pamphlets as *On the (alleged) League of Nations* (c. 1936). In 1941 he wrote to a Birmingham friend that he had not changed his views about the League. It was he said, 'constructed by statesmen and for statesmen; and the business of such persons is not to put something into the common stock of mankind, but to best one another by all means so as to get something out, each for his own particular state or ruling class' (letter to Herbert Timmington, 15.III.1941, archives of Birmingham Museum and Art Gallery). Other Quakers thought the fledgling League should be supported and there was a lively exchange of views in the letter pages of the Quaker journal, *The Friend*.

18. V Massey, *A Testimony to the Life of Joseph Edward Southall*, Warwickshire Monthly Meeting of the Society of Friends, Birmingham, June, 1945 (no pagination). These sentences also reproduced in *Quaker Faith & Practice*, section 18.15, in the chapter "Faithful lives".

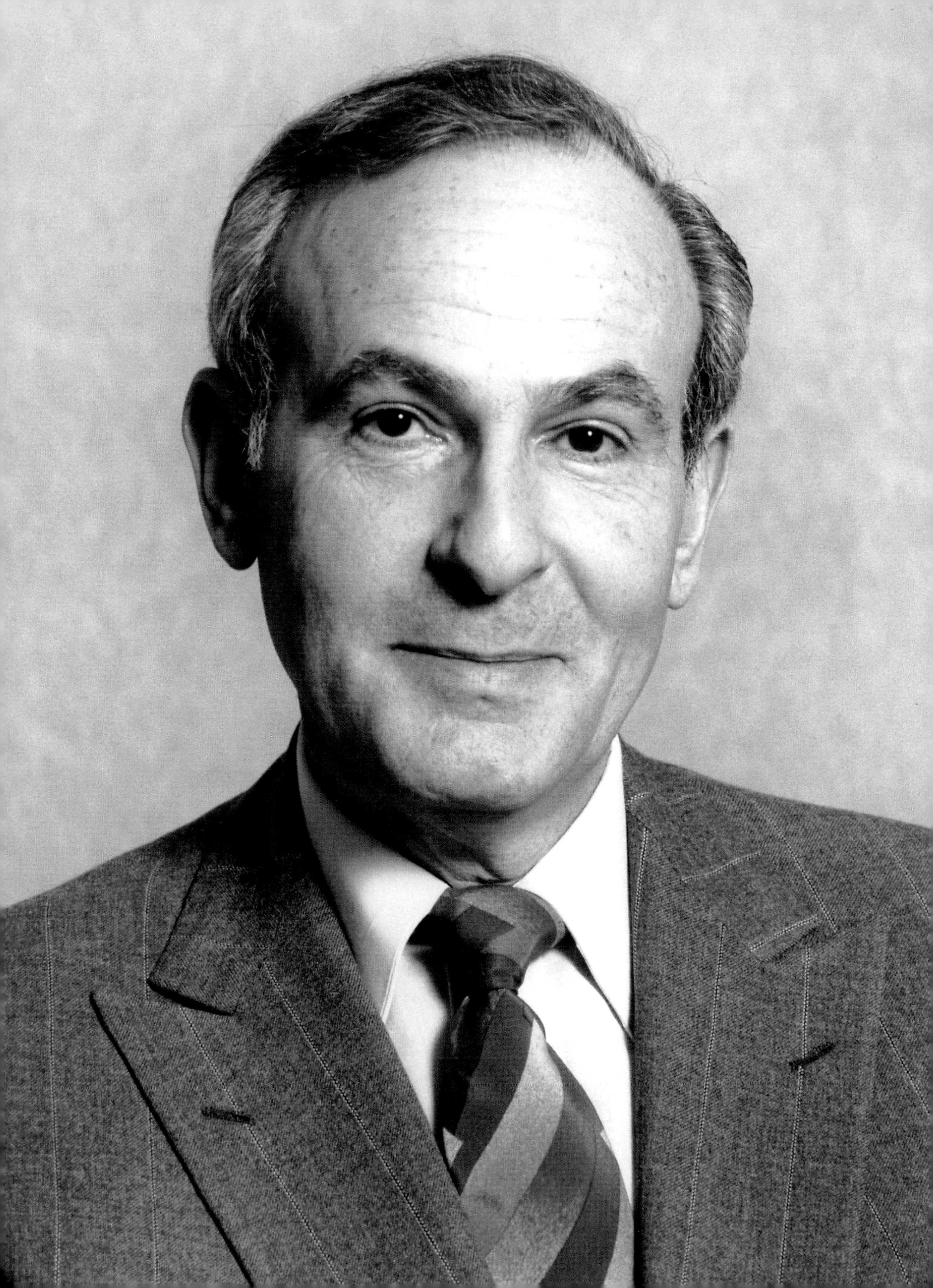

Alan Fortunoff, 1932–2000
Profile of a Collector
Peyton Skipwith

Alan Fortunoff, a second-generation New Yorker, was a cultured and sensitive man with a love of nineteenth-century English literature and a serious interest in British art of the late nineteenth and early twentieth-century. His father, Max, had emigrated from Russia as an eight-year-old to join two older siblings in the New World. Like many such Jewish émigré families the Fortunoff brothers started trading in a modest way, gradually prospering and, by degrees, opening several small specialist stores in Brooklyn selling hardware, household-goods, jewellery, gifts etc., thus Alan was born into the retail business, starting at an early age sweeping the floor and assisting customers at his parents' store in Livonia Avenue under the elevated railway. However, as a boy he did not enjoy good health, and was frequently confined to bed and it was at this period he discovered such authors as Dickens, Wilkie Collins, Herman Melville and, of course, Mark Twain. Interest in literature led naturally to an interest in those artists who had illustrated his favourite novels, but in parallel he also developed a fascination for nineteenth-century design with Owen Jones' *Grammar of Ornament* as a seminal text. Copies of this and others of Jones' magnificently illustrated books, along with works by the Audsleys, Christopher Dresser and Viollet-le-Duc were included in the sale of his books at Bloomsbury Auctions in June last year.

In many ways the story of the Fortunoffs in New York epitomises 'the American Dream' that inspired so many displaced and impoverished peoples who arrived in the New World with few worldly possessions, but, equally, unencumbered by the prejudices and cultural baggage of the Old World that they had left behind. In the early 1950s Alan got an undergraduate degree at New York University in business studies, going on to take a law degree and following this some years later with an advanced degree in international law, all at NYU. By 1964, conscious that many of their customers were moving from the inner city to the suburbs of Long Island, Alan was instrumental in merging the nine small stores into a single business and relocating to Westbury on Long Island. Later, he opened additional stores in New Jersey as well as the flagship store on Manhattan's prestigious Fifth Avenue. Although he obviously thrived on the organisational challenge of all this activity and involved himself personally in every aspect of the store's business, his daughter Andrea feels that it did not challenge him sufficiently either intellectually or aesthetically, which was why, in the mid 1970s, he drove himself to get his masters' degree in Jurisprudence despite already having a Doctor of Law degree, and also why his art collection became so important to him.

I first met Alan in January 1970 when he bought several works from The Fine Art Society, including his first Southall, *Fisherman and Boat* , (cat.no.19) as well as an austere male portrait by Gerald Brockhurst, both artists whose work was to become central to his collection. Early the following year he bought Southall's *Camogli* (cat.no.21) as well as works by Charles and Margaret Gere and Maxwell Armfield, fellow-members with Southall of the Birmingham Group, who had first exhibited together at The Fine Art Society in 1907; in addition he purchased two works by Cayley Robinson, including *Lesson Time* (fig.1). He was back in London at the end of August with his wife, Helene, when he added further works by Southall and Armfield's *Pacific Portrait* to his burgeoning collection. On this occasion his

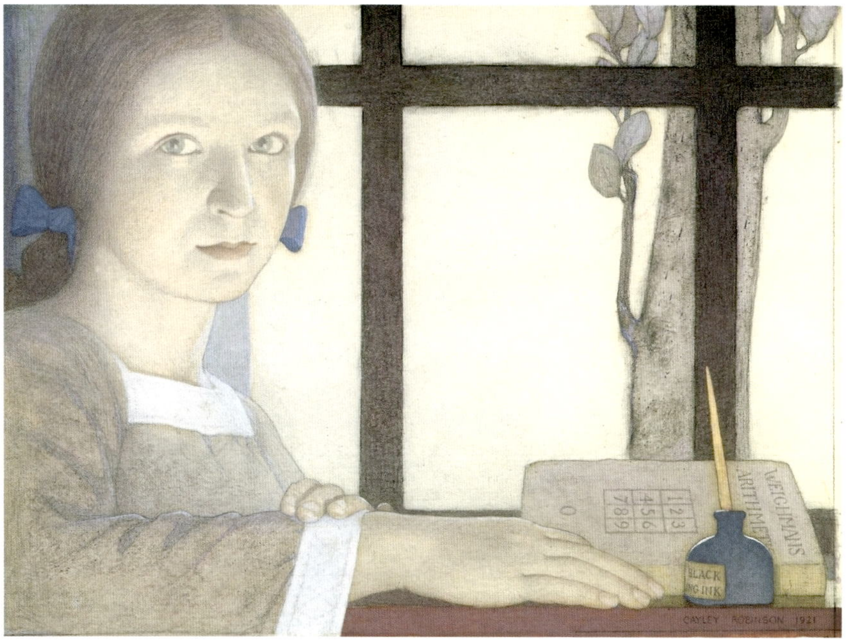

Fig. 1. Frederic Cayley Robinson, 1862–1927
Lesson Time
Watercolour over pencil, 10 x 13 1/2 (25.4 x 34.3)
The Fine Art Society

and Helene's visit coincided with the bank-holiday and my wife and I took pity on them being stuck in London at a time when all English businesses were firmly closed. Our pity was misplaced. Helene, who had by then built up the antique jewellery side of Fortunoff's, told us at dinner that she had arranged for various suppliers to open specially, and had made several-hundred purchases. A lasting friendship developed alongside the shared interest in the works of particular artists, and I became aware of the rhythm which dictated the timing of their visits to London; these always coincided with trade-fairs either in the UK or Italy. With a growing family at home, Alan was frequently on his own but always with a busy schedule; a pattern developed over time and I would always entertain him to lunch in London, and he would entertain me to dinner in New York. In addition to art he loved good food and fine wine. Indeed, he not only collected wine, but, much against his son David's instincts, set up a wine business as an adjunct to Fortunoff's. That first dinner had been at Bianchi's, an old-fashioned, first-floor, Italian restaurant in Soho, where Logie Baird had demonstrated television. Later the Tate Gallery's restaurant, with its excellent wine-list became a favourite, along with Langan's. I acquired a wholly undeserved reputation for *sang froid* when, on a visit to the latter, we were offered complimentary drinks due to a bomb-scare; Alan suggested we should go elsewhere but I pointed out that we would not be allowed to leave the restaurant as the street had been sealed off, and accepted the offer.

Style and clarity, often coupled with a sense of sophisticated innocence, informed the background to Alan's aesthetic taste. Style was, of course, the hallmark of works such as Owen Jones' *Grammar of Ornament* and Dresser's *Studies in Design*, both clearly laid out and beautifully printed by the chromolithographic process, which had been perfected in the mid-nineteenth century. The extra dimension of sophisticated innocence was reflected in the works of Joseph Southall, Harry Epworth Allen, Maxwell Armfield, Gerald Brockhurst, C.R.W. Nevinson, Ethelbert White and the engravings of Eric Gill, Paul Nash and Buckland Wright, which formed the core of his collection. All artists whose work had a kinship with the great American regional painters and illustrators such as Grant Wood, Andrew Wyeth and Maxfield Parish. Indeed, Maxwell Armfield had spent the years from 1916 to 1921 in America and had lectured in New York on the techniques of tempera painting, before moving to California, so there was a

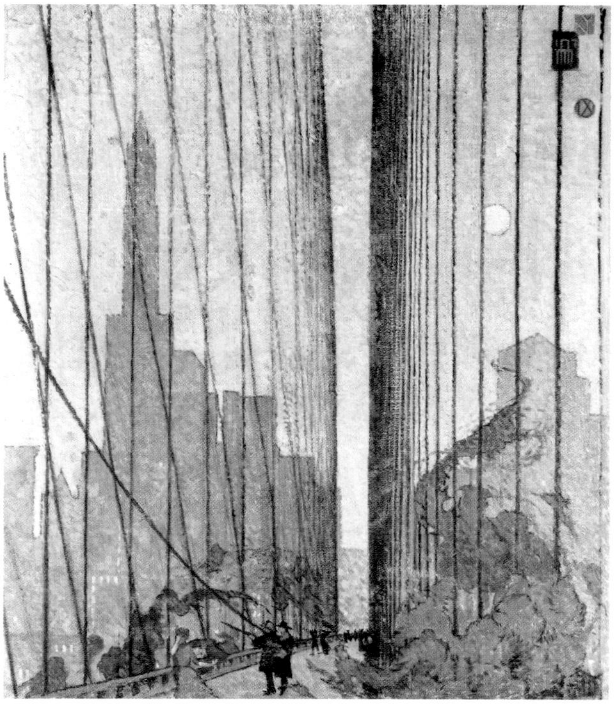

Fig. 2. Maxwell Armfield, 1882–1972
Brooklyn Bridge
Oil on canvas, 34 x 30 (86.4 x 76.2)
Private Collection

direct link between Southall's Birmingham and the United States. Armfield's great oil painting of Brooklyn Bridge (fig.2) hung prominently in the Fortunoffs' art-deco New York apartment, flanked by two large and stylish works by William Strang (fig.3). Laurence Binyon, writing in the introduction to one of Strang's memorial exhibition catalogues, noted that 'something of the ugliness of all his [Strang's] sitters shows through the beauty of his draughtsmanship', and it was this quality of uncompromising, puritanical directness which appealed to Alan and provided the link between the works in the Fortunoff collection and made Alan's selection of them so personal.

Over the years, as my own family needs dictated, our shared enthusiasms led to four works from my collection passing through The Fine Art Society into the Fortunoff Collection: Southall's *Coral Necklace* (cat.no.2), Mark Gertler's *Homage to Roger Fry*, and two works by Nevinson, *Night Club, Marseilles*, which had previously belonged to Ethelbert White, and a pen and chalk drawing for *Column on the March*. Southall, Nevinson and Brockhurst were probably the three artists Alan most admired. The Fitzwilliam

Museum, Cambridge, was the recipient of a gift of a substantial group of Brockhurst etchings, whilst at one time or another he owned several of Nevinson's greatest paintings including *On the Road to Ypres* and *Aerial View (from a Paris Plane)*, but the one that probably resonated most strongly for personal reasons was a New York scene – the *Third Avenue, Elevated Railway* – which he must have linked with the Livonia Avenue store where he started his working life. Like most serious collectors, Alan parted with works either to fund or make room for other acquisitions. Not even Southall was exempt: *On the Beach* and *Lady in a Green hat*, both of which were lent by the Fortunoffs to the 1980 exhibition, were de-acquisitioned in the intervening years. *Lady in a Green Hat* was based on the pencil study of Janet Hutchinson – later Lady Ilford – (cat.no.41), who was also the dedicatee of Southall's lithographic self-portrait (cat.no.14); all three works dating from 1918.

Alan's collecting ranged wider than art, books and wines; on several occasions I had calls from him asking me to look at, and bid on, vintage cameras coming up for sale at Christie's South Kensington. These were not

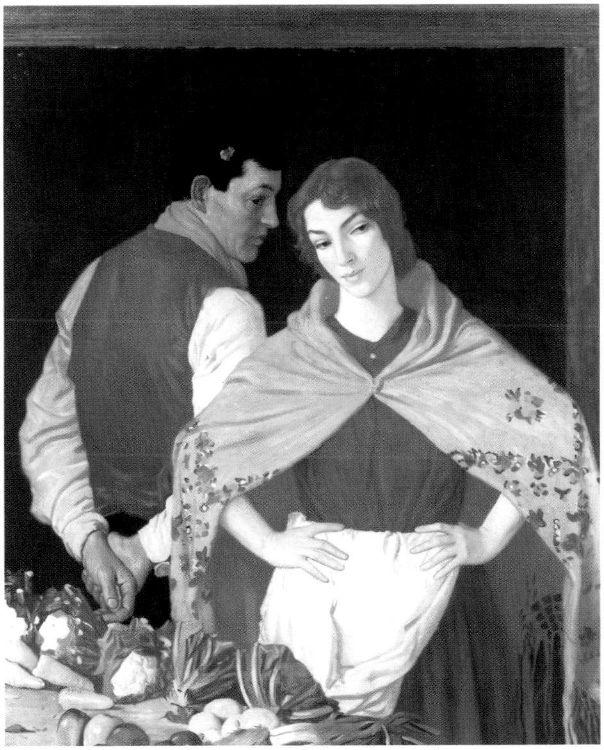

Fig. 3. William Strang, 1859–1921
The Listener
Oil on canvas, 45 x 39 (114.3 x 99)
Private Collection

for decoration but for use; they had to be in good working order; Alan was a fine and exacting photographer, who appreciated the varied quality of image and print that could be obtained by the use of different apparatuses. The landscape studies he made whilst hiking, usually with one of his sons, in the great unspoilt open spaces – those glories of of the North American continent – reveal another side of Alan's love of art and that was his appreciation of nature, they also reveal him as an artist in his own right. His love of nature also found an outlet nearer home with his active involvement in the preservation of the Old Westbury Gardens.

True collectors are rare. Collecting is a passion involving many sacrifices; whilst money is useful, what is more important is that special combination of heart and eye. Alan Fortunoff possessed that combination and the collection of Joseph Southall's work, which he made will probably never be equalled; whilst his and Helene's names will appear in the provenance of many works of art, no future literature concerned with Southall and the Birmingham School will be complete without mention of the Fortunoff Collection.

Opposite cat.no.6. Cleaning the lines, 1900 (detail)

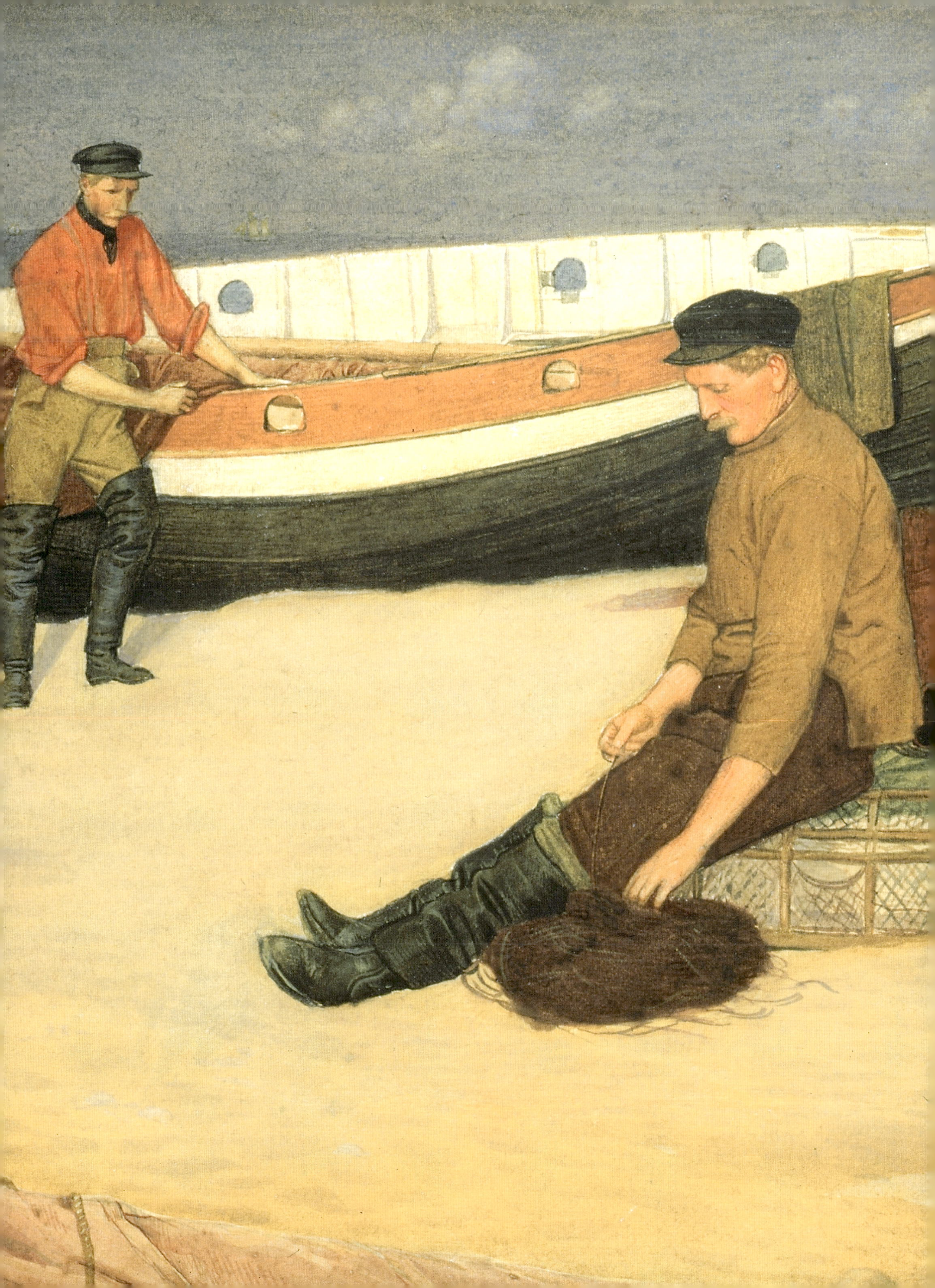

Notes on the Catalogue

Sizes are given in inches and (centimetres), height preceding width.
All works are for sale unless otherwise stated.
Copyright strictly reserved in all cases.

Southall's dating: It was normal Quaker practice in Southall's day to use Roman numerals rather than the names of the month when writing a date and to call a month by its number rather than its name. Southall invariably followed this practice.

With regard to the studies, (catalogue numbers 28–60), the titles used here are modern. The provenance for all studies marked with an asterisk after the number is: Estate of Mrs AE Southall: Mrs Elizabeth Baker: The Fine Art Society: Mr & Mrs Alan Fortunoff. Mrs Elizabeth Baker was married to the artist's nephew, Edward Martin Baker (known as Ned), who inherited much of Southall's widow's estate, where it did not pass through the sale rooms.

Abbreviations

ACES: Arts and Crafts Exhibition Society
Aldeburgh, 1981: Refers to the exhibition 'Southall in Suffolk' organised by The Fine Art Society for the Aldeburgh Festival, 1981.
Birmingham & FAS, 1980: Refers to the exhibition and catalogue 'Joseph Southall, 1861–1944: Artist Craftsman', City Museum & Art Gallery, Birmingham, 8 August – 30 September and at The Fine Art Society, London, 14 October – 7 November, 1980.
ILP: Independent Labour Party
RA: Royal Academy
RBSA: Royal Birmingham Society of Artists.
RWS: Royal Society of Painters in Watercolour

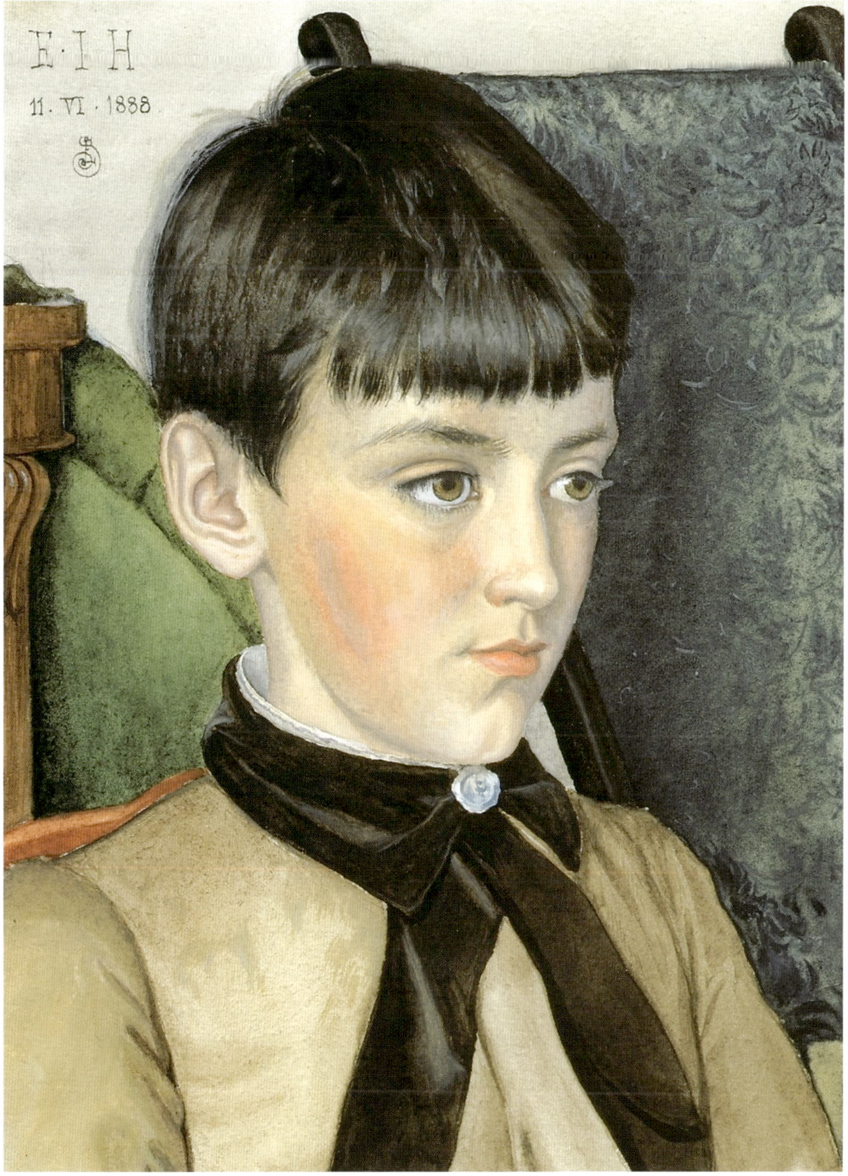

1. Portrait of Isabella Harlock, 1888
Watercolour & bodycolour, 8 3/4 x 6 1/2 (22.2 x 16.5)
Signed in early form of monogram, inscribed *E.I.H.* & dated (twice) *II.VI.1888* (tl & br)

Provenance: Bourne Fine Art: The Fine Art Society:
Mr & Mrs Alan Fortunoff

The sitter was a relation of Southall's future wife, Anna Elizabeth Baker.

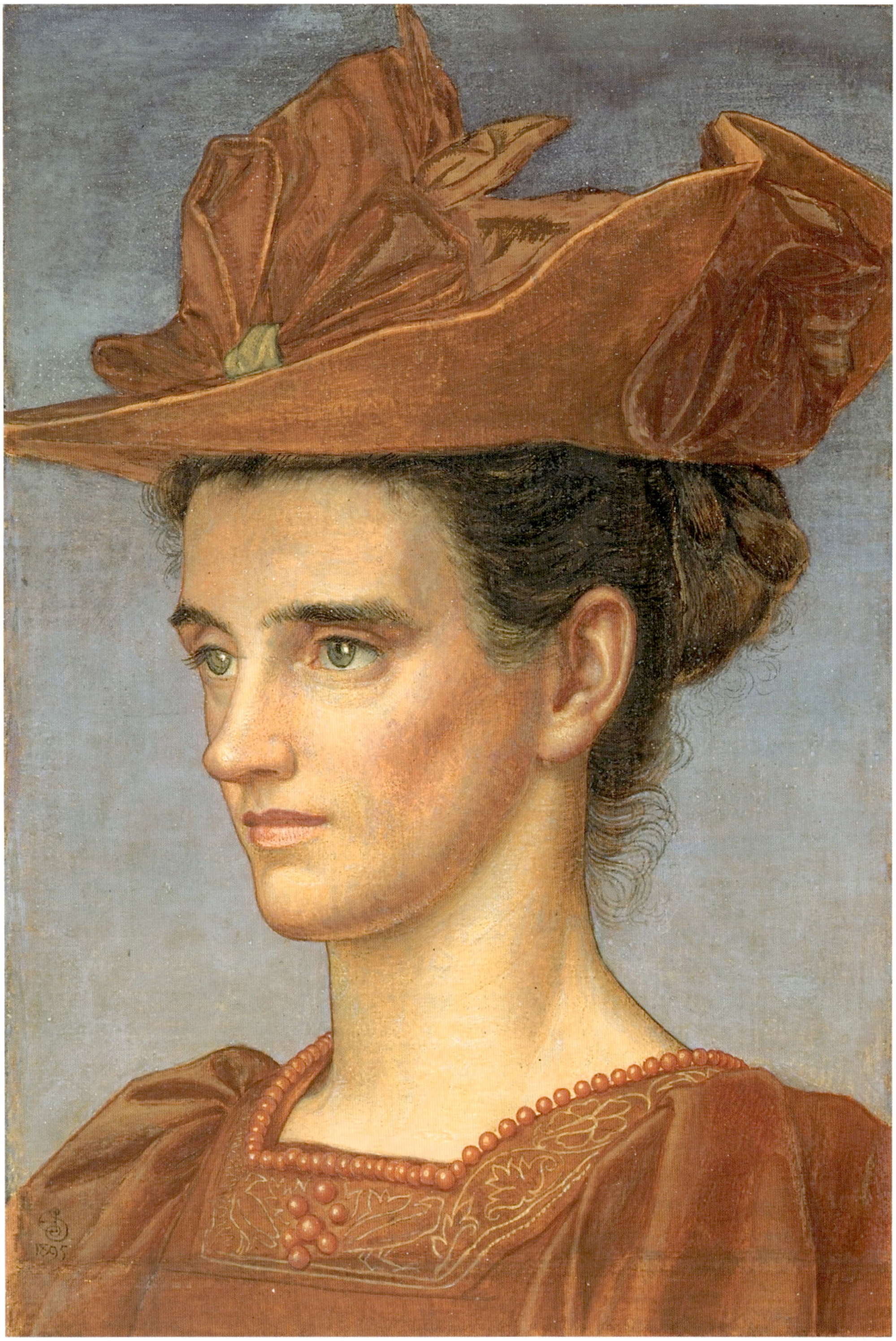

2. The Coral Necklace, 1895

Tempera on panel, 11 1/2 x 8 3/4 (29.5 x 22.1)
Signed in monogram & dated *1895* (bl), and inscribed around the edge *Yolk tempera colour begun 29.IX.1894 Almost finished XII.1894 Antiseptic on this corner of sky* and (on far sleeve) *30.XII.1897. Gesso never smoothed I think JES V.'05.* Other inscriptions are partly obscured by paint layer. Inscribed (verso): Experiments with colour and medium as used in this portrait, with comprehensive colour notes, painted with strips of colour used, and notes on technique.

Provenance: Peyton Skipwith: The Fine Art Society: Mr & Mrs Alan Fortunoff

Exhibited: Birmingham & FAS, 1980 (E8)
This is a portrait of the artist's first cousin and future wife, Anna Elizabeth Baker (1859–1947).

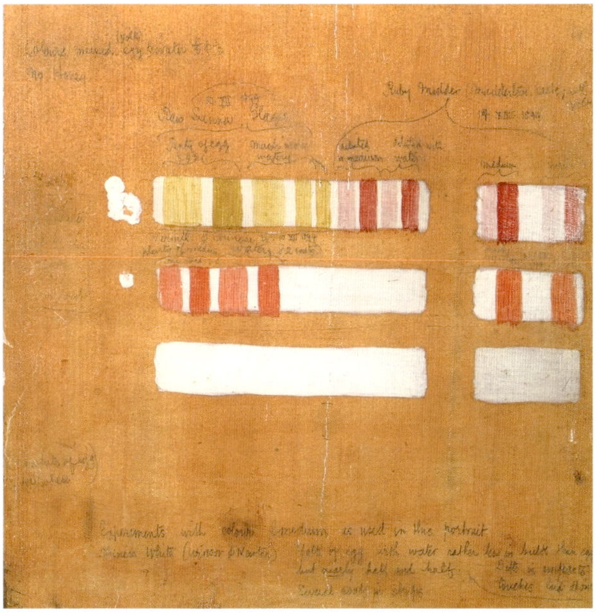

The painting is a major document of Southall's working methods: nothing else in his output contains so many notes inscribed on the work of art itself. In this documentation he was following the practice of the Pre-Raphaelite painters. For example Holman Hunt provided similar strips of colour, with notes on them and his technique, in the spaces to left and right of the painted arched top of his picture *The Two Gentlemen of Verona* (1851) (Birmingham Museum & Art Gallery).

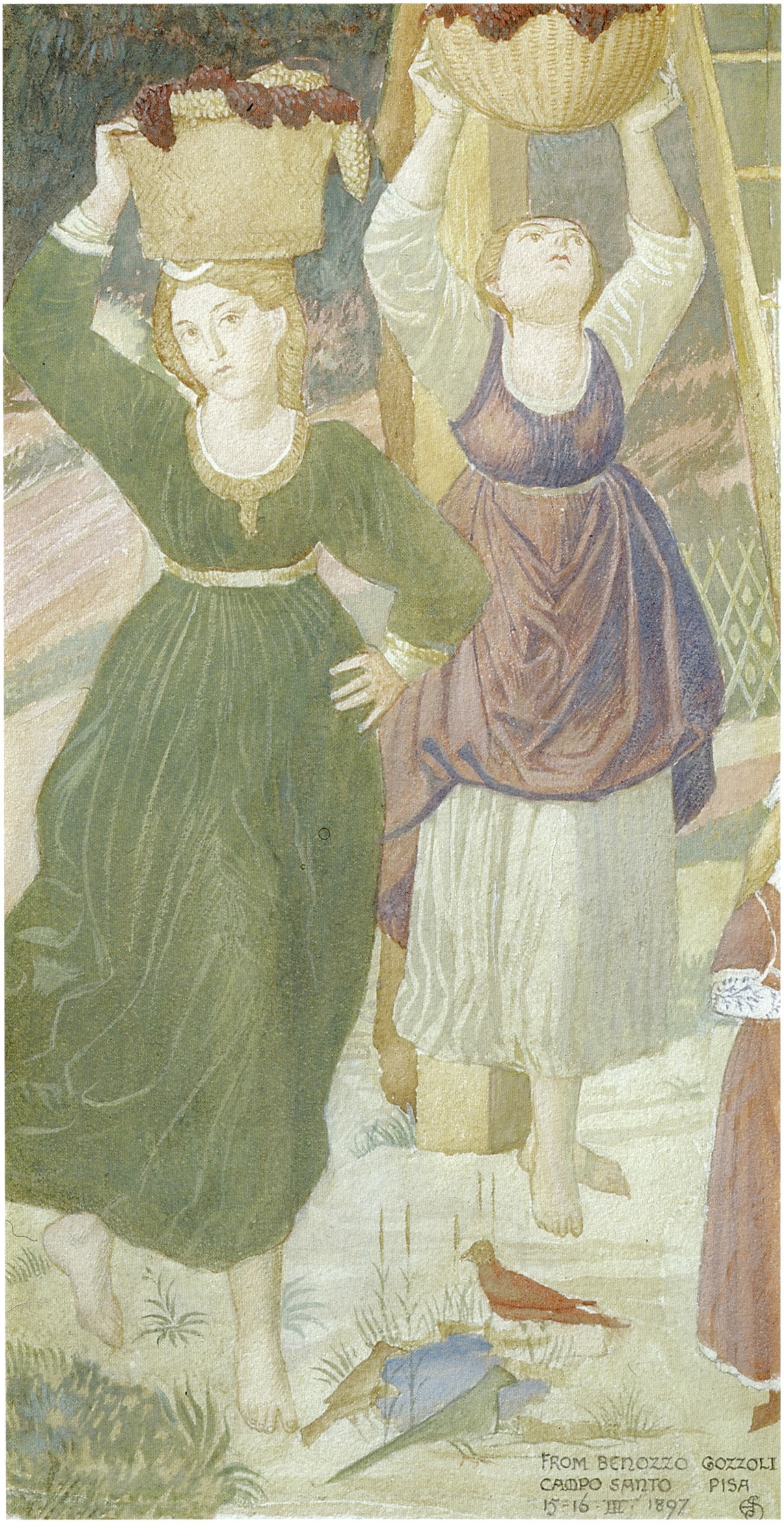
FROM BENOZZO GOZZOLI
CAMPO SANTO PISA
15-16 · III · 1897

3. From Benozzo Gozzoli, Pisa, 1897

Watercolour over pencil, 10 1/8 x 5 3/4 (25.7 x 14.5)
Signed in monogram & inscribed
FROM BENOZZO GOZZOLI/CAMPO SANTO PISA/15–16.III.1897

Provenance: Mrs A E Southall, sale of her estate, Edwards, Son & Bigwood & Mathews, Birmingham (23 Mar. 1948, lot 247): The Fine Art Society: Mr & Mrs Alan Fortunoff

This detail from the frescoes in the Campo Santo at Pisa comes from the far left of Benozzo Gozzoli's depiction of the vintage and drunkenness of Noah. Gozzoli (1421–1497) executed this fresco between 1469 and 1484; it is one of 23 scenes from the Old Testament carried out here by the artist, completing a series that had been incomplete since the previous century. The frescoes were badly damaged in 1944 when a shell set the building on fire, causing the lead on the roof to melt and run down the frescoed walls.

In an article for The Friend's Quarterly Examiner, written many years later, Southall recalled the thrill of his first visit to Pisa, at the age of twenty-one: 'Never can I forget the thrill of joy which I experienced when, without any knowledge of what I was about to see, I stepped inside the enchanting cloisters of the great Campo Santo of Pisa. There I found myself at 21 years of age face to face with a vast series of frescoes, so quiet and yet so gay, so reticent in manner and so lively in essence that words must ever fail to convey even the faintest expression of what I felt. Here we have hundreds of feet of wall twenty-five feet high covered all over with the work of the early Italian masters from the scholars of Giotto onward – culminating in the great series of Biblical histories by the pupil of Angelico, Benozzo Gozzoli, who with his pupils, worked for fourteen years consecutively to make this last resting place of the dead as full of life as art could make it. For, after all, the value of these histories is not in their chronology but in their lessons to us as human beings of whatever race.' (Friend's Quarterly Examiner, No.234, Fourth Month, 1925, pp.142–3)

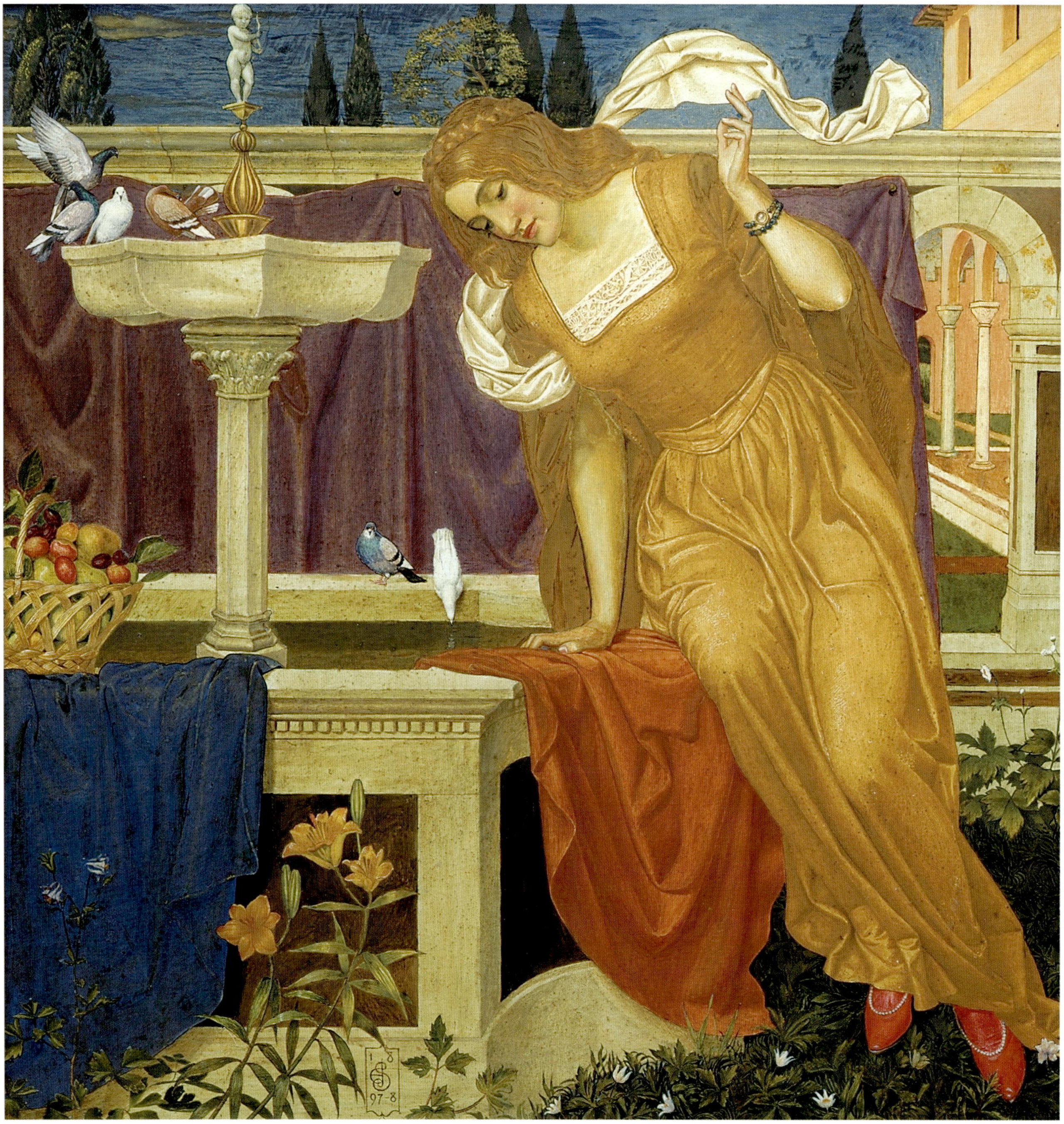

4. Beauty Seeing the Image of Her Home in the Fountain (Beauty at the Fountain), 1897 8

Tempera on wood panel, 18 3/4 x 18 1/2 (47.5 x 47.0)
Signed in monogram & dated *18/97–8* (bc)

Provenance: Bought New Gallery, 1898 by Laurence Hodson: by descent (with Lillian Hodson, 1929): Christie's, London (6 Nov. 1992, lot 5): The Fine Art Society: Mr & Mrs Alan Fortunoff

Exhibited: London, New Gallery, *Summer Exhibition*, 1898 (290); London, Leighton House, *Modern Paintings in Tempera*, 1901 (13); Wolverhampton, *Art & Industrial Exhibition*, 1902 (116); Paris, Galeries Georges Petit, *Joseph Southall*, 1910 (6); Birmingham & FAS, 1980 (B3)

Literature: The Studio, vol. xxiii, 1901, p. 158, repr. p.160

Beauty and the Beast was the folk tale most illustrated by Southall. The artist's notes record an (untraced) painting in oils of *Beauty and Her Father in the Beast's Palace* (1894). A large painting of *Beauty Receiving the White Rose From Her Father* (1898–9) (Birmingham Museum & Art Gallery) depicts an earlier episode while this painting here is of a later one. Southall's closest friend, Arthur Gaskin, had illustrated the fable for Baring-Gould's *Book of Fairy Tales* in 1894.

Both the shape of the panel and the design of the frame are unusual for one of Southall's works. From manuscript notes (private colln.) it seems likely that the artist found the frame in Italy and then created a panel to match. Be that as it may, this is surely the most outstanding painting in the Fortunoff collection, highly constructed and finished, and a *tour de force* in both its colouring and decorative effect.

Southall discussed the painting with Sir Edward Burne-Jones on 24 November 1897 (manuscript note, private collection.): 'Went to lunch with EB-J again and took Beauty at the Fountain a good way towards completion. Philip B-J was there. He EB-J did not quite like the face but admired the rest very much & said the red drapery she sits upon was "a heavenly red" – liked "the little chap" on the fountain and the pigeons very much also her hands and arms he praised most warmly & the jewel on bracelet.'

The lace on Beauty's bodice is very close to a design for Greek Lace by Southall (Cheltenham Art Gallery & Museum, inv. no.1987.113r, with thanks to Mary Greensted and Sophia Wilson).

Cheltenham Art Gallery & Museum (Margaret Bellwood Bequest) purchased with the generous assistance of the National Art-Collections Fund, 2004

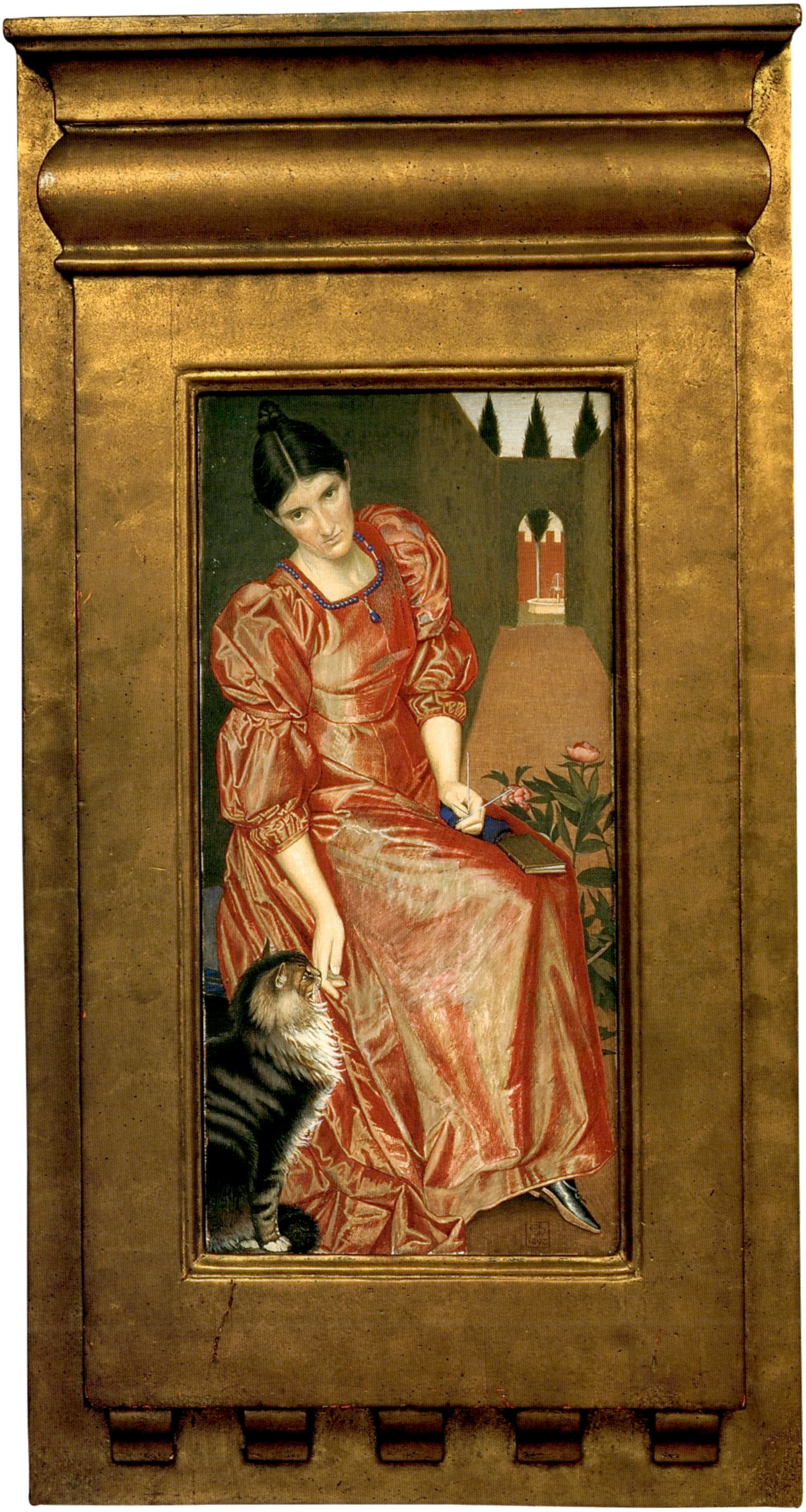

5. Hortus Inclusus, 1898

Watercolour on vellum, 17 x 8 1/2 (43.0 x 21.4)
Signed in monogram & dated *1898* (br) and inscribed with the title and date on the top fold over edge of the vellum

Provenance: The Estate of Mrs A E Southall: Mrs Elizabeth Baker: Sotheby's Belgravia (5 Nov 1974, lot 46): The Fine Art Society: Mr & Mrs Alan Fortunoff

Exhibited: London, New Gallery, *Summer Exhibition*, 1905 (48): Liverpool, *Autumn Exhibition*, 1905 (493): Bradford, *Spring Exhibition*, 1906 (21): Paris, Galeries Georges Petit, *Joseph Southall*, 1910 (19): Birmingham, RBSA, *Joseph Southall*, 1933 (44): Dudley, *Joseph Southall*, 1934 (30): Birmingham; London, RWS & Bournemouth, *Memorial Exhibition*, 1945 (54): Birmingham & FAS, 1980 (E10)

This exquisitely rich watercolour depicts Southall's future wife and the cat, Colin. *Hortus Inclusus* or 'Garden Enclosed' was a popular Renaissance subject, where the private garden, particularly that belonging to a prince, was overlaid with complex symbolic significance.

Anna Elizabeth Baker records in a note book (private collection.) that it took eighty two hours from December 1899 to March 1900 to apply the gesso, gild and burnish the 'Frame for Joe for portrait of myself and Colin', at a total cost of £2/2s./6d, (£2.12 1/2p) including the gold leaf. (See *Joseph Southall, 1861–1944: Artist-Craftsman*, Birmingham, 1980, p.58, for details.)

Cheltenham Art Gallery & Museum (Margaret Bellwood Bequest) purchased with the generous assistance of the MLA/V&A Purchase Grant Fund and the National Art-Collections Fund, 2004

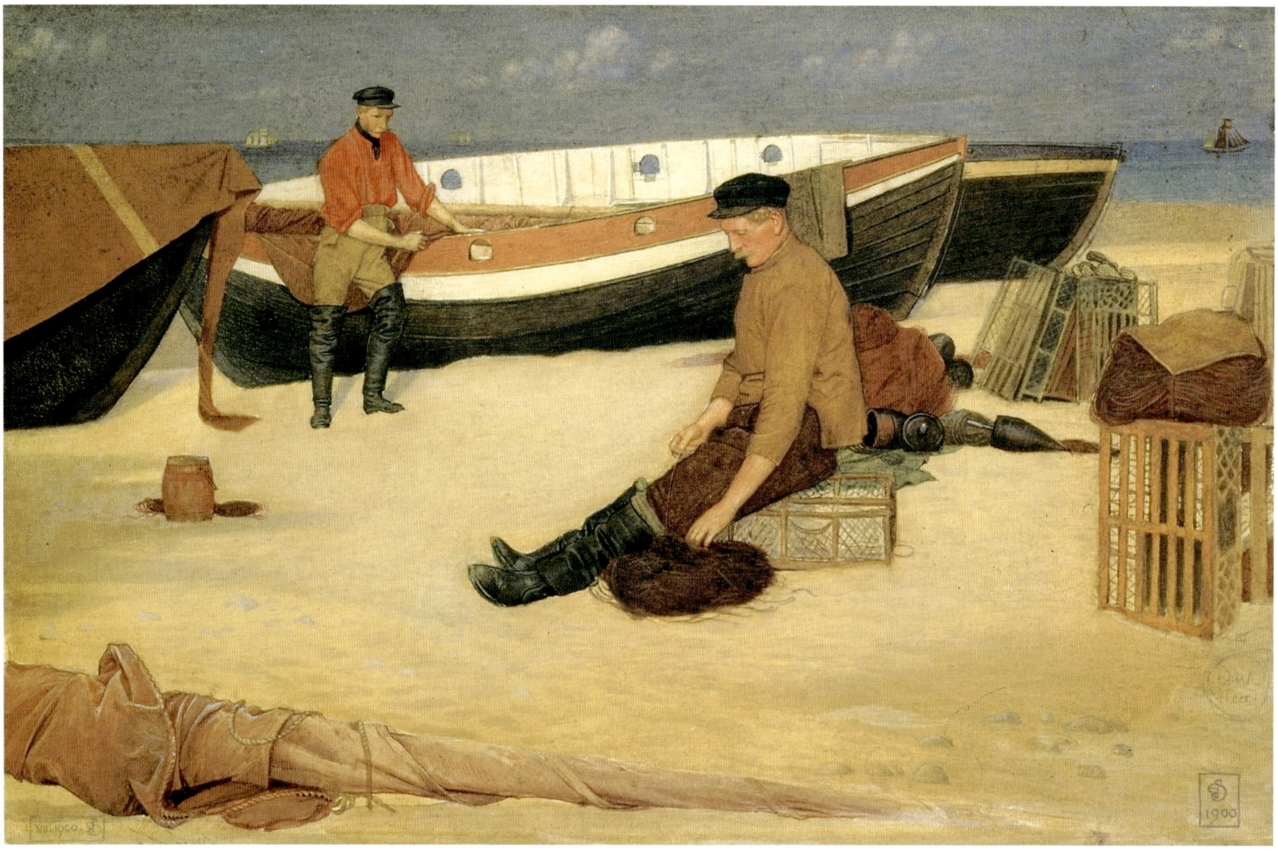

6. Cleaning the Lines, 1900

Watercolour, 8 3/4 x 13 3/4 (22.4 x 35.1)
Signed in monogram & dated *VII.1900* (bl) and again *1900* (br).
Annotated *Dark / here* (lr) and inscribed (verso) *Formalin 9.IX.1933*

Provenance: Maxwell Armfield, RWS: Alexander Ballard: The Fine Art Society: Mr & Mrs Alan Fortunoff

Exhibited: Birmingham, Art Circle, *Summer Exhibition*, 1900 (51): Birmingham, RBSA, *Autumn Exhibition*, 1901 (367): Birmingham, RBSA, *Spring Exhibition*, 1908 (296): Paris, Galeries Georges Petit, *Joseph Southall*, 1910 (14): London, NEAC, *Summer Exhibition*, 1918 (180): Birmingham, RBSA, *A Birmingham Group*. 1919 (87): London, Alpine Club Gallery, *Joseph Southall*, 1922 (10): Manchester, *Joseph Southall*, 1922 (37): London, Leicester Galleries, *Joseph Southall*, 1926 (108): Birmingham, Ruskin Galleries, *Joseph Southall*, 1927 (18): Birmingham, RBSA, *Joseph Southall*, 1933 (67): Dudley, *Joseph Southall*, 1934 (32): possibly West Bromwich, 1937: Birmingham; London, RWS and Bournemouth, *Memorial Exhibition*, 1945 (51): FAS, *The Arts and Crafts Movement*, 1973 (P117): Birmingham & FAS, 1980 (F1)

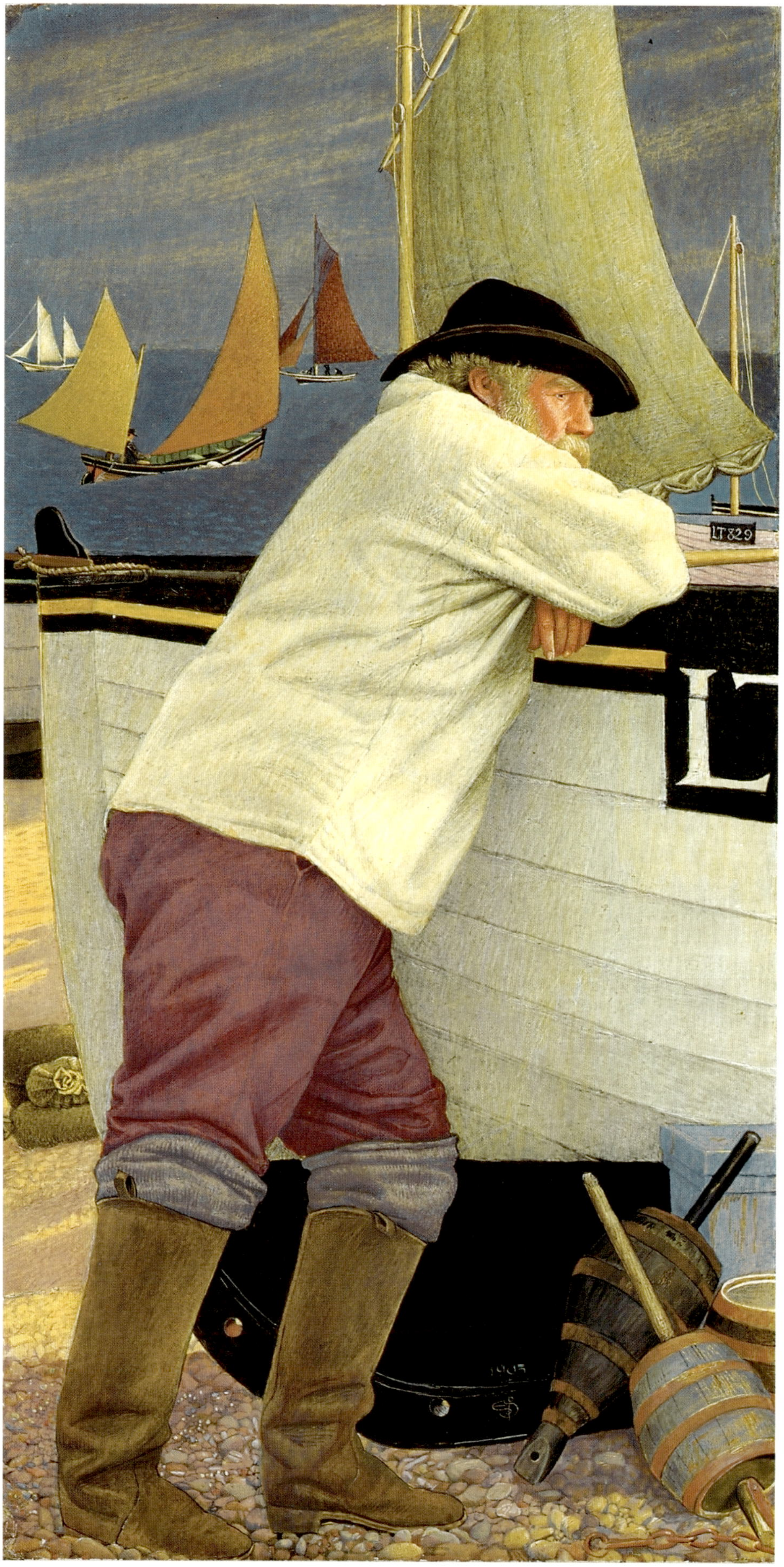
LT829

7. The Old Fisherman, 1903

Tempera on card, 15 x 8 (38.1 x 20.3)
Signed in monogram & dated *1903* on the keel of the boat

Provenance: Arthur Gaskin (1909) and by descent: Sotheby's, London (11 Oct. 1989, lot 119): The Fine Art Society: Mr & Mrs Alan Fortunoff

Exhibited: London, New Gallery, *Summer Exhibition*, 1904 (268): Manchester, Manchester Academy of Fine Arts, *Autumn Exhibition*, 1904 (118): Birmingham, Art Circle, 1905 (14): Stockport, *Spring Exhibition*, 1905 (168): FAS, *Spring '90*, 1990 (33)

Literature: Laurence W. Hodson "The Birmingham Group: Arthur J. Gaskin and Joseph Southall", *Studio*, Vol. Lxxix, 1920, repr. p.9

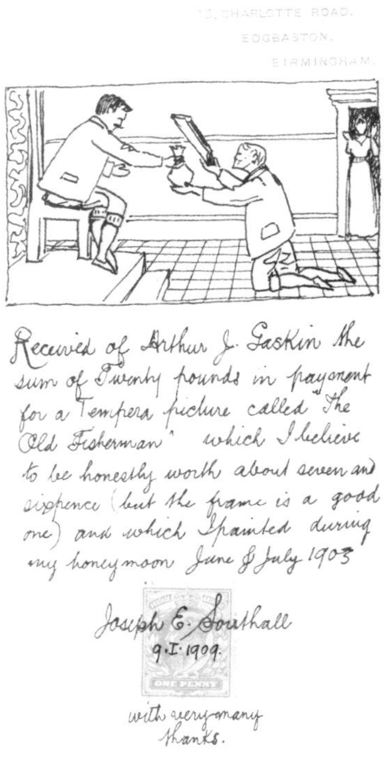

CHARLOTTE ROAD,
EDGBASTON,
BIRMINGHAM.

Received of Arthur J. Gaskin the sum of Twenty pounds in payment for a Tempera picture called "The Old Fisherman" which I believe to be honestly worth about seven and sixpence (but the frame is a good one) and which I painted during my honeymoon June & July 1903

Joseph E. Southall
9.I.1909.

with very many thanks.

Southall's formal receipt dated *9.I.1909* is drawn on his headed notepaper from 13 Charlotte Street, Edgbaston, and depicts an enthroned Arthur Gaskin handing over a bag of money to the supplicant artist, whilst Mrs Southall, with both hands raised with pleasure, watches from the doorway.

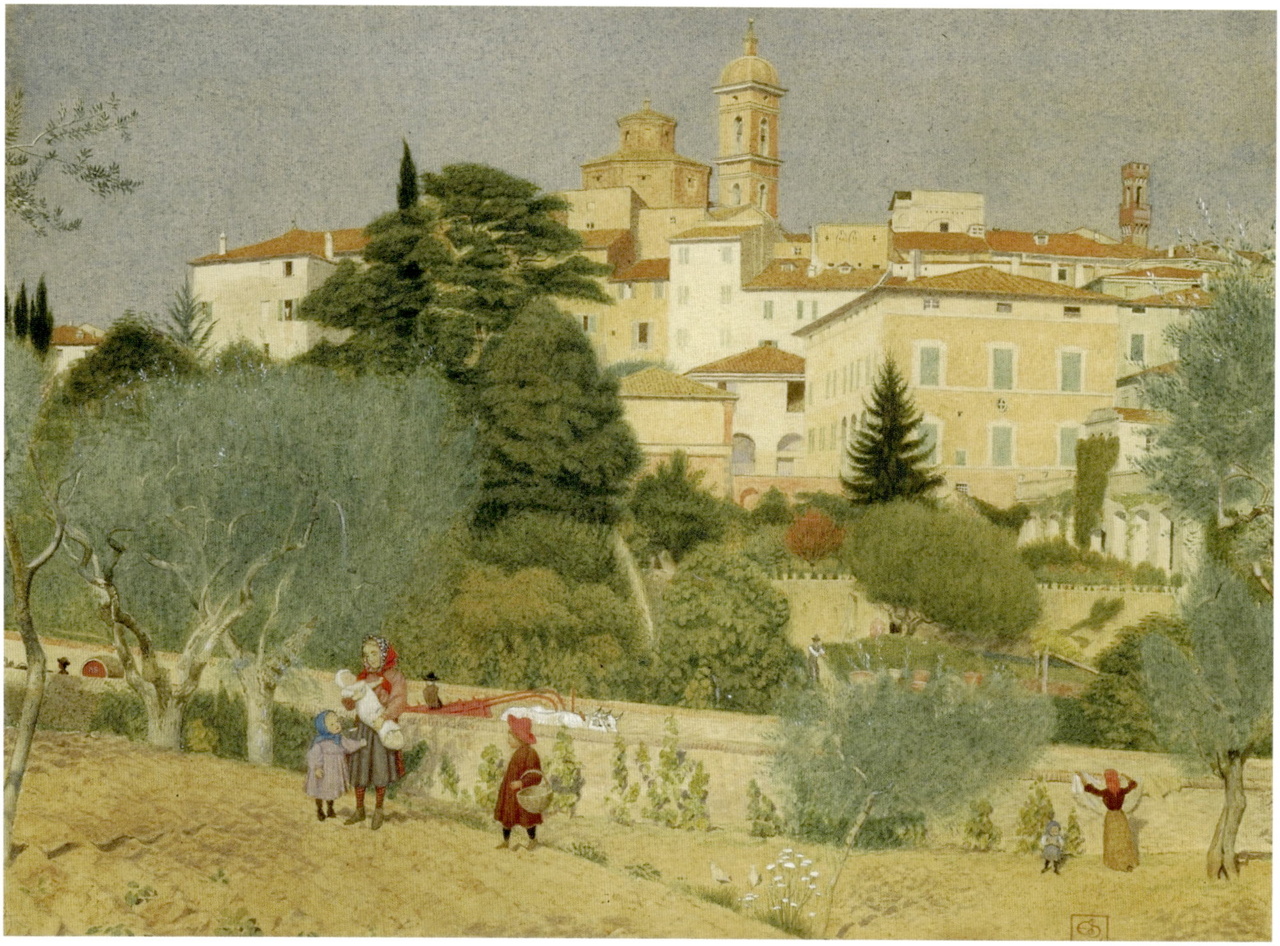

8. In Tuscany, 1906

Watercolour, 11 1/4 x 15 1/2 (28.5 x 39.4)
Signed in monogram & dated *1906* (br)

Provenance: Bought NEAC, 1945, by Miss D Goddard: Sotheby's Belgravia (9 Mar. 1976, lot 37): The Fine Art Society: Mr & Mrs Alan Fortunoff

Exhibited: London, New Gallery, *Summer Exhibition*, 1907 (371): Birmingham, RBSA, *Autumn Exhibition* 1907 (245): Paris, Galeries Georges Petit, *Joseph Southall*, 1910 (27): London, *Coronation Exhibition*, 1911 (79): London, Alpine Club Gallery, *Joseph Southall*, 1922 (14): Manchester, *Joseph Southall*, 1922 (33): Birmingham, Ruskin Galleries, *Joseph Southall*, 1927 (16): Birmingham, RBSA, *Joseph Southall*, 1933 (34): Dudley, *Joseph Southall*, 1934 (23): London, NEAC, *Autumn Exhibition*, 1945 (298): London, RWS and Bournemouth, *Memorial Exhibition*, 1945 (103)

The town depicted is Sinalunga (ESE of Siena and WSW of Cortona) (letter from Mrs Southall to Miss Goddard, 11 November 1945) (private collection.)

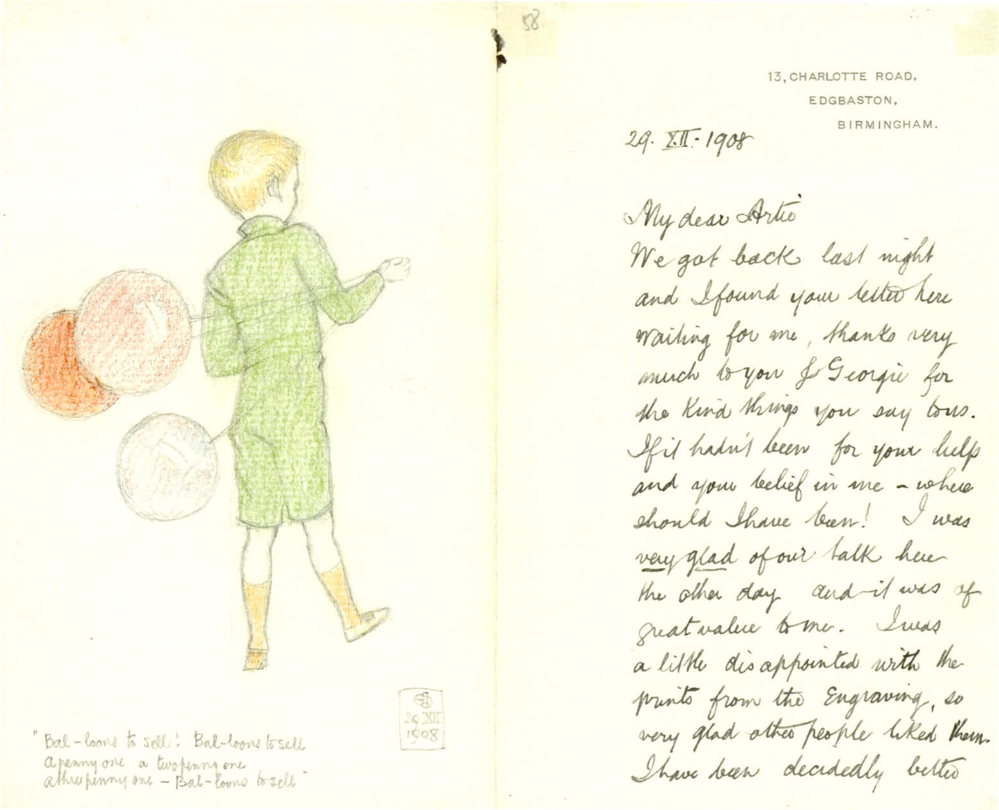

9. Balloons to Sell! – Illustrated Letter to Arthur Gaskin, 1908

Pencil & chalks, the letter in ink, 7 x 8 3/4 (17.8 x 23.4)
The letter (folded sheet), from 13 Charlotte Road, Edgbaston, Birmingham (Southall's home). The illustration signed in monogram, dated *29.XII.1908* (br) and inscribed *"Bal-loons to sell! Bal-loons to sell / a penny one a tuppeny one / a threepenny one – Bal-loons to sell"* (ll)

Provenance: Arthur Gaskin, to whom sent: by descent through his daughter, Joscelyne Charlewood-Turner; Sotheby's, London (19 Jul. 1989, lot 83): The Fine Art Society: Mr & Mrs Alan Fortunoff

Exhibited: Birmingham & FAS, 1980 (E25(i))

Southall begins the letter thanking the Gaskins for "the kind things you say to us. If it hadn't been for your help and your belief in me – where should I have been!" He goes on to discuss other matters – weather, friends, a possible commission and a recent visit to relatives in Croydon – ending: "Here is a little sketch of my little Allen nephew at Croydon marching round the dining room chanting his little musical chant 'balloons to sell' – If only I could paint him!!"

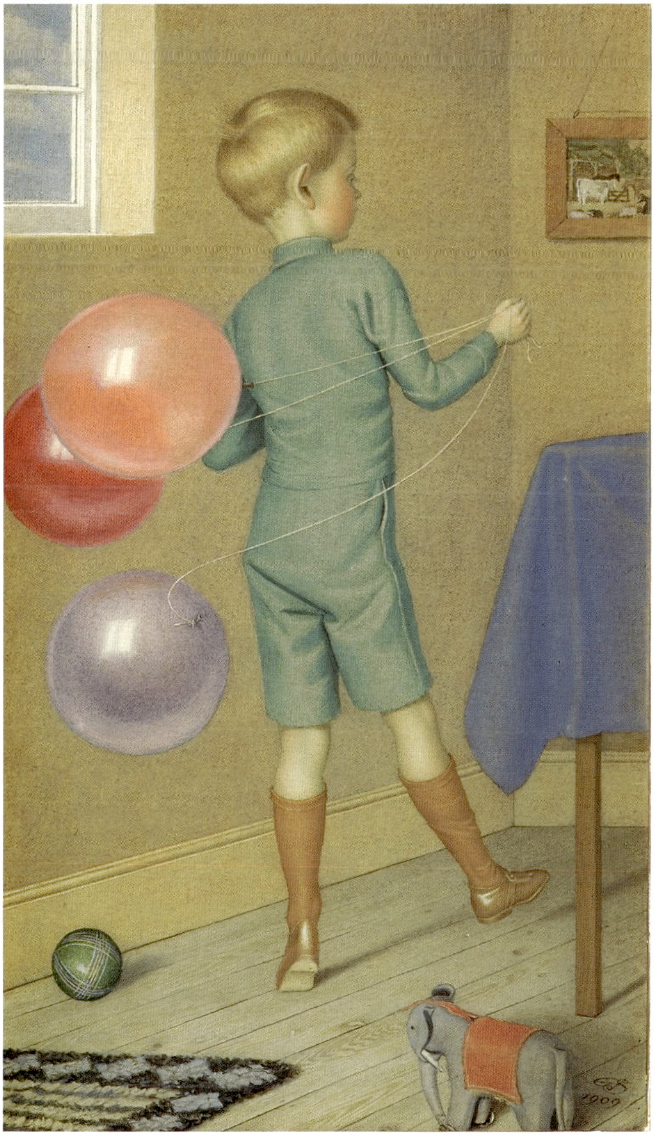

10. Balloons to Sell!, 1909
Tempera on paper, 19 1/4 x 11 1/4 (48.8 x 28.6)
Signed in monogram & dated *1909*, (br)

Provenance: Mrs A E Southall, sale of her estate, Edwards, Birmingham (23 Mar. 1948, lot 139): Miss Enid Allen: Julian Hartnoll: The Fine Art Society: Mr & Mrs Alan Fortunoff

Exhibited: Paris, Galeries Georges Petit, *Joseph Southall*, 1910 (15): Birmingham, Art Circle, *Summer Exhibition*, 1910 (17): Birmingham, London, RWS and Bournemouth, *Memorial Exhibition*, 1945 (57): Birmingham & FAS 1980 (E25)

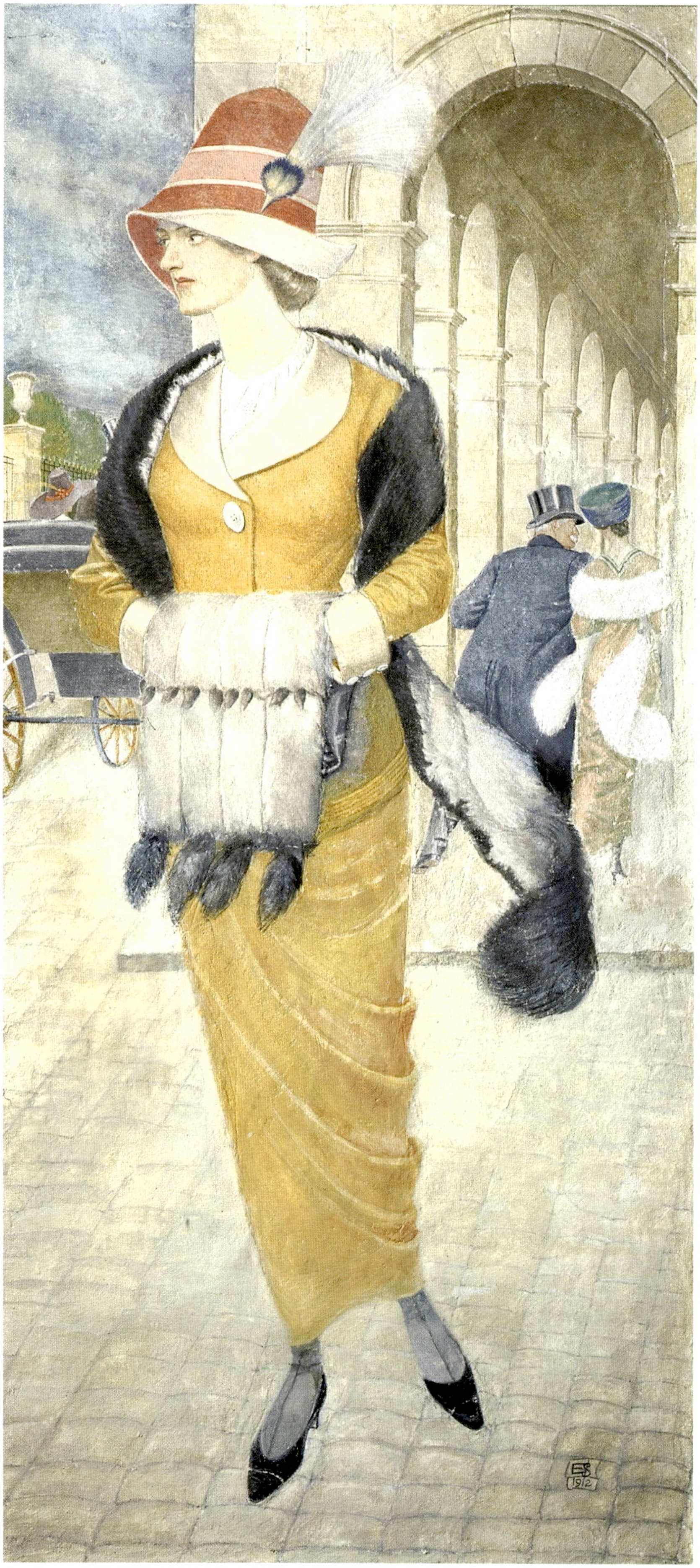

11. In the Rue de Rivoli, 1912

Buonfresco, 48 x 22 1/2 (121.9 x 57.2)
Signed with monogram & dated *1912* (br)

Provenance: Mrs A E Southall, sale of her estate, Edwards, Son & Bigwood & Mathews, Birmingham (6 Apr. 1948, lot 199-part): Mrs Bridgwater: The Fine Art Society: Mr & Mrs Alan Fortunoff

Literature: *Joseph Southall, 1861–1944: Artist-Craftsman,* Birmingham, 1980, pp.90–1, ill.p.91.

The stance of the central figure is almost identical to that of the main figure in Southall's fresco, *Corporation Street, Birmingham, 1914*, in Birmingham Museum & Art Gallery; the lady being based on a buonfresco portrait of Mrs William Smedley-Aston, now in Kidderminster Art Gallery. However, according to family legend the elegant lady in the rue de Rivoli is a portrait of Georgie Gaskin.

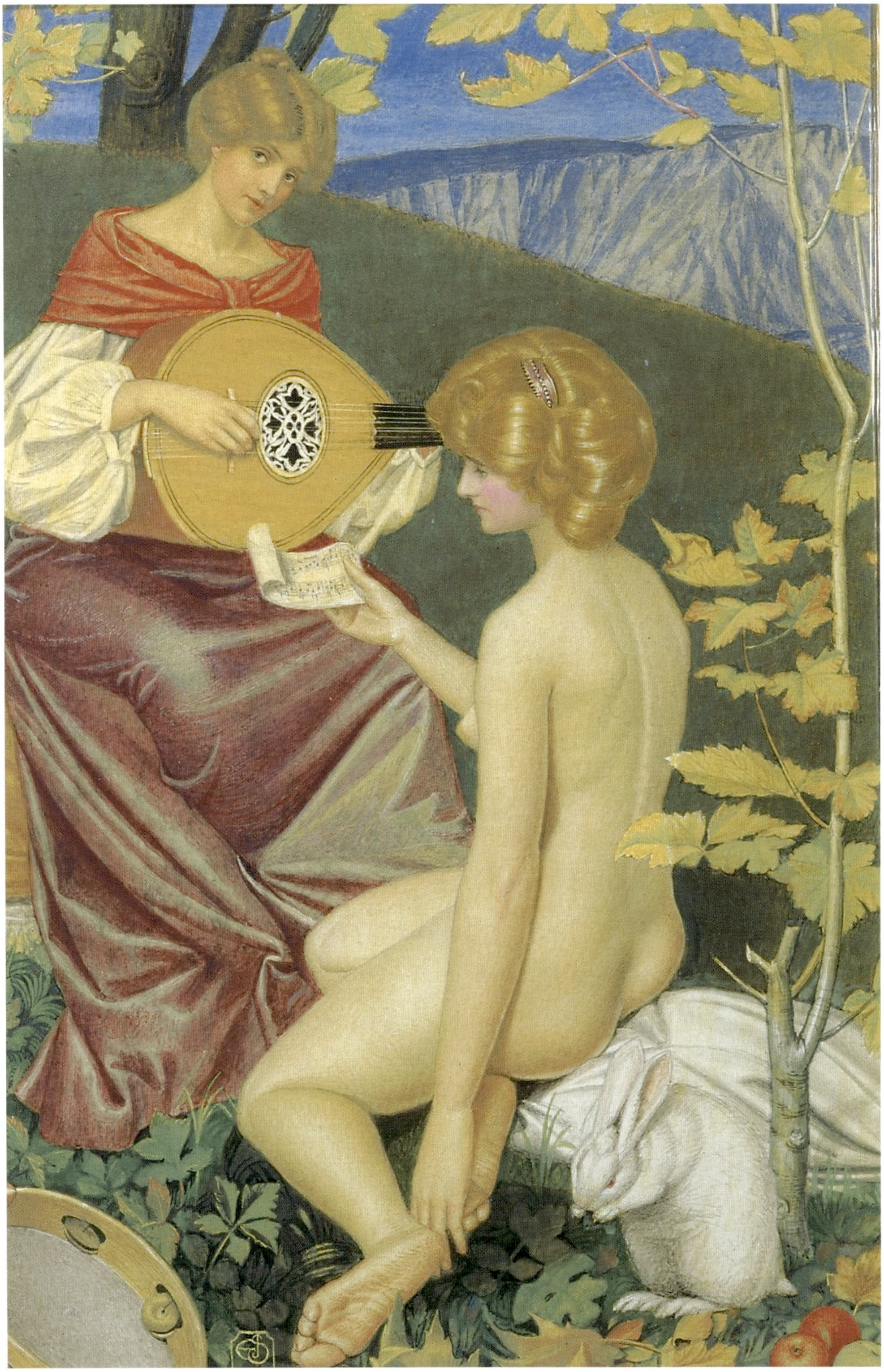

12. Music, 1912

Tempera and pencil on card, 14 x 9 1/4 (35.2 x 23.7)
Signed in monogram & dated *1912* (bc)

Provenance: Mrs A E Southall: Ernest Allen: Miss Enid Allen: Julian Hartnoll: The Fine Art Society: Mr & Mrs Alan Fortunoff

Exhibited: Birmingham & FAS, 1980 (B9)

This is a curious, if finely coloured, picture, which the artist never seems to have exhibited. Little is recorded of Southall's interest in music, though he owned a spinet and a harpsichord and references occur in surviving correspondence, as well as sketchbook drawings of such performers as Edith Ryland, Joseph Camenzina and Lillian Burman (see Joseph Southall, 1861–1944: Artist-Craftsman, Birmingham, 1980, p. 42). The music on the sheet in the painting appears to be only representational.

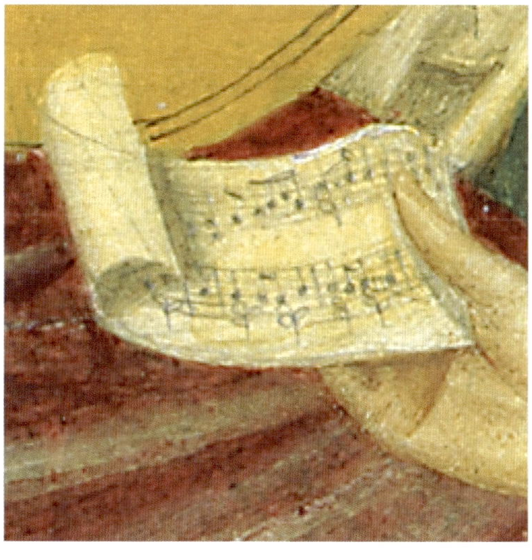

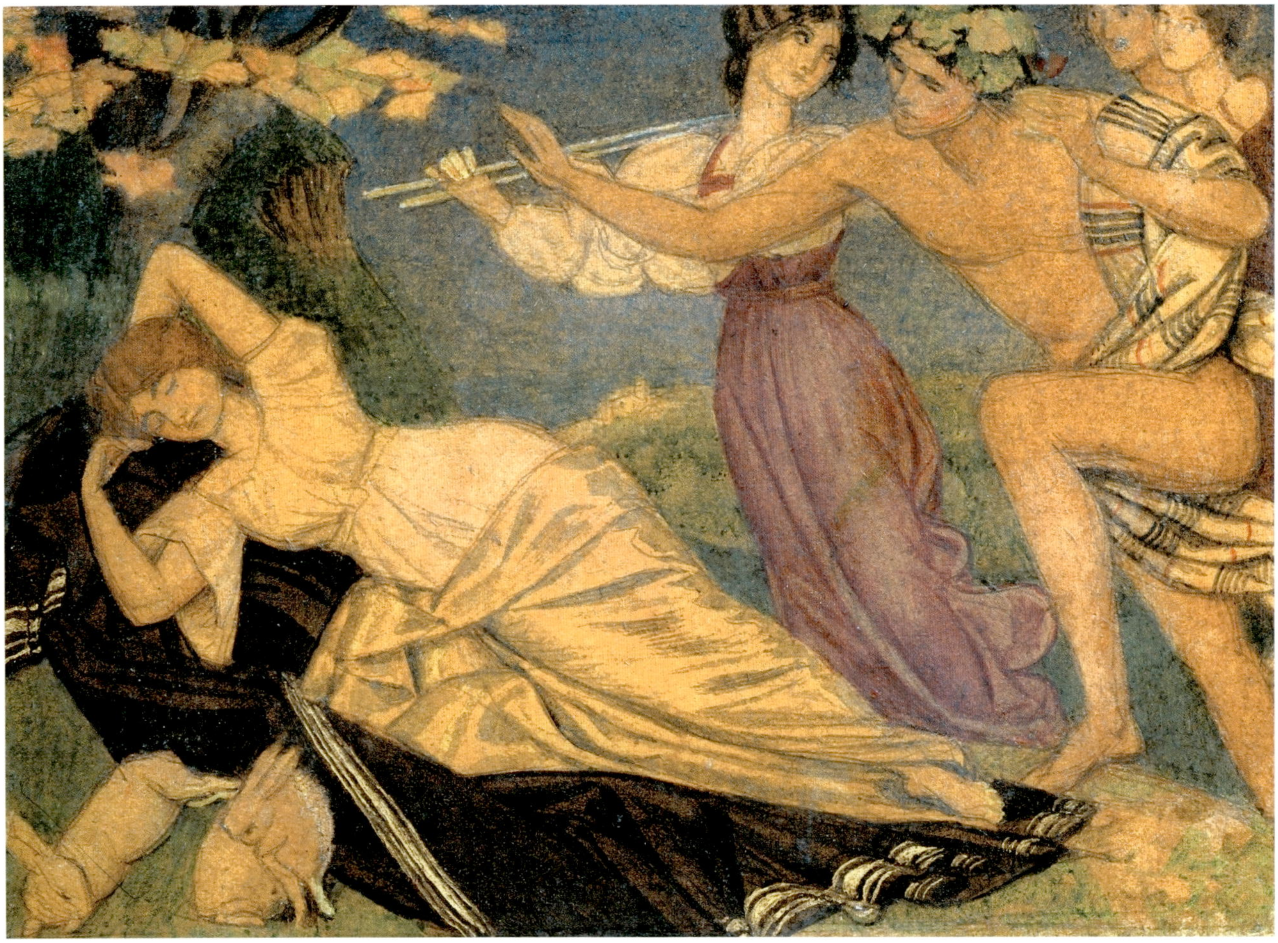

13. Study for Bacchus and Ariadne, circa 1912
Watercolour over pencil on card, varnished, 7 x 9 1/2 (18 x 24.2)

Provenance: The Fine Art Society: Mr & Mrs Alan Fortunoff

A quarter-size study for the tempera painting first exhibited at the 1913 Salon of the Société National des Beaux-arts, Paris (see *Joseph Southall 1861–1944: Artist-Craftsman*, Birmingham, 1980, p.42, cat.no.B10). Ariadne was quite a frequent subject for the artist, particularly as Ariadne in Naxos.

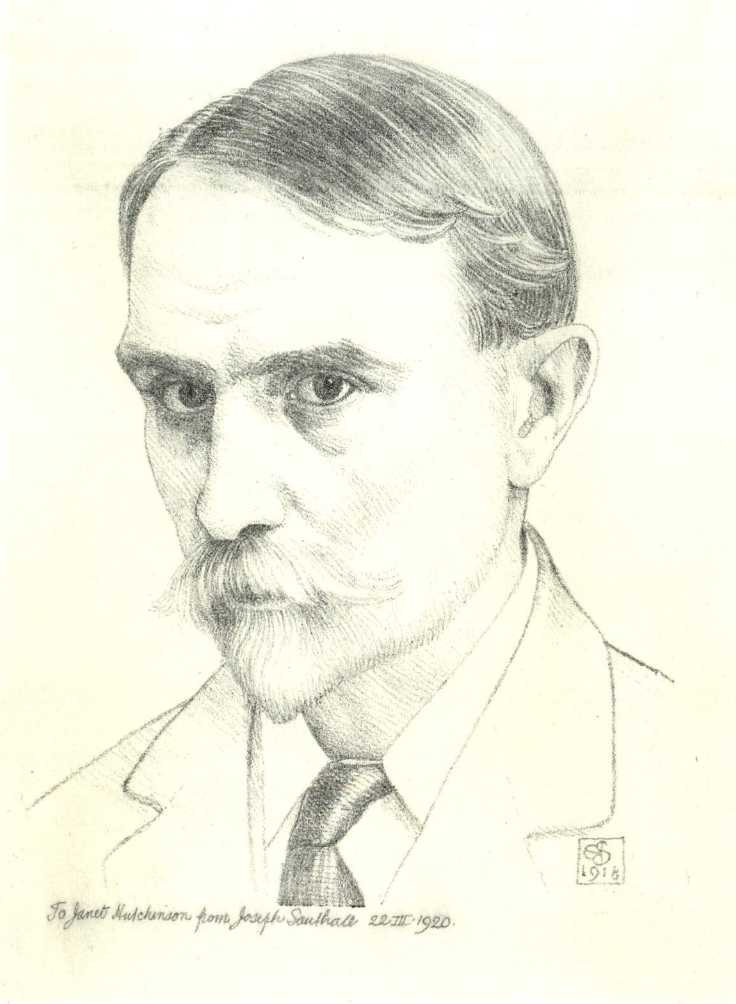

14. Self-Portrait, 1918

Lithograph, 16 x 10 1/8 (41 x 26)
Signed in monogram & dated *1918* in the stone (br) and inscribed in pencil *To Janet Hutchinson from Joseph Southall 22.III.1920* (ll)

Provenance: Janet Hutchinson (Lady Ilford): The Fine Art Society: Mr & Mrs Alan Fortunoff

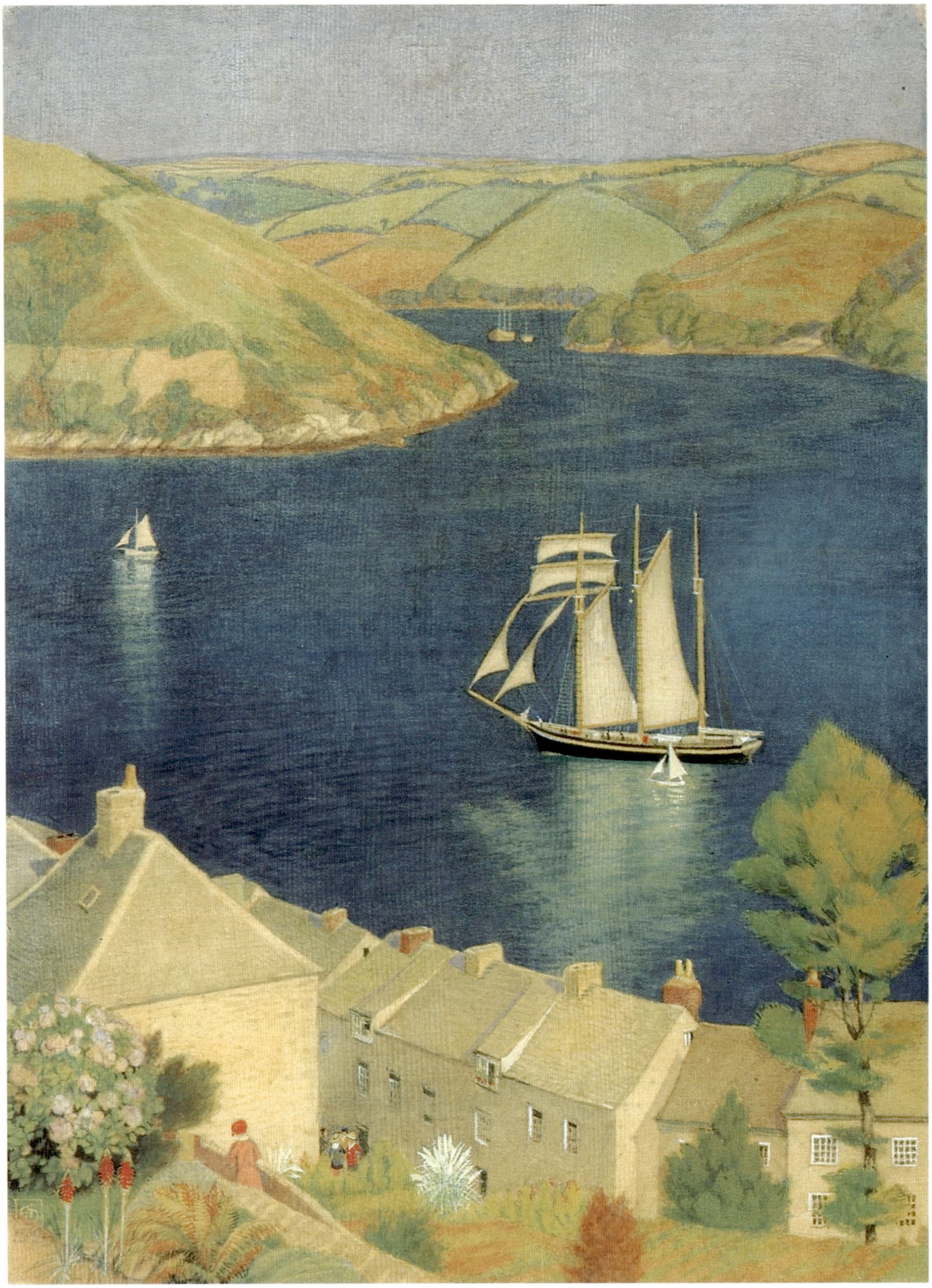

15. The Three-Masted Schooner, 1919

Tempera on silk 15 3/4 x 11 3/4 (40.7 x 30.5)
Signed in monogram & dated 1919 (bl)

Provenance: Donald Hope: Michael Hope: The Fine Art Society: Mr & Mrs Alan Fortunoff

Exhibited: Birmingham, RBSA, *Joseph Southall*, 1933 (24): Birmingham; London, RWS and Bournemouth, *Memorial Exhibition*, 1945 (76)

Over several decades Southall painted a number of views of the Fowey Estuary, mostly taken from the same elevated vantage-point around St. Catherine's Point to the left of the harbour entrance, with the blockhouse at Polruan to the right, and featuring old-fashioned sailing vessels. The intense stillness of these scenes, with schooner, brig or barque frozen in time, evoke Coleridge's lines 'As idle as a painted ship / Upon a painted ocean.' However, the idyllic beauty of Southall's dreamlike, and essentially optimistic, images could not be further removed from Coleridge's hallucinatory and doom-laden vision as conjured up in *The Rhyme of the Ancient Mariner.*

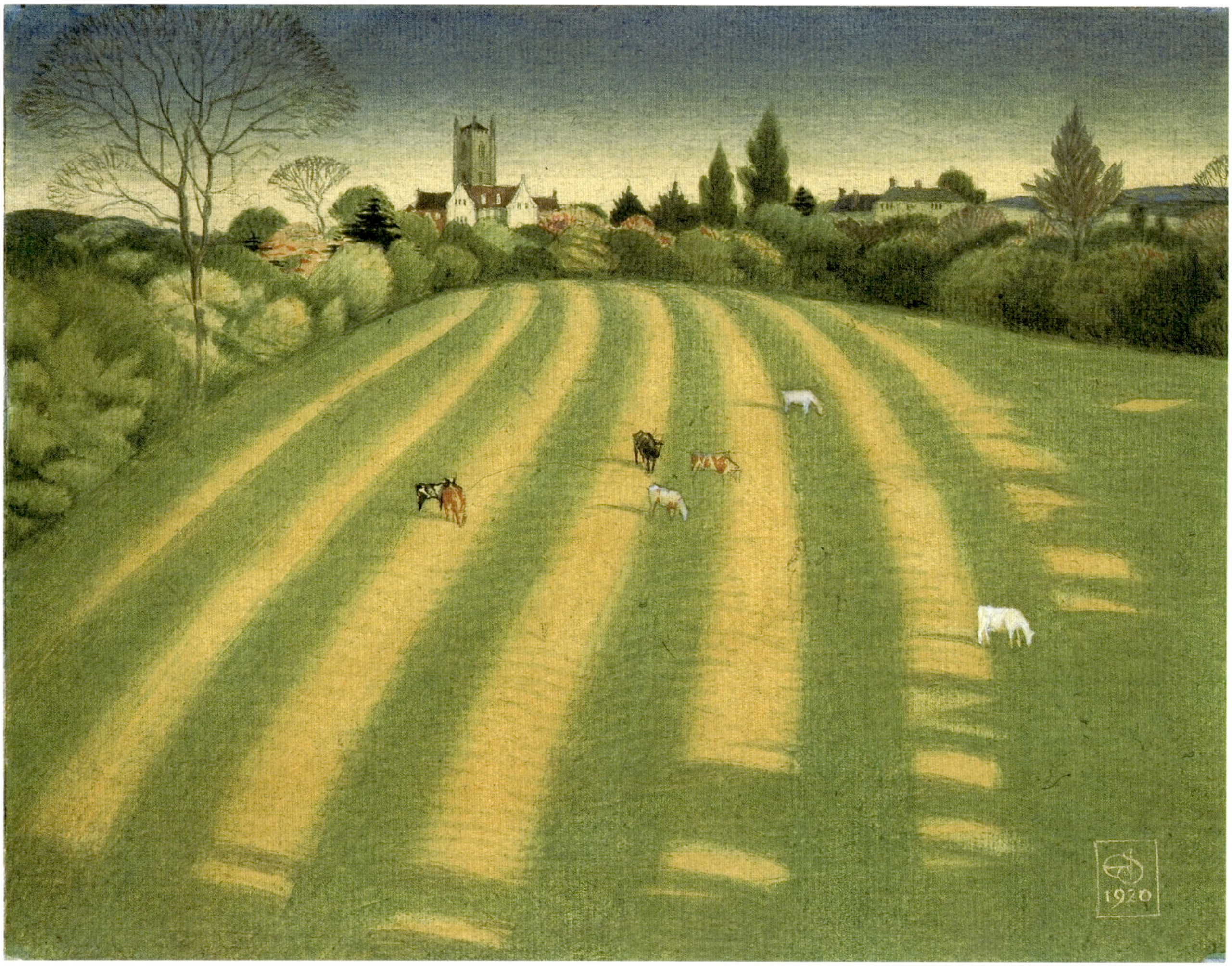

16. The Meadow, 1920
Watercolour, 7 5/8 x 10 (19.4 x 25.4)
Signed in monogram & dated *1920* (br)

Provenance: Geoffrey & Janet Hutchinson (Lord & Lady Ilford): The Fine Art Society: Mr & Mrs Alan Fortunoff

Exhibited: London, NEAC, *Summer Exhibition*, 1921 (153): London, Alpine Club Gallery, *Joseph Southall*, 1922 (6), Manchester, *Joseph Southall*, 1922 (33): London, *Memorial Exhibition*, 1945 (D)

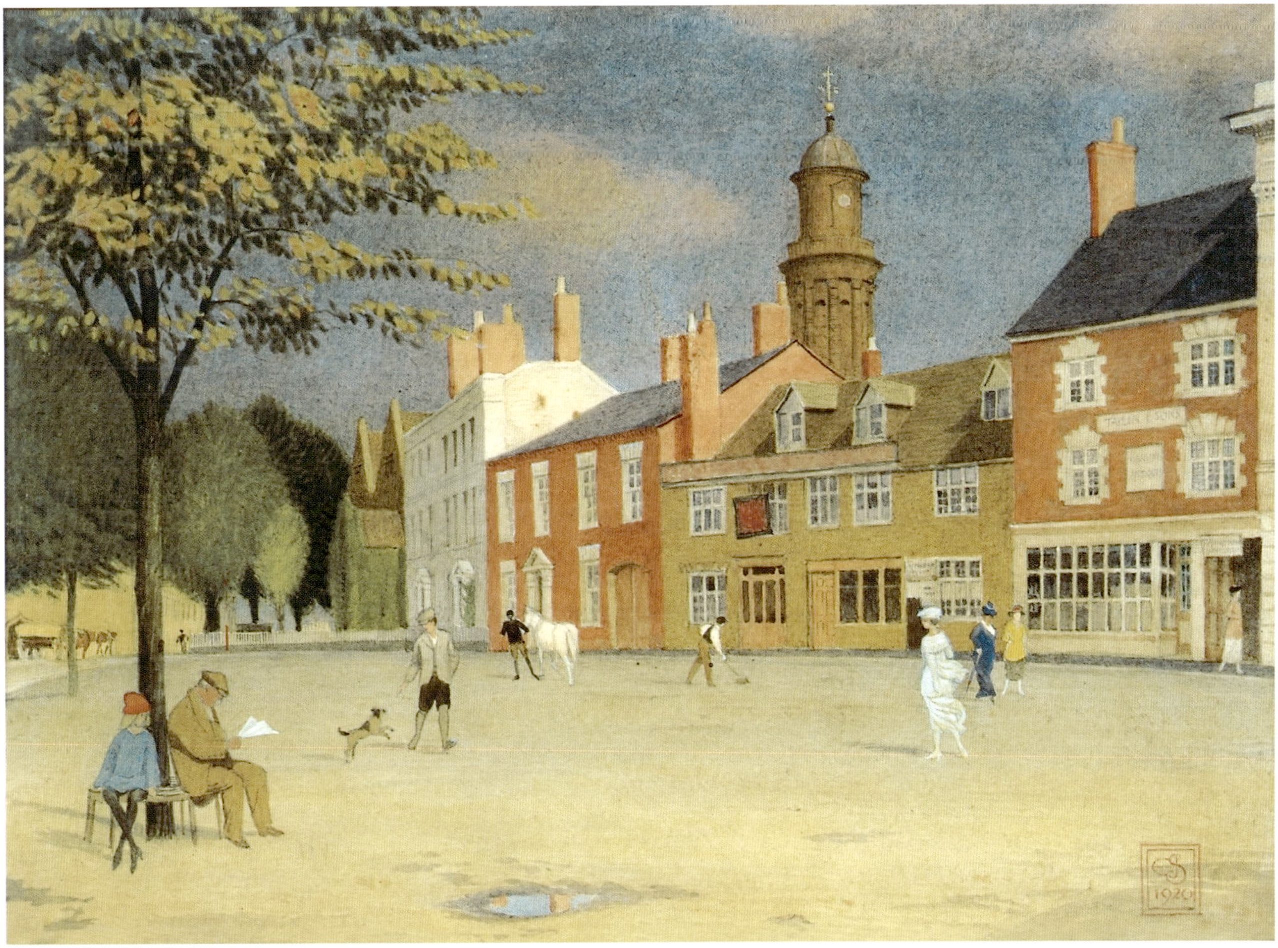

17. The Green at Banbury, 1920
Watercolour and bodycolour, 9 1/4 x 13 1/4 (23.5 x 33.5)
Signed in monogram & dated *1920* (br)

Provenance: Geoffrey and Janet Hutchinson (Lord & Lady Ilford): Phillips, Marylebone (7 July 1978, lot 523): The Fine Art Society: Mr & Mrs Alan Fortunoff

Exhibited: London, NEAC, *Winter Exhibition,* 1920–21 (85); Birmingham & FAS, 1980 (F20)

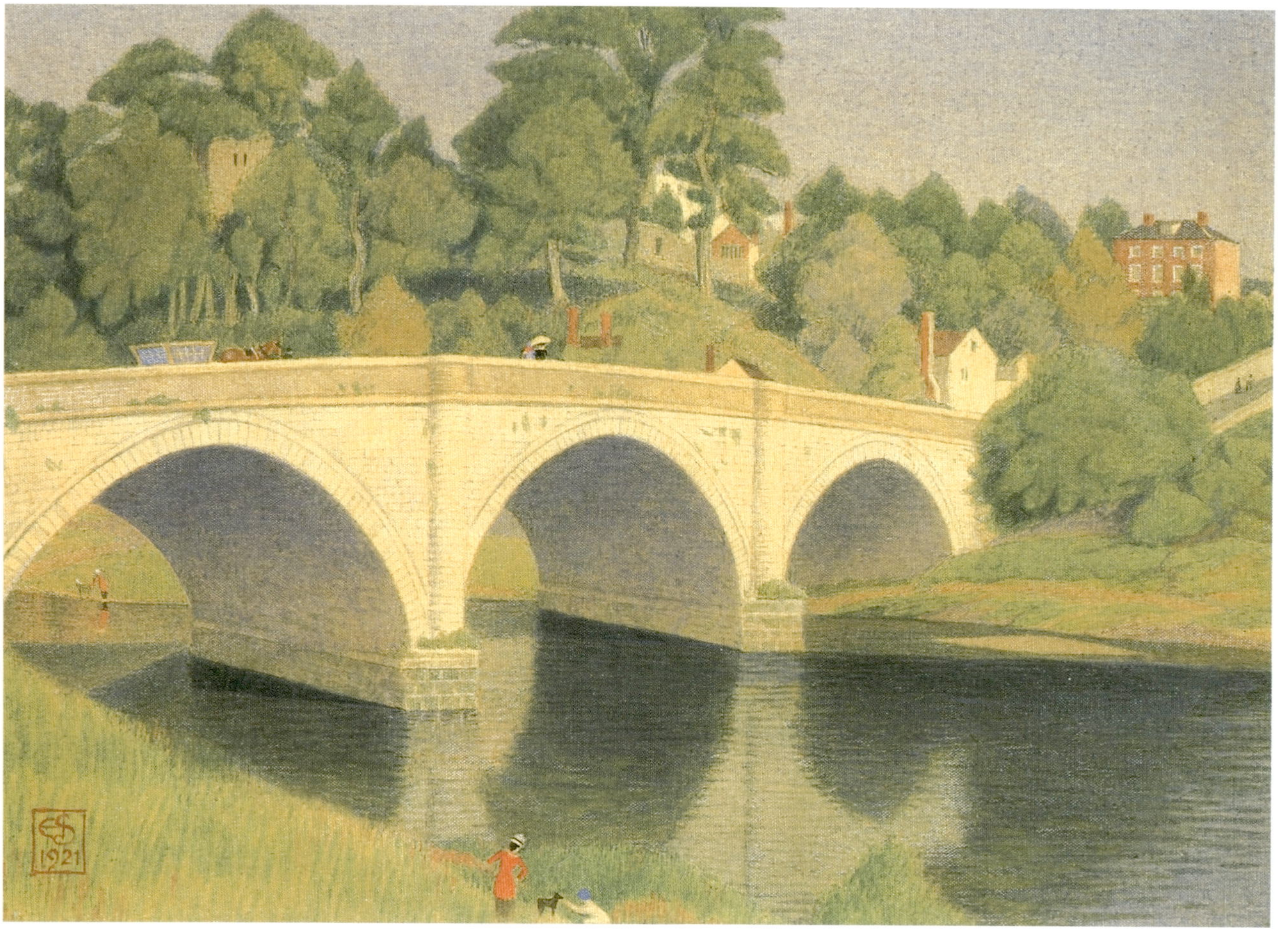
1921

18. Dinham Bridge, Ludlow, 1921

Tempera on linen, 8 1/2 x 12 (21.3 x 30.1)
Signed in monogram & dated *1921* (bl)

Provenance: Miss Enid Allen: Julian Hartnoll: The Fine Art Society: Mr & Mrs Alan Fortunoff

Exhibited: London, *Memorial Exhibition*, 1945 (E)

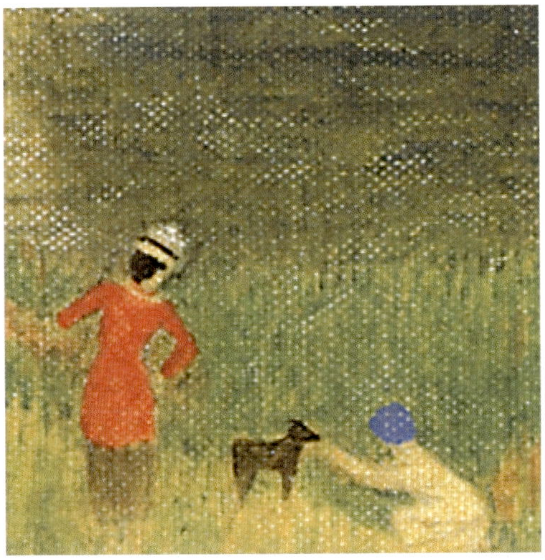

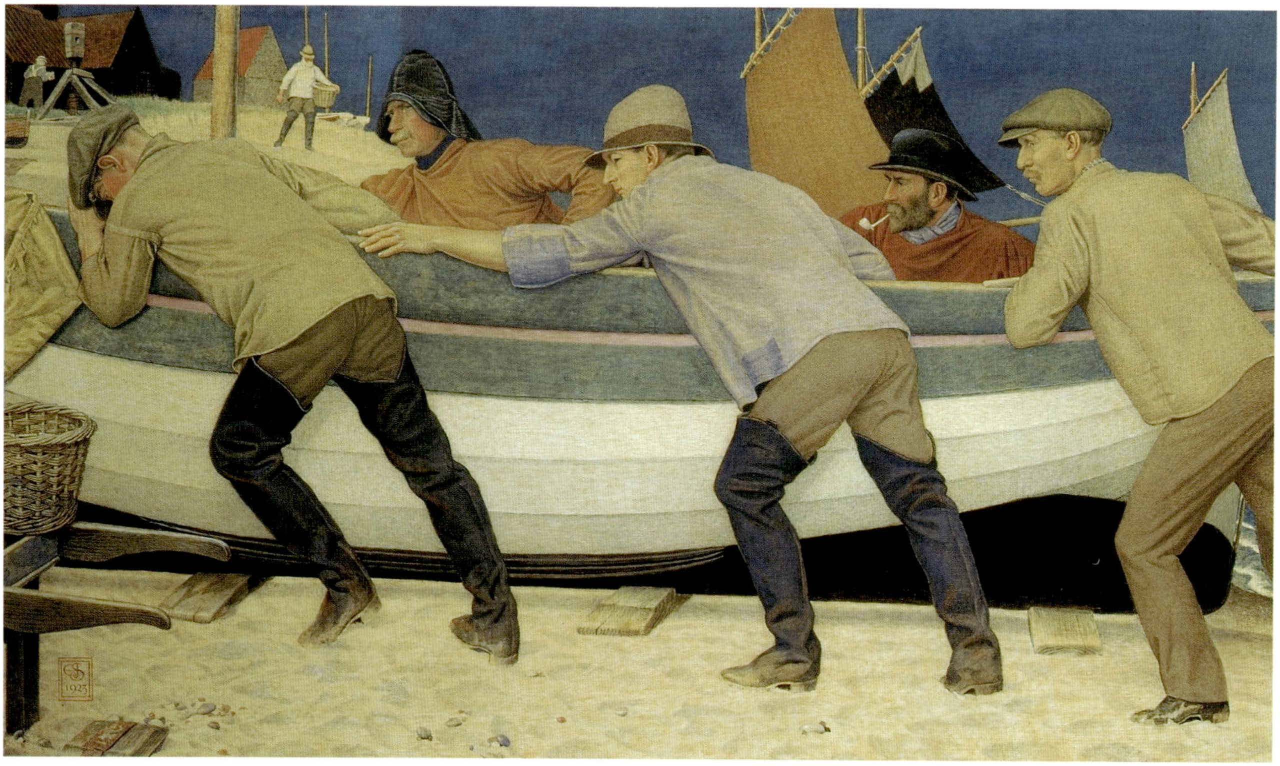

19. Fishermen and Boat, 1923

Tempera on linen, 19 1/2 x 33 3/4 (49.5 x 85.7)
Signed in monogram & dated *1923* (bl)

Provenance: Lord Blanesburgh: The Royal Caledonian Schools: The Fine Art Society: Mr & Mrs Alan Fortunoff

Exhibited: Wembley, *British Empire Exhibition*, 1924 (R.38): London. FAS, *The Earthly Paradise*, 1969 (172)

This is a larger version of *Up From The Sea*, 1920 (Castle Museum, Nottingham), with the same three figures on the right, meant to represent three generations of a fishing family, but without the boy who appears in the foreground of the former. See cat.no.50 for a study for the left hand front figure.

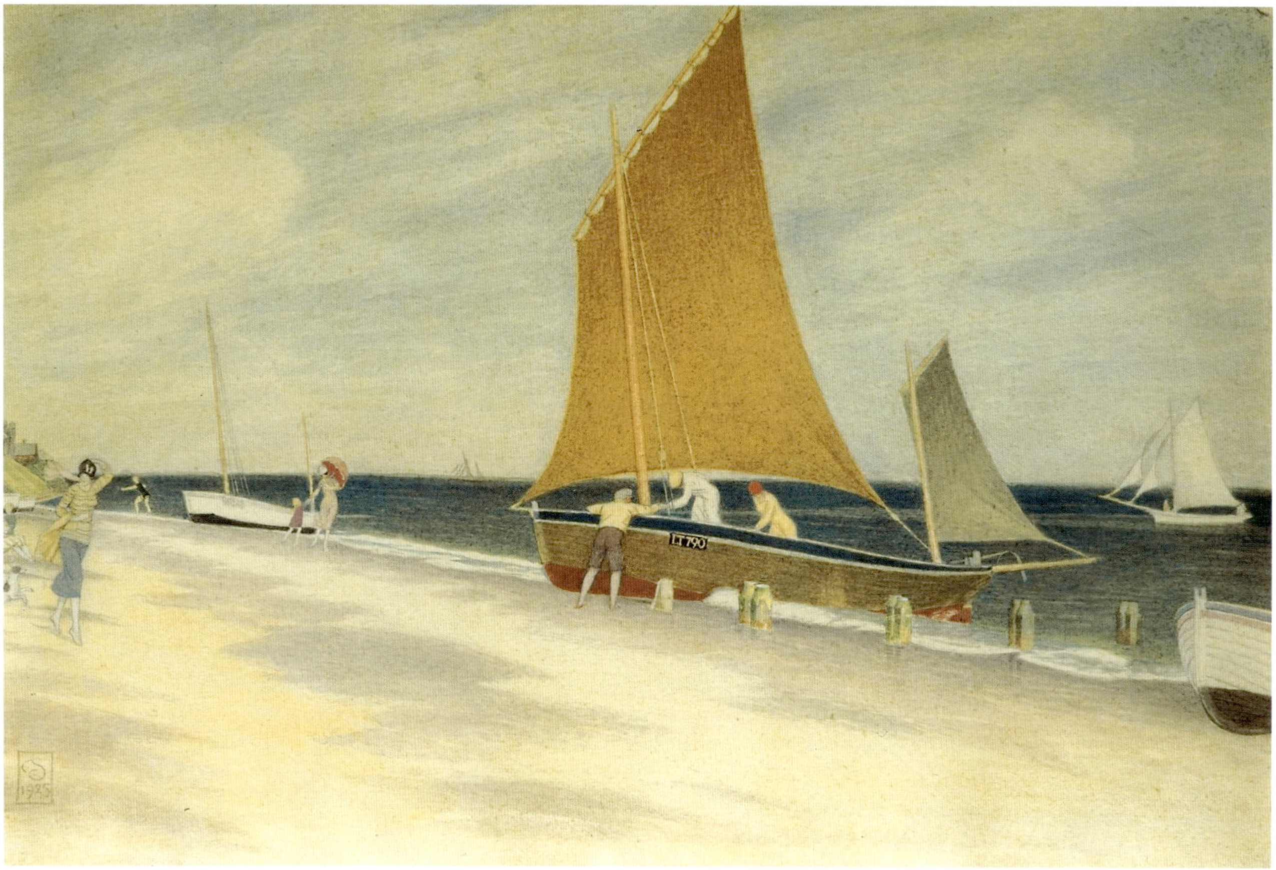
LT790

20. Pleasures of the Seaside, 1925

Watercolour, 12 x 17 1/2 (30.5 x 44.5)
Signed in monogram & dated *1925* (bl)

Provenance: Sotheby's, London (10 Nov. 1981, lot 81): The Fine Art Society: Mr & Mrs Alan Fortunoff

Exhibited: London, Leicester Galleries, *Joseph Southall,* 1926 (98): London, RWS, *Winter Exhibition,* 1926 (6): Birmingham, Ruskin Galleries, *Joseph Southall,* 1927 (25): Dudley, *Joseph Southall,* 1934 (46): (possibly) Birmingham, RBSA, *Autumn Exhibition,* 1942 (47)

The setting is Southwold beach.

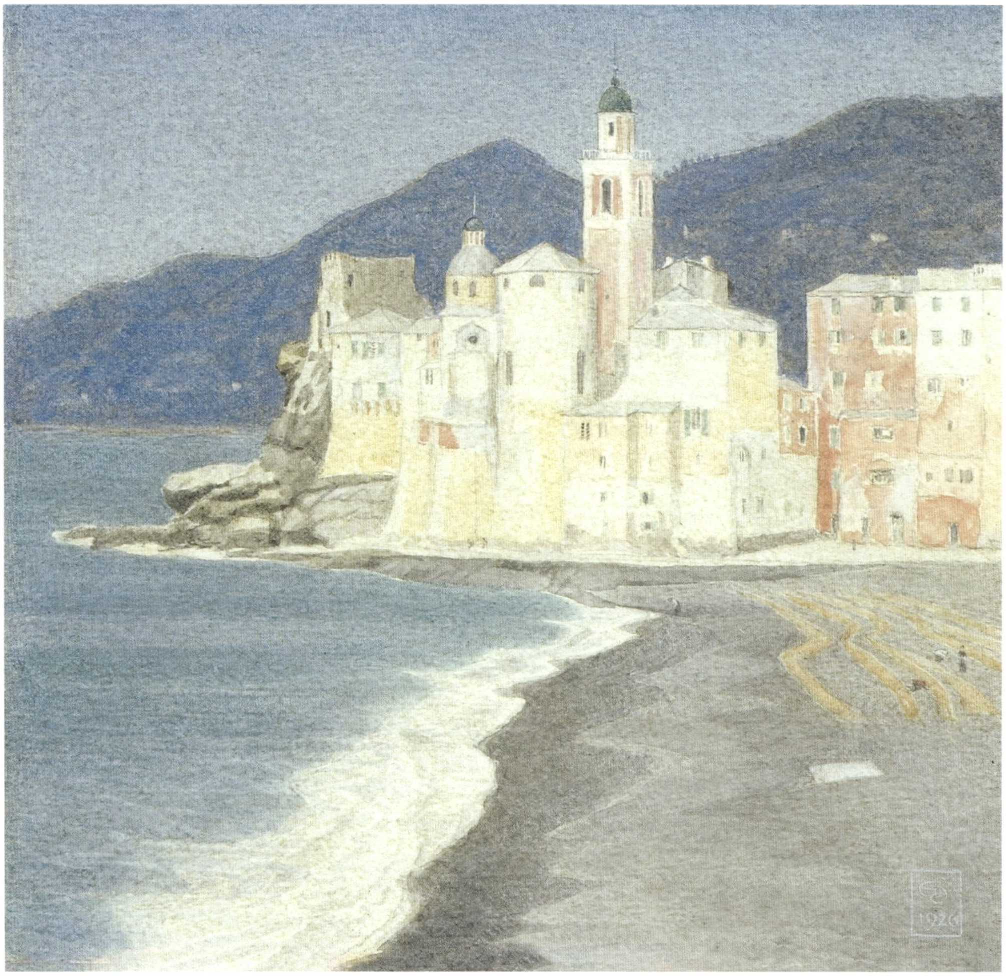

21. Camogli, 1926
Watercolour, 8 x 8 1/4 (20 x 21.2)
Signed in monogram & dated *1926* (br) and inscribed *CAMOGLI / 28.IV.1926* in right-hand margin

Provenance: Lord Blanesburgh: The Royal Caledonian Schools: The Fine Art Society: Mr & Mrs Alan Fortunoff

Exhibited: London, RWS, *Summer Exhibition,* 1927 (98); London, FAS, *The Earthly Paradise,* 1969 (176)

Camogli is a small fishing village on the Italian Riviera between Nervi and Portofino, SE of Genoa.

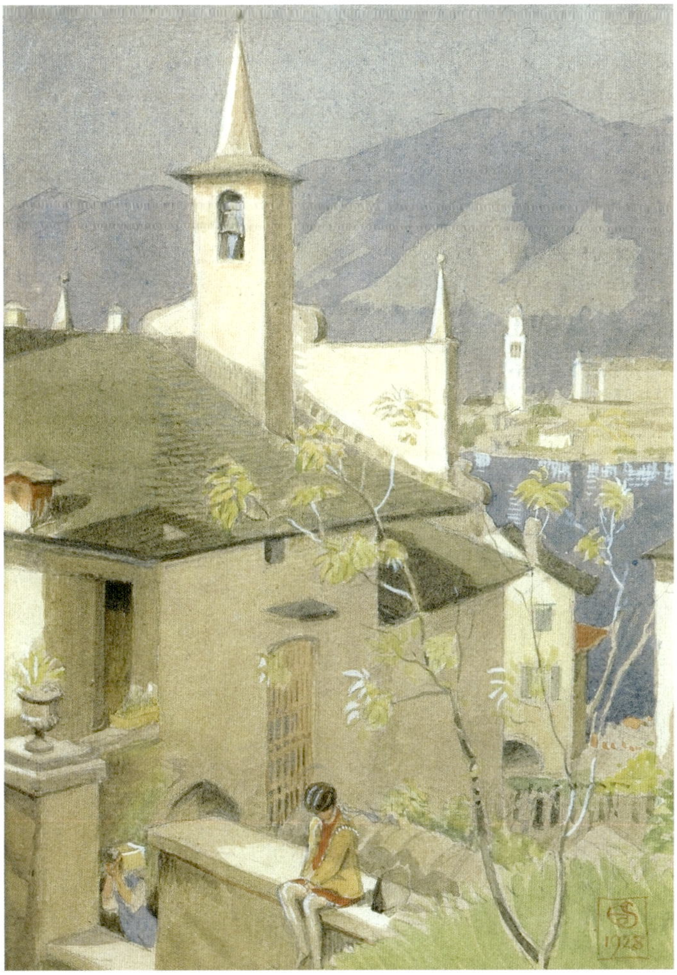

22. North Italian Townscape, 1928
Watercolour over pencil, 8 x 5 3/4 (20.3 x14.6)
Signed in monogram & dated 1928 (br)

Provenance: Miss Enid Allen: Julian Hartnoll: The Fine Art Society: Mr & Mrs Alan Fortunoff

Southall's original title for this work is lost, but the scene is probably a small town in the Italian Alps, possibly on the River Adige.

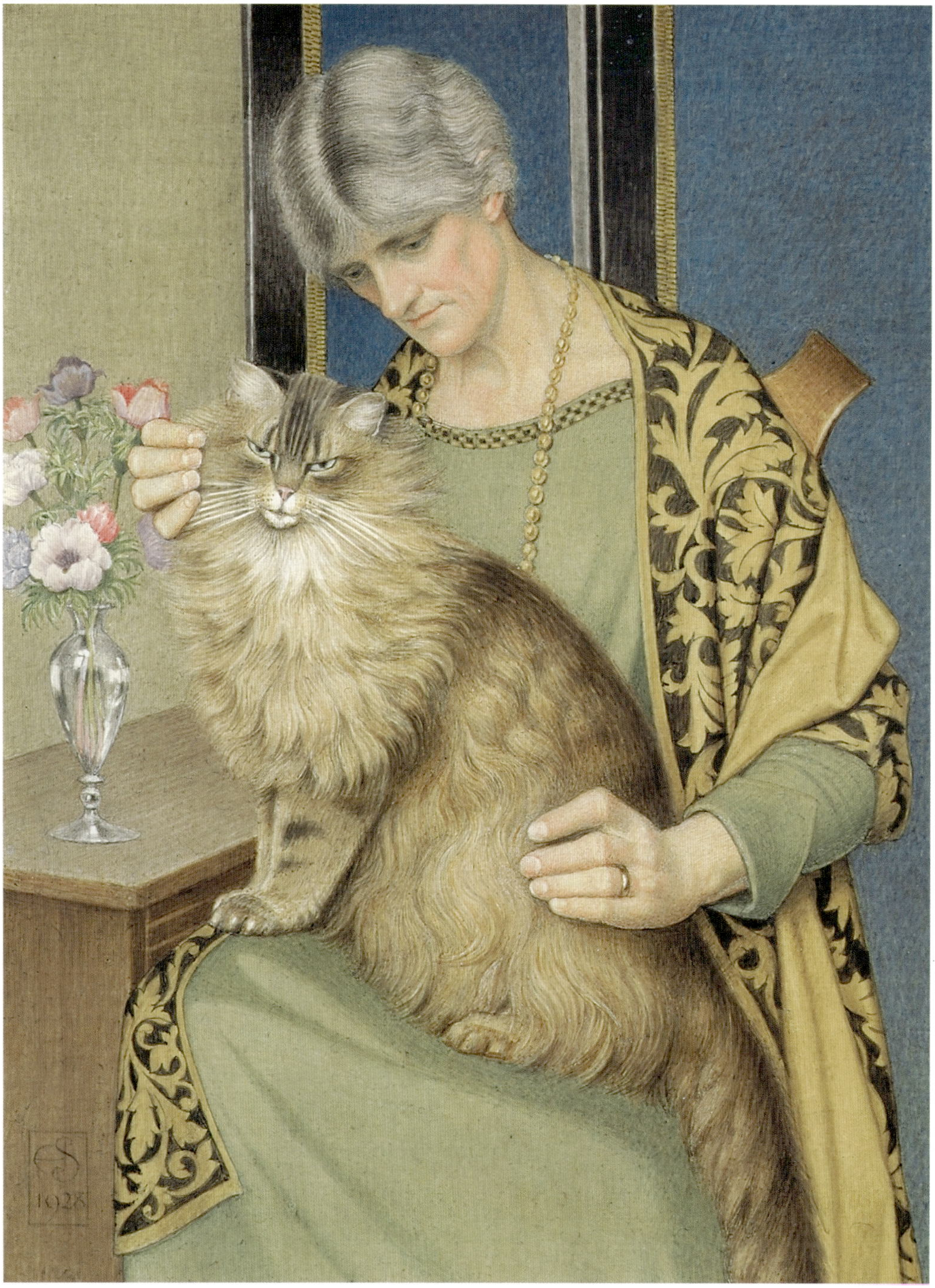

23. Contentment, 1928

Watercolour on vellum nailed to a linen-covered stretcher
14 1/2 x 10 3/4 (36.7 x 27.5)
Signed in monogram & dated *1928* (br) and inscribed (verso) *PORTRAITS OF BESSIE & TODDIE / watercolour on Vellum / Joseph Southall 1928*

Provenance: Mrs A E Southall, her sale, Edwards, Birmingham (23 Mar. 1948, lot 249): Sotheby's, Belgravia (19 March 1979, lot 17): The Fine Art Society: Mr & Mrs Alan Fortunoff

Exhibited: London, NEAC, *Summer Exhibition*, 1928 (99): Birmingham, RBSA, *Autumn Exhibition*, 1928 (143): Paris, Société National des Beaux-arts, Salon, 1929 (1573): London, Leicester Galleries, *Joseph Southall*, 1931 (46): Birmingham, RBSA, *Joseph Southall*, 1933 (57): Birmingham; London, RWS & Bournemouth, *Memorial Exhibition*, 1945 (65): Birmingham & FAS, 1980 (E12)

Literature: 'Up Front', The Observer Colour Magazine, 18 March 1979, p.23

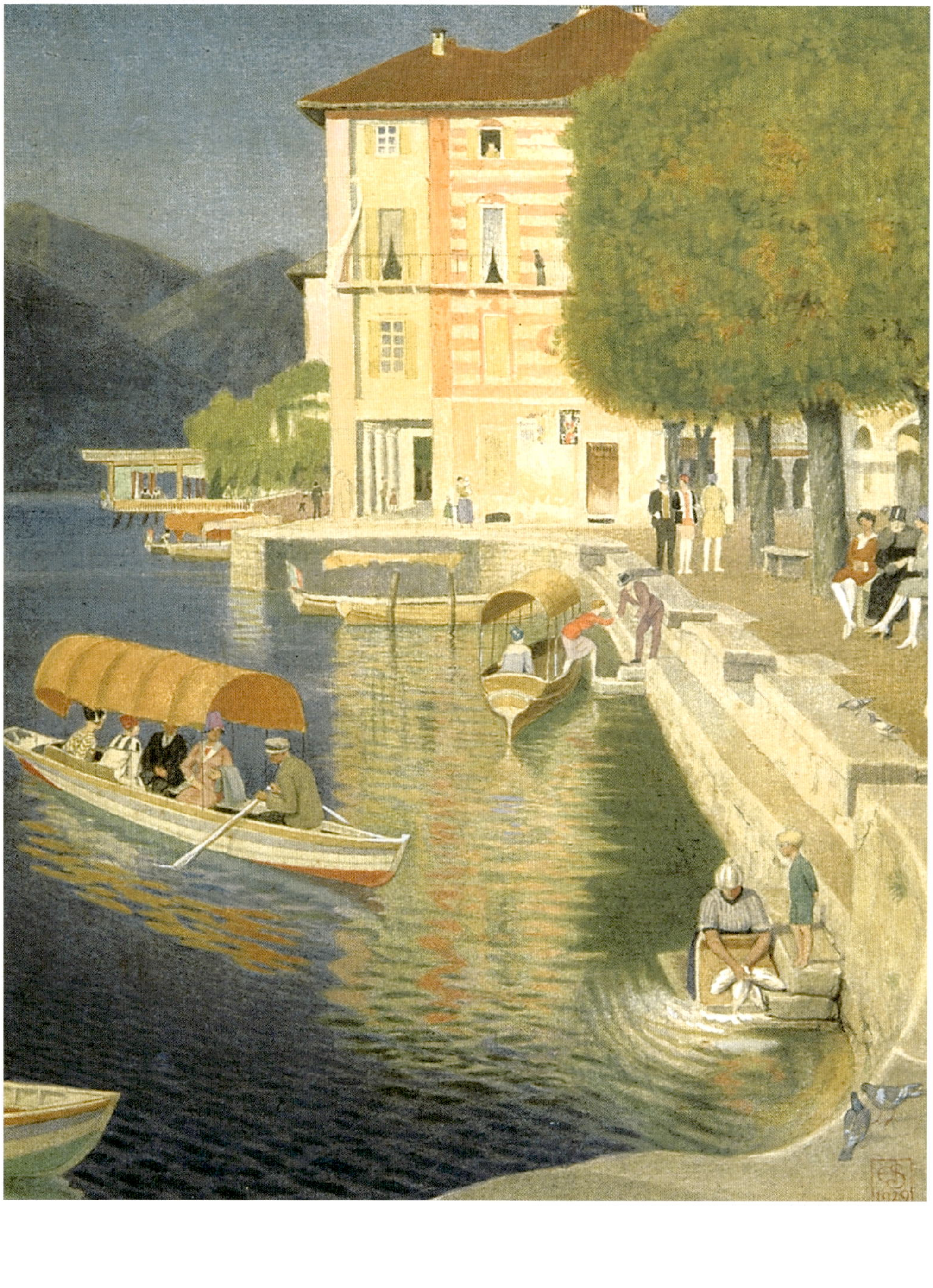

24. The Quay, Orta, 1929
Watercolour on silk, 15 x 12 1/4 (38 x 30.9)
Signed in monogram & dated *1929* (br)

Provenance: J B Clark: The Fine Art Society: Mr & Mrs Alan Fortunoff

Exhibited: Paris, Société National des Beaux-arts, Salon, 1930 (1730): London, Leicester Galleries, *Joseph Southall,* 1931 (44)

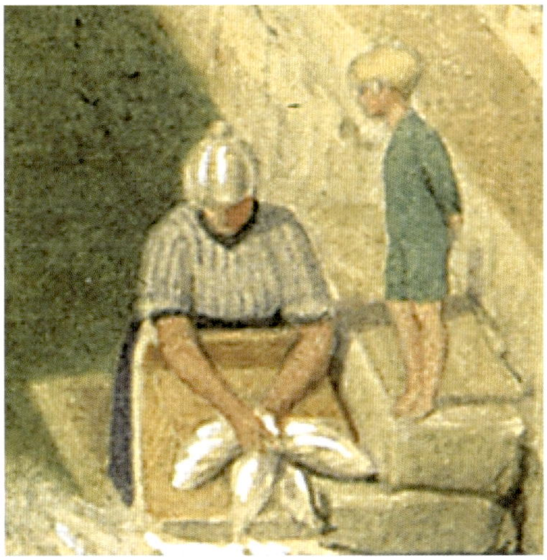

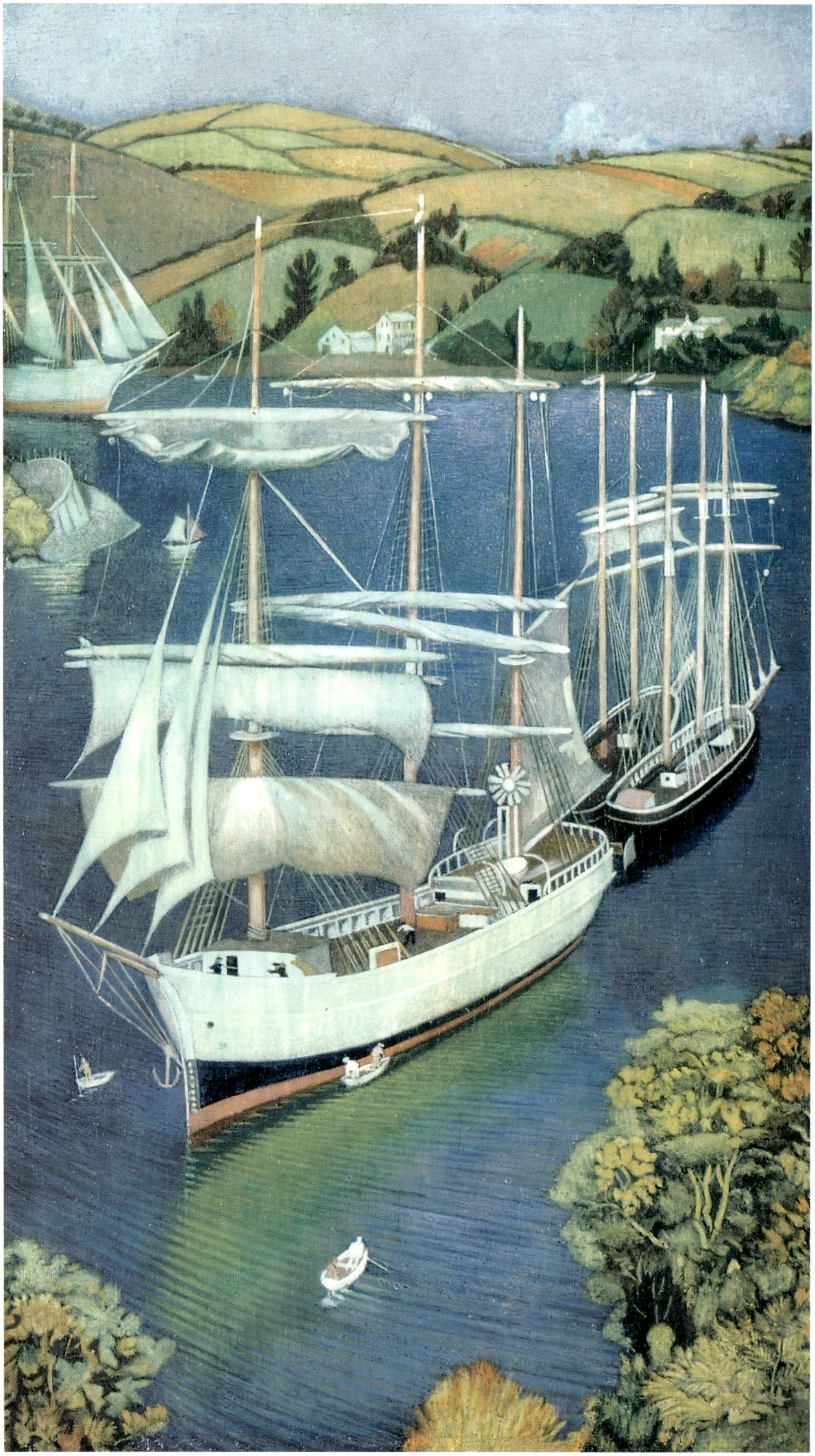

25. Brigs on the Fowey Estuary, late 1920s

Oil on panel, 14 x 8 (35.5 x 20.3)

Provenance: Lady Head: The Fine Art Society: Mr & Mrs Alan Fortunoff

Exhibited: FAS, *Spring '89*, 1989 (41)

The scene is of Mixtow on the Fowey Estuary upstream of the town of Fowey. There is some artistic licence in the landscape just as there is in the size of the sailing ships, which were used to carry china clay (with thanks to Lynn Goold, Fowey). Southall's original title for this work is lost.

This is the only oil painting in the collection but the technique is more akin to that of tempera than oils. Very unusually, it is neither signed nor dated. Scraps of newspaper glued to the back suggest a date in the late 1920s. Certainly it appears to be a later rather than an earlier work. It is a curiosity but shows how the artist has become so assimilated to handling tempera

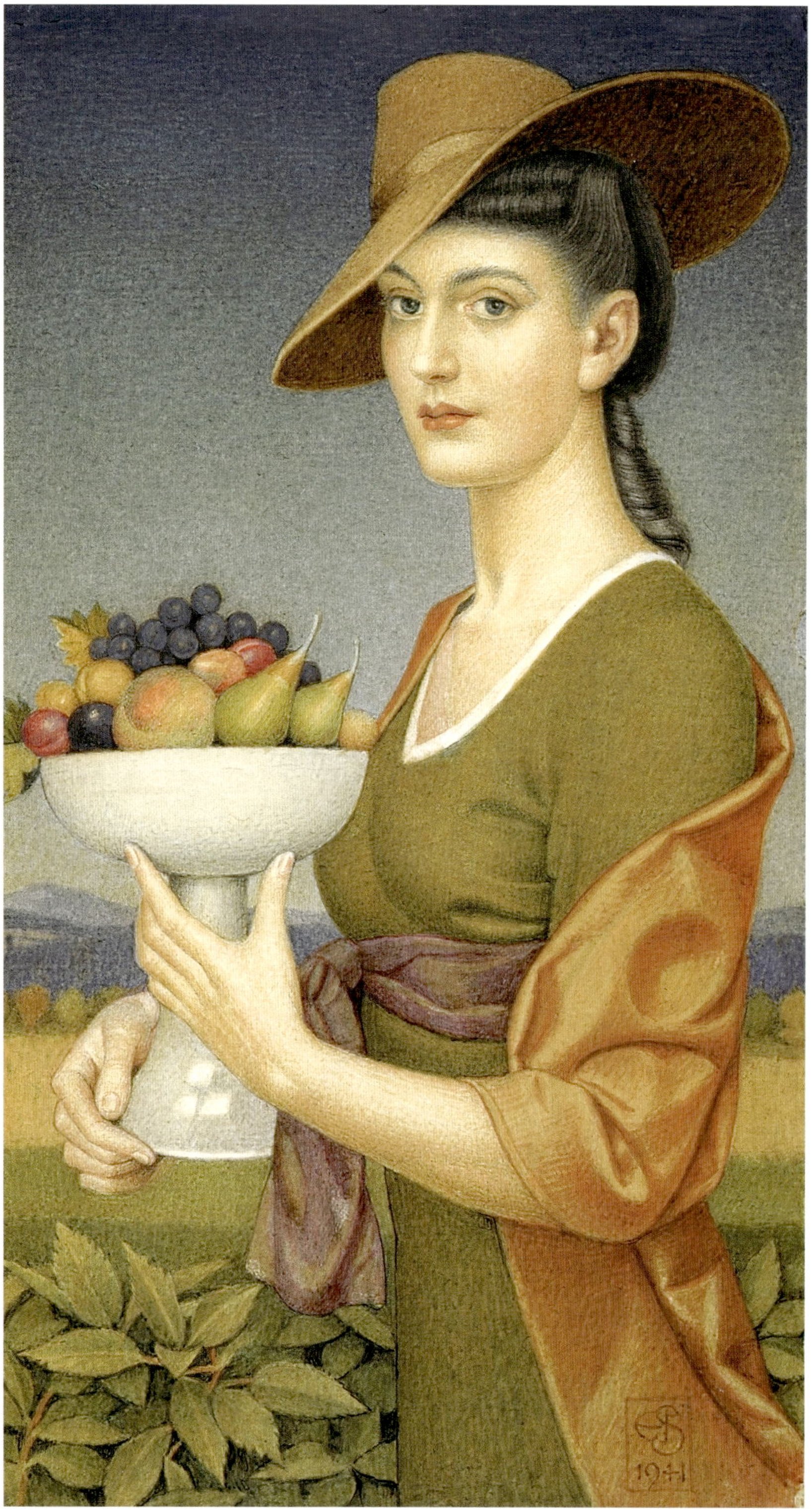

26. A Dish of Fruit, 1922–1941

Watercolour over pencil, 14 1/2 x 8 (36.5 x 20.5)
Signed in monogram & dated *1941* (br). Inscribed (verso) *Newman Whatman on double Bristol Board 1922 / formalin both sides 26.IX.40 / no spots*

Provenance: The Estate of Mrs A E Southall: Mrs Elizabeth Baker: The Fine Art Society: Mr & Mrs Alan Fortunoff

Exhibited: (Possibly) Birmingham, RBSA, Spring Exhibition, 1944 (241)

The strong Art Deco feel to this work, surprising for 1941, is possibly explained by the earlier date of 1922 on the reverse. It is probable that it was conceived at the earlier date and put aside unfinished. For a related semi-nude study dated both 1940 and 1941 see cat.no.58.

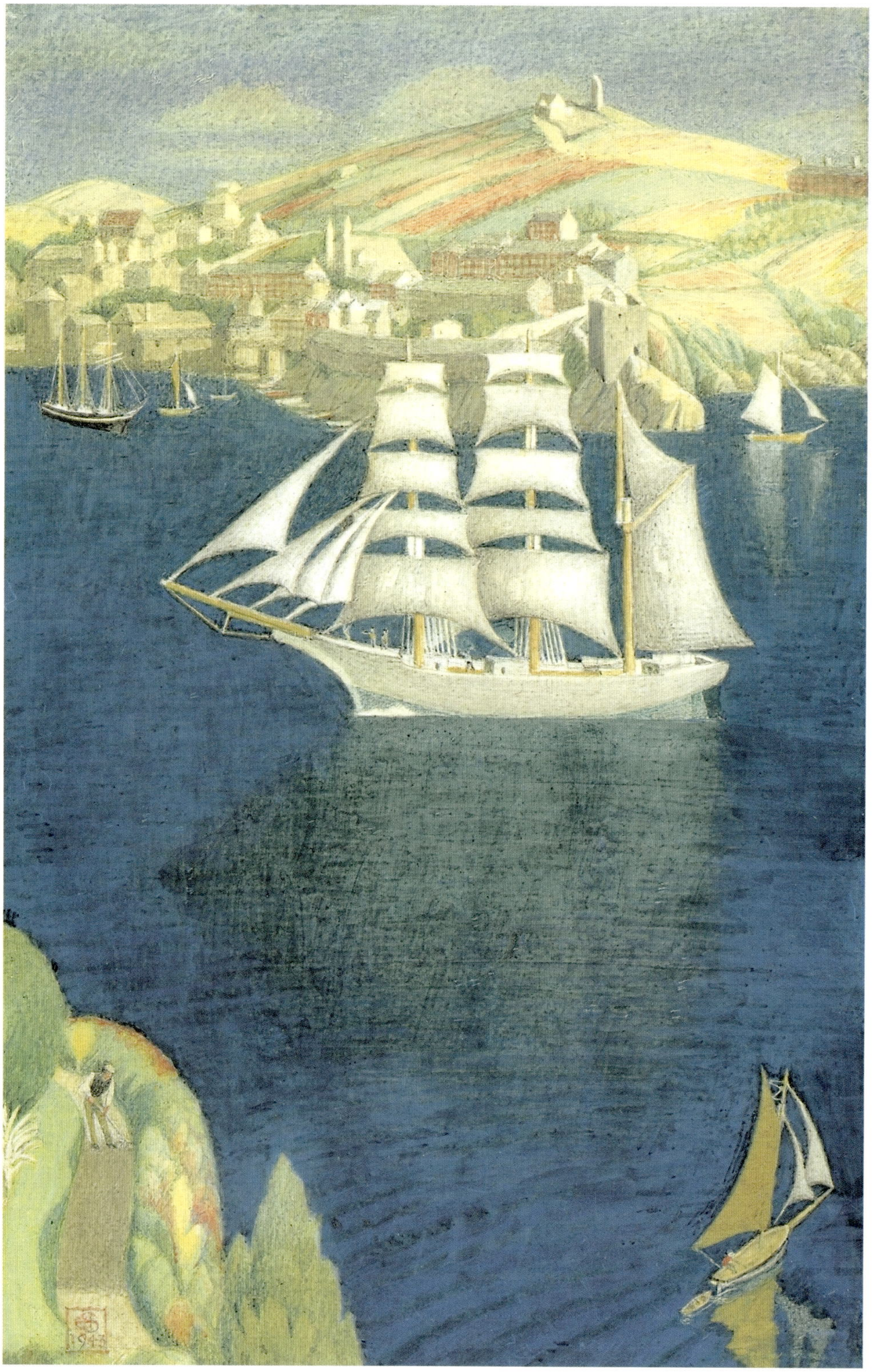

27. The White Barque at Fowey, 1943

Tempera on board, 14 x 9 (35.6 x 22.8)
Signed in monogram & dated *1943* (bl)

Provenance: Miss Enid Allen: Julian Hartnoll: The Fine Art Society: Mr & Mrs Alan Fortunoff

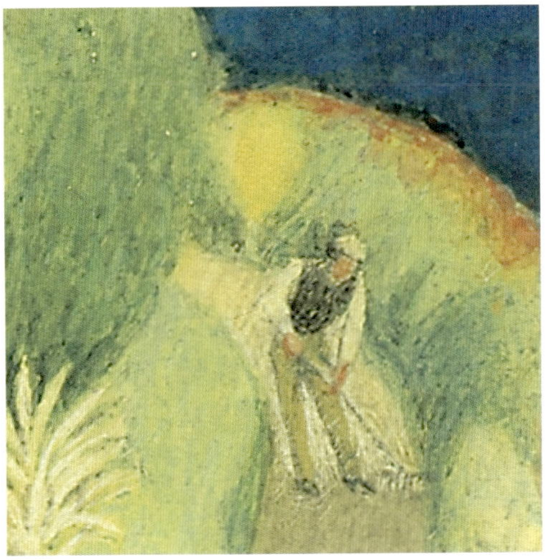

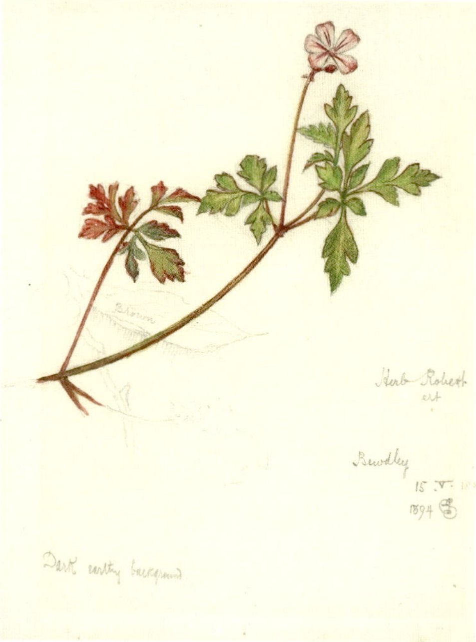

28. Plant Study, 1894

Watercolour over pencil, 6 1/4 x 5 (16 x 12.6)
Signed in monogram & dated *Bewdley 15.V.1894* (lr). Annotated *Brown* (c),*Herb Robert / ert / Dark earthy background* (cr).

Provenance: The Fine Art Society: Mr & Mrs Alan Fortunoff

Bewdley was close to the home of Southall's uncle, George Baker, who introduced him to John Ruskin in 1884.

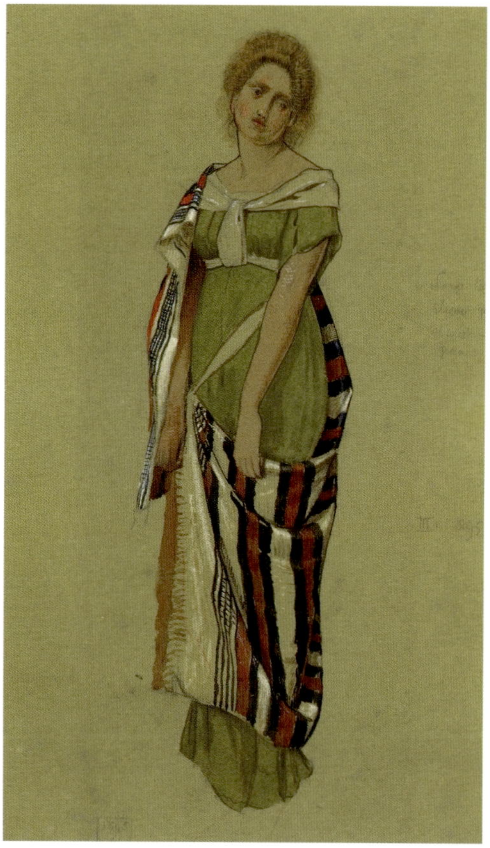

29. Study for 'The Mystic Burial', 1895

Watercolour over pencil on olive green paper, 12 x 8 1/2 (30.6 x 21.8)
Signed in monogram & dated *1895* (bl), dated again *III.1895* (cr). Annotated *Large loose/ sleeve gathered/ at waist – / green* (cr)

Provenance: The Fine Art Society: Mr & Mrs Alan Fortunoff

One of a number of studies with mediaeval themes, depicted in rich glowing colours, at about his time, and clearly influenced by the artist's visits to Italy. This work is a preliminary study for the central figure of the composition of this title: for further details see *Joseph Southall, 1861–1944: Artist-Craftsman*, Birmingham, 1980, p. 28 (A9).

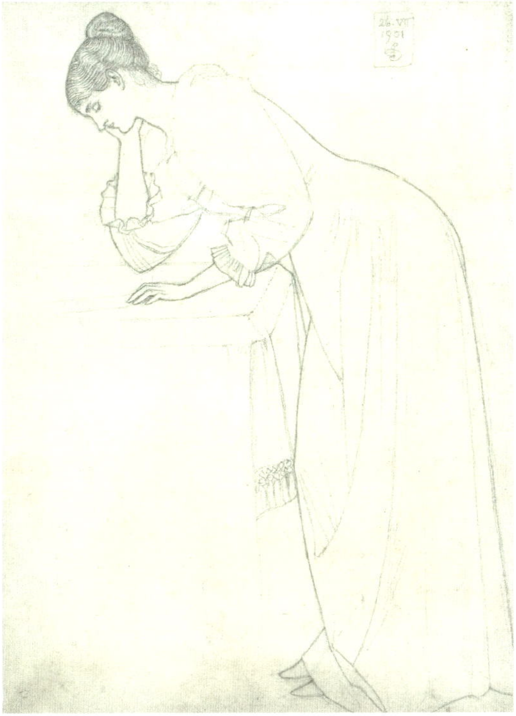

30. Study of Anna Elizabeth Baker, 1901

Pencil, 7 1/8 x 5 1/4 (18.1 x 13.3)
Signed in monogram & dated *26.VII.1901* (tr)
and (verso) *F[ormalin] 1936*

31.* Mending the Net, 1904

Pencil & watercolour, 5 3/4 x 9 1/2 (14.8 x 24)
Signed in monogram & dated 5*.VII.1904* (bl).
Annotated *grey / blue* (on seated child).

Exhibited: (possibly) London, New Gallery, *Summer Exhibition*, 1909 (63): Aldeburgh, 1981 (22)

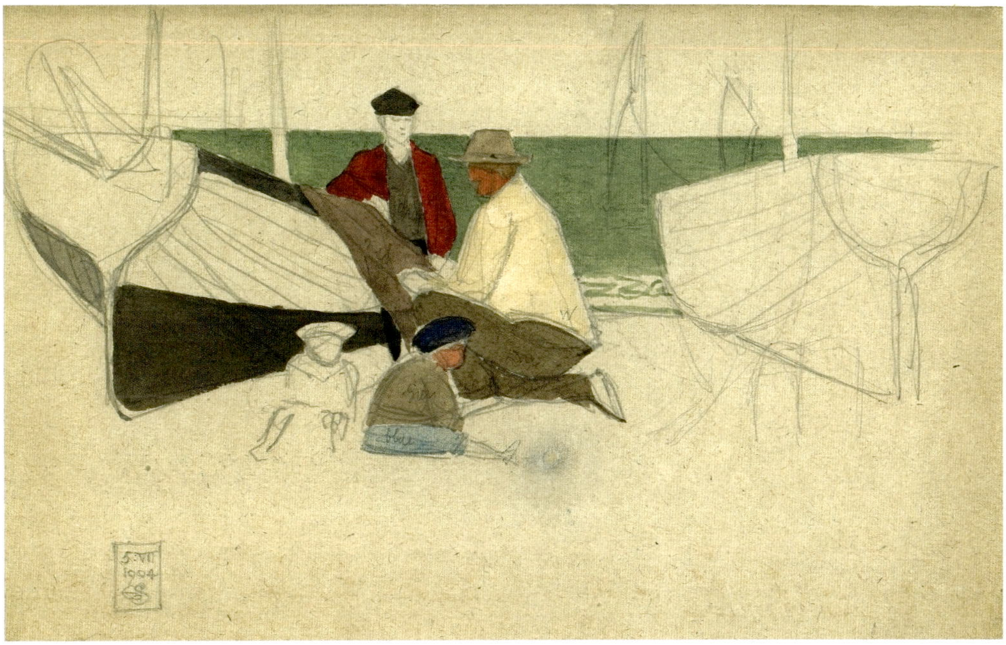

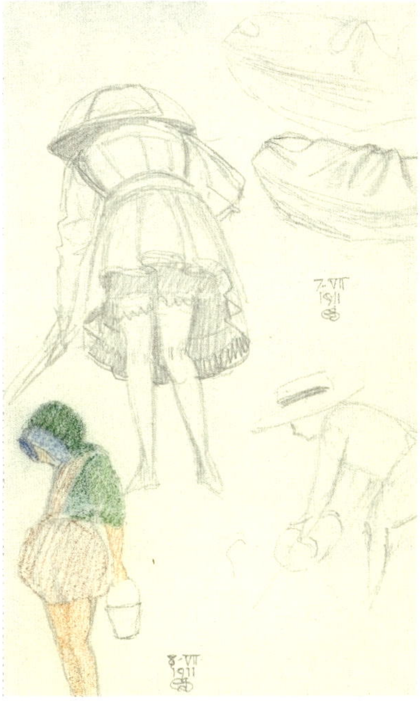

32.* Girls on the Shore, 1911
Pencil & watercolour, 7 x 4 1/4 (17.8 x 11)
Signed twice in monogram & dated
7.VII.1911 and again *8.VII.1911*

Exhibited: Aldeburgh, 1981 (29)

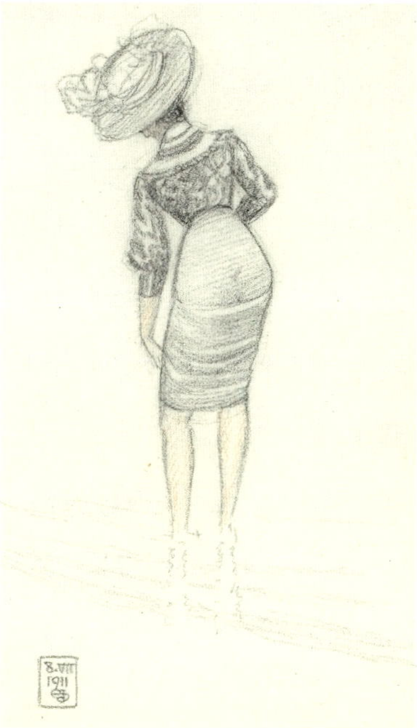

33.* Elegant Young Woman Paddling, 1911
Pencil & chalk, 7 x 4 1/4 (10.8 x 17.5)
Signed in monogram & dated *8.VII.1911* (bl)

Exhibited: Aldeburgh, 1981 (2)

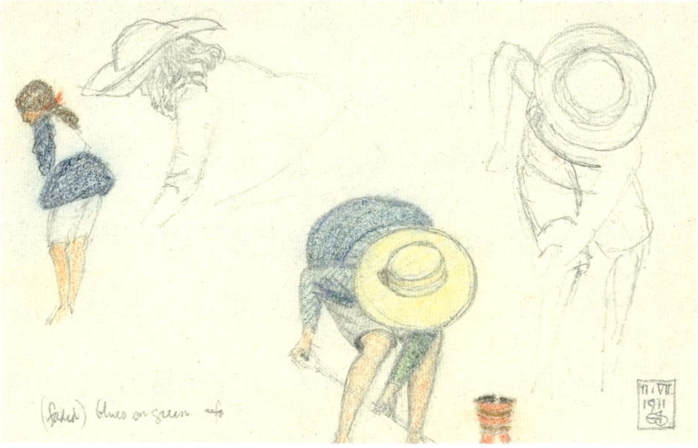

35.* Girls Digging, 1911
Pencil & chalks, 4 1/4 x 7 (10.8 x 17.5)
Signed in monogram & dated *11.VIII.1911* (br)
and annotated (faded) *blues on green* (bl)

Exhibited: Aldeburgh, 1981 (13)

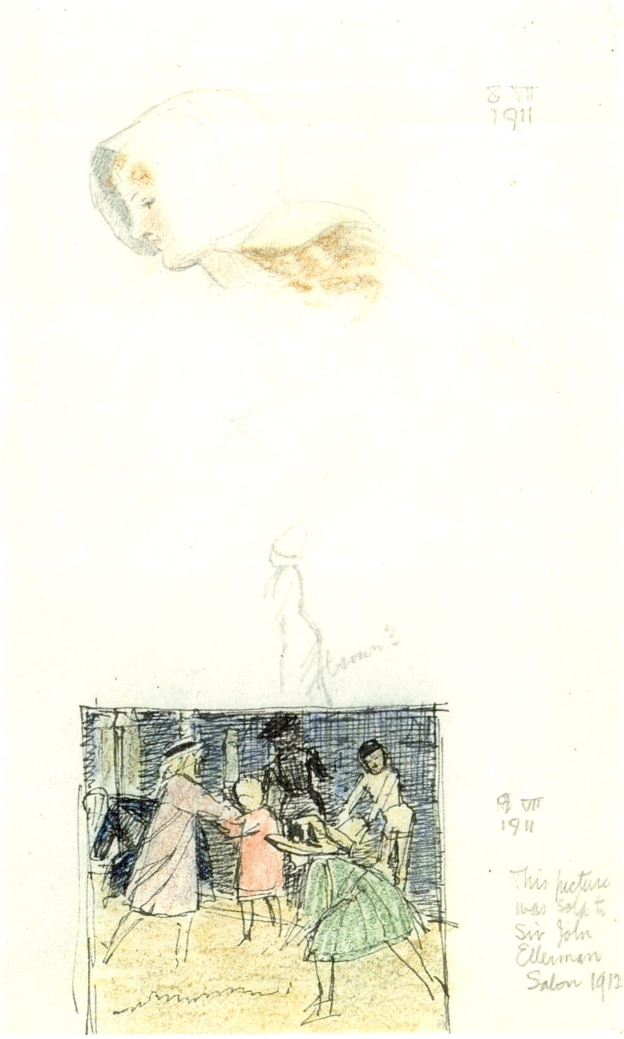

34.* Two Studies, 1911

Pencil, pen & ink & pastel, 7 x 4 1/4 (17.5 x 11)
Dated *8.VII.1911* (tr) by upper study & again *9.VII.1911* & inscribed (alongside lower study) *This picture / was sold to / Sir John / Ellerman / Salon 1912* (br)

Exhibited: Aldeburgh, 1981 (47)

This drawing and the three studies opposite are for *On The Beach*, 1911. *On The Beach* belonged to Mr and Mrs Alan Fortunoff at the time of the 1980 exhibition and was lent by them to it (cat.no.F2). It has since been sold at Sotheby's, London, 7 Nov. 1990, Lot 16, and Sotheby's, London, 2 Oct. 1991, Lot 50. This tempera painting on silk, one of Southall's best Southwold beach scenes, was originally bought by Sir John Ellerman, the shipping magnate, at the Salon of the Société National des Beaux-arts, Paris, in 1912 (no.1188, as *Au Bord de la Mer*, reproduced in colour in catalogue).

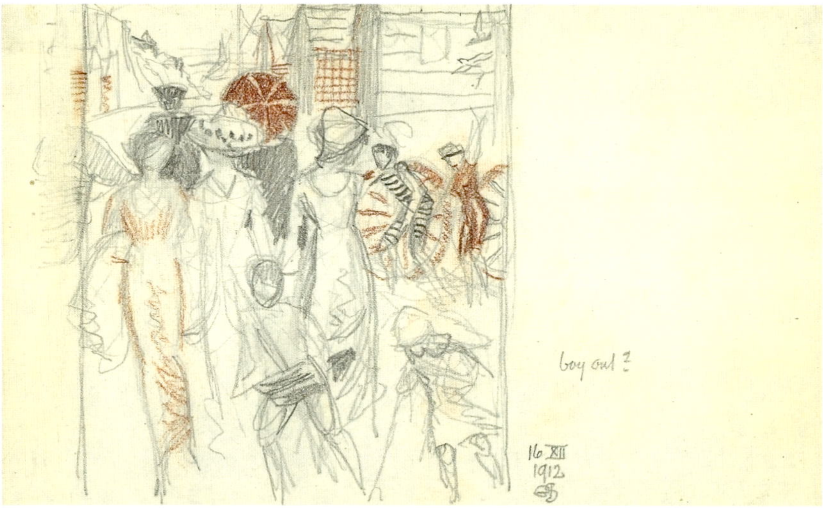

36.* Southwold – Composition Study for Painting, 1912
Pencil & chalk, 4 x 6 1/2 (10.2 x 16.70)
Signed in monogram & dated *16.XII.1912* and annotated *boy out?*

Exhibited: Aldeburgh, 1981 (40)

This sketch-book sheet is clearly an idea for a multi-figure composition based on sketches and recollections of summers in Southwold.

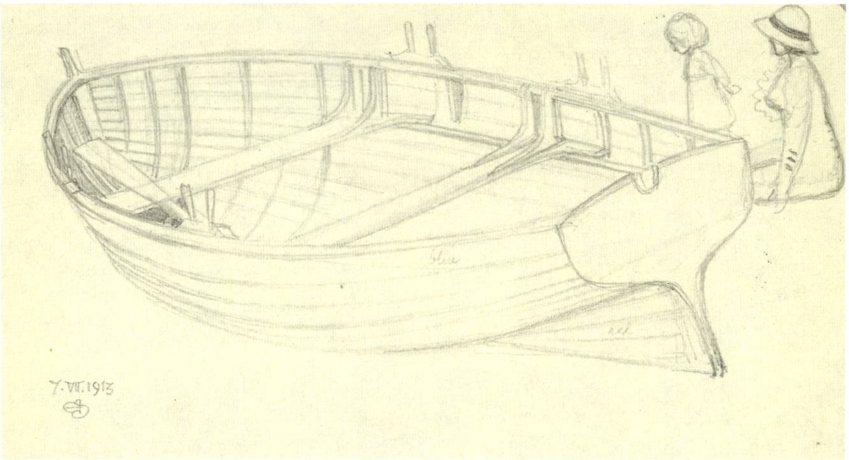

38.* Beached Boat and Figures, Southwold, 1913
Pencil, 4 1/8 x 6 7/8 (10.5 x 17.6)
Signed in monogram & dated *7.VII.1913* (bl)

Exhibited: Aldeburgh, 1981 (44)

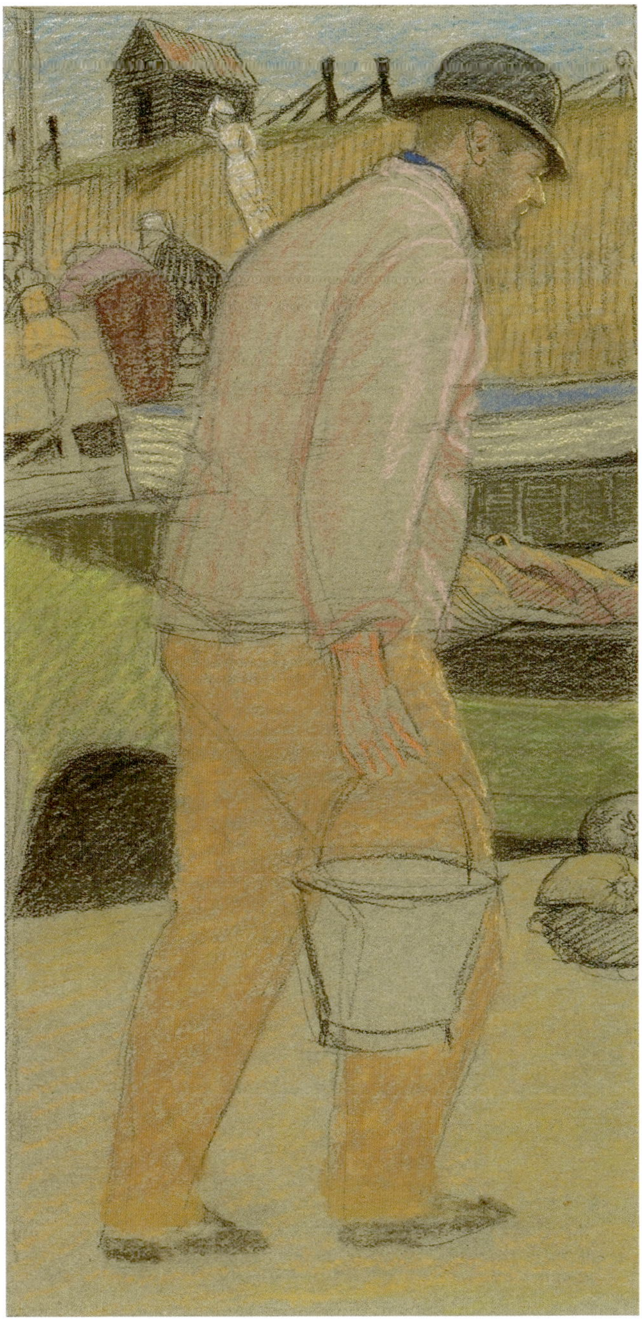

37. Fisherman with Bucket, Southwold, 1912
Pastel over pencil on buff paper, 11 x 5 1/2 (28 x 23), sheet size 12 x 9 (30.5 x 22.9)
Signed in monogram & dated *VII.1912* (lr margin under mount)

Provenance: John Gere

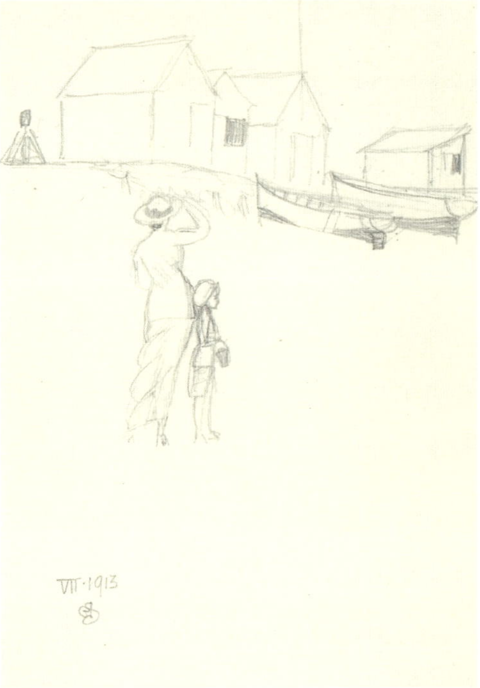

39.* Beach Scene, Southwold, 1913

Pencil, 7 x 4 1/4 (10.8 x 17.5)
Signed in monogram & dated *VII.1913* (ll)

Exhibited: Aldeburgh, 1981 (21)

40. Grazing Sheep, Watchet, Somerset, 1915

Pastel over pencil, 9 x 12 (22.7 30.6)
Signed in monogram & dated *24.IX.1915* (br)

Provenance: Phillips Son & Neale, London (30 Oct. 1978, lot 134b): The Fine Art Society: Mr & Mrs Alan Fortunoff

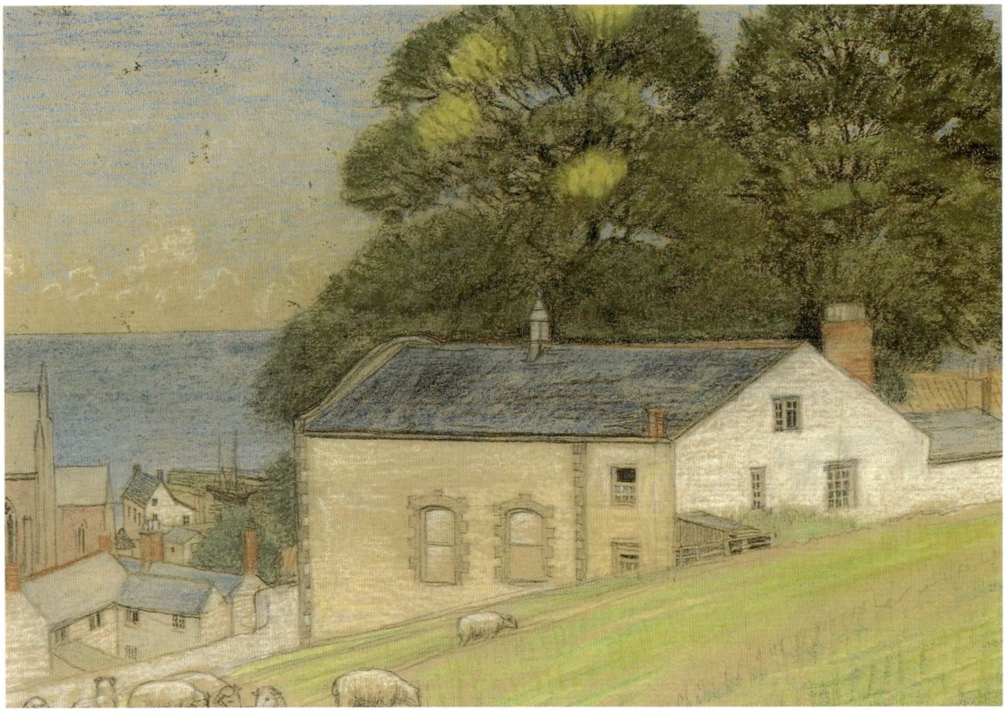

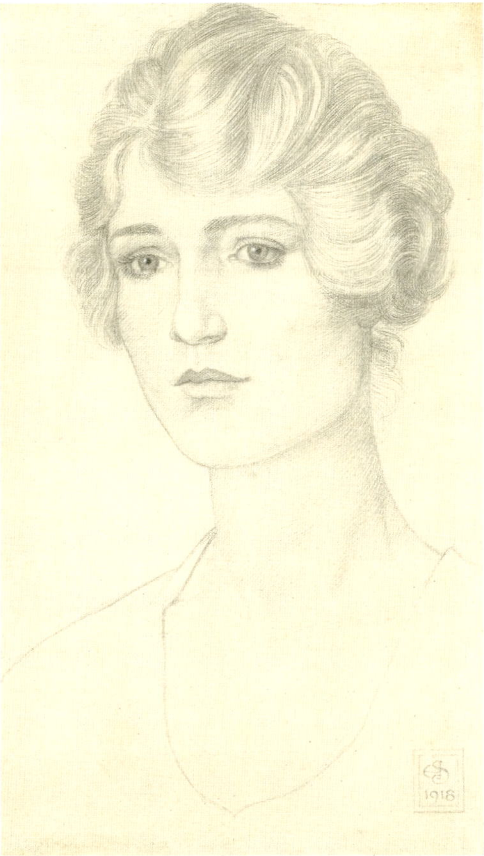

41. Portrait Study of Janet Hutchinson, 1918
Pencil, 12 x 7 1/2 (30.5 x 18.7)
Signed in monogram & dated *1918* (br)

Provenance: Geoffrey & Janet Hutchinson (Lord & Lady Ilford): The Fine Art Society: Mr & Mrs Alan Fortunoff

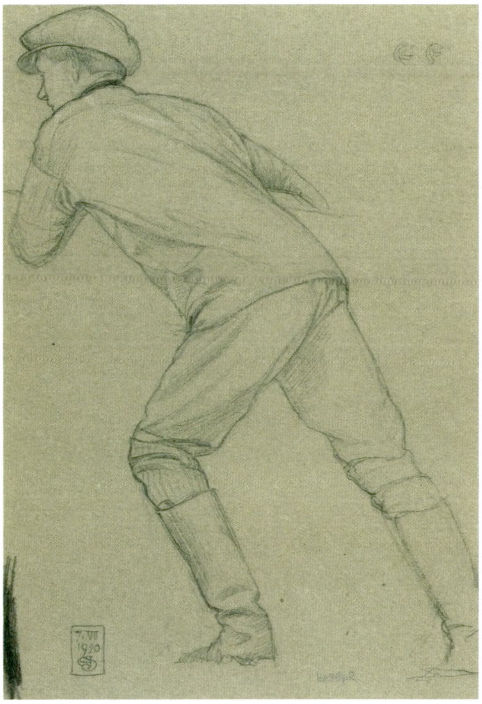

42.* Fisherman Study, 1920
Pencil on buff paper, 12 x 8 1/2 (30.6 x 21.8)
Signed in monogram & dated *7.VII.1920* (bl) also inscribed *BARBER* (lr)

Exhibited: Aldeburgh, 1981 (31)

Southall executed a number of portrait studies of Janet Hutchinson – later Lady Ilford. He created a tempera portrait of her (which was formerly in the Fortunoff collection) entitled Lady in a Green Hat in the same year as this study. Janet Hutchinson came from an important Birmingham family by the name of Keep. She and her husband were noted patrons and collectors, owning fine works by Southall, Wilson Steer, Augustus John, William Nicholson and Gilbert Spencer. Southall dedicated his self-portrait, cat.no.14, to her.

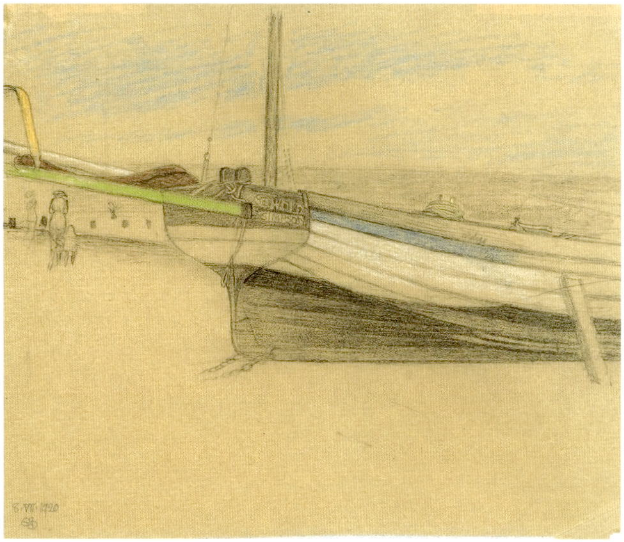

43.* Beached Fishing Boat, Southwold, 1920

Charcoal & pastel, 8 1/4 x 10 (20.8 x 25.7)
Signed in monogram & dated *8.VII.1920* (bl).
Inscribed *SOWOLD / SIMPSON* on stern of boat.

Exhibited: Aldeburgh,1981 (7)

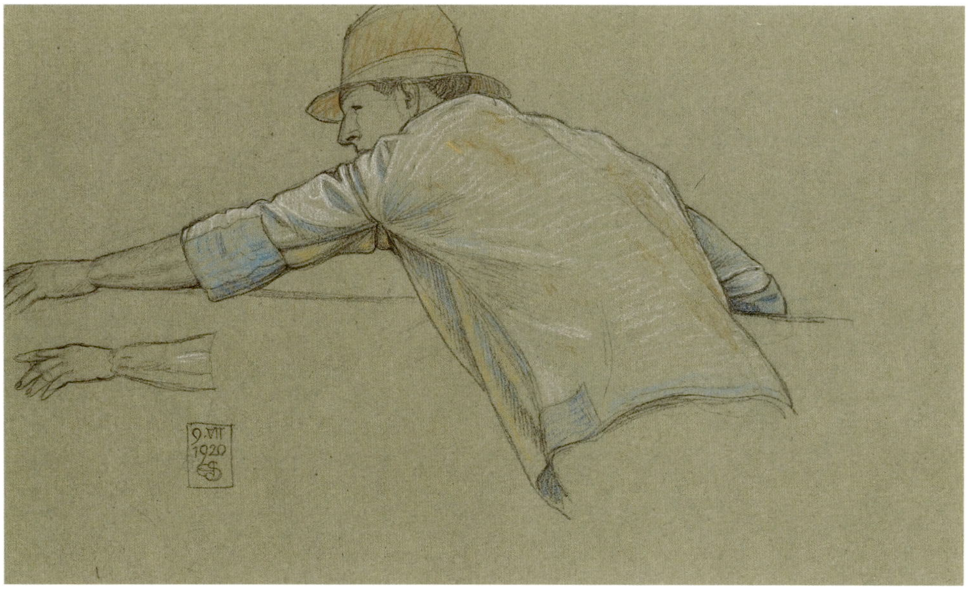

44.* Study for Up From The Sea, 1920

Pastel over pencil on buff paper, 8 1/2 x 12 (21.8 x 30.6)
Signed in monogram & dated 9.VII.1920 (ll)

Exhibited: Aldeburgh, 1981 (32)

Study for the central front figure, repeated in *Fisherman and Boat* (cat.no.19).

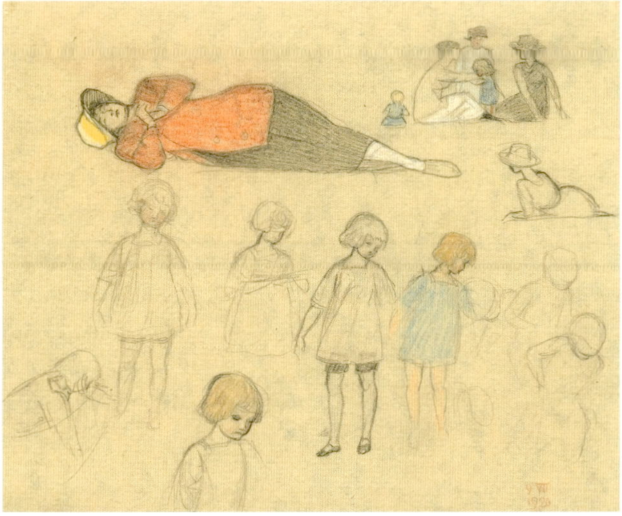

45.* Figures on the Shore, Southwold, 1920

Charcoal & pastel on buff paper,
8 3/4 x 10 1/8 (22 x 25.8)
Signed in monogram & dated *9.VII.1920* (br)

Exhibited: Aldeburgh, 1981 (27)

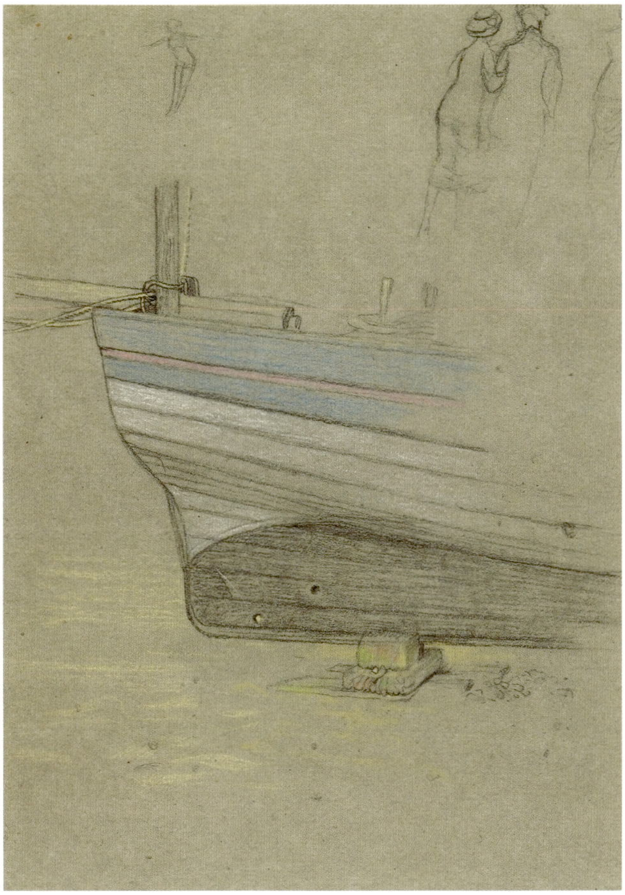

46.* Study of the Stern of a Fishing Boat, 1920

Pastel over pencil on buff paper,
12 x 8 1/2 (30.6 x 21.8)
Signed in monogram & dated *20.VII.1920* (bl)

Exhibited: Aldeburgh, 1981 (28)

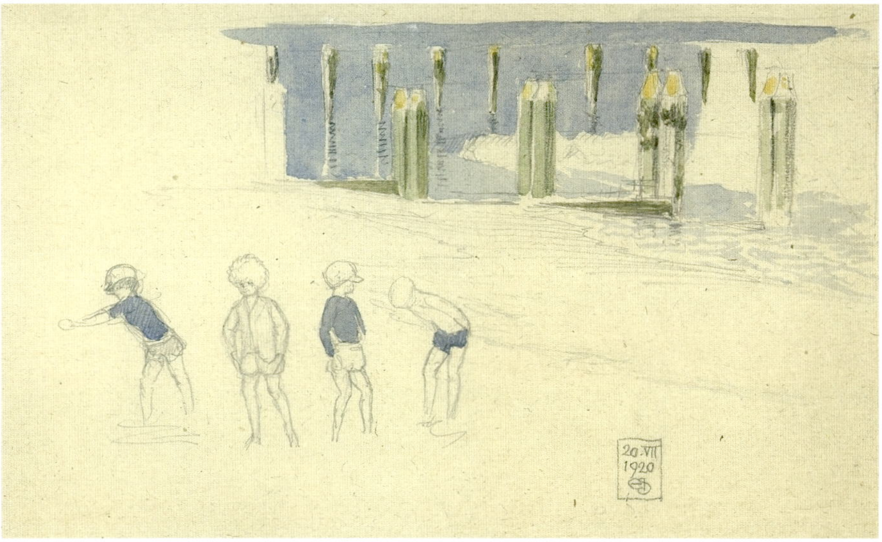

47.* Four Children and Breakwater, 1920
Pencil & watercolour, 5 3/4 x 9 1/2 (14.8 x 24)
Signed in monogram & dated *20.VII.1920* (lr)

Exhibited: Aldeburgh, 1981 (33)

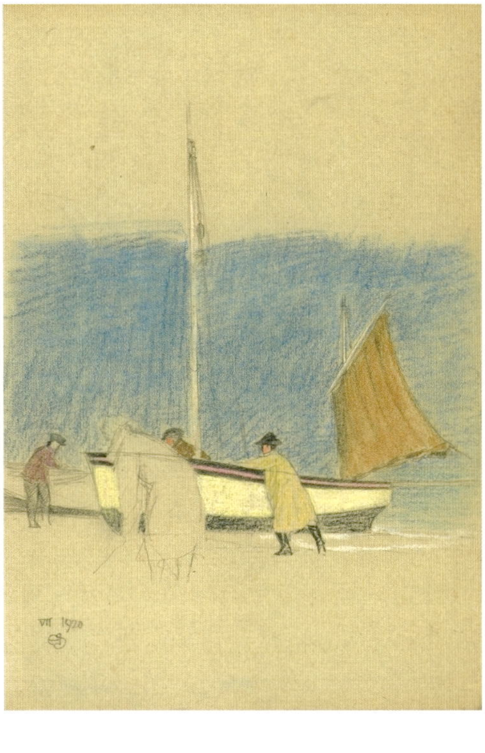

48.* Fishermen and Boat on the Shore, 1920
Pastel over pencil, 12 x 8 1/2 (30.6 x 21.8)
Signed in monogram & dated *VII.1920* (bl)

Exhibited: Aldeburgh,1981 (43)

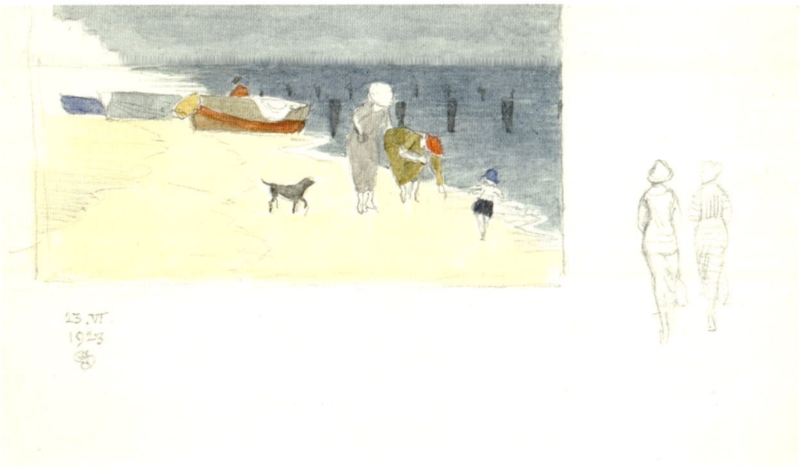

49.* Shore Scene, Southwold – Idea for a Painting – 1923
Pencil & watercolour, 4 x 6 7/8 (10 x 17.5)
Signed in monogram & dated *23.VI.1923*

Exhibited: Aldeburgh,1981 (43)

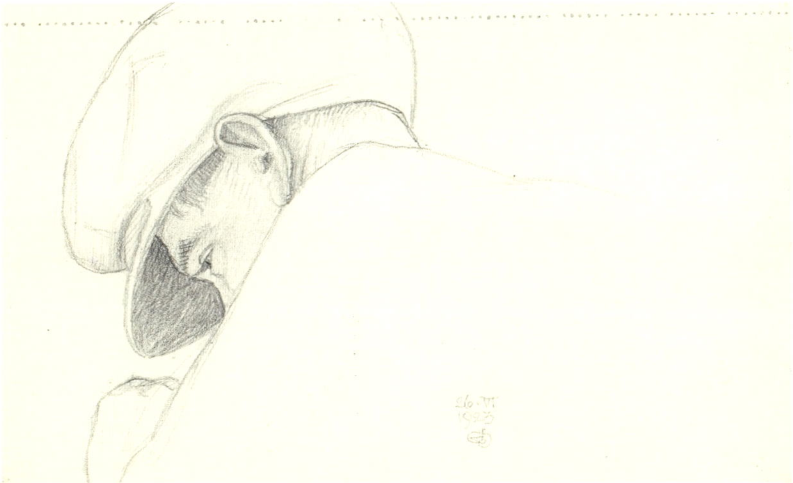

50.* Study for Fishermen and Boat, 1923
Pencil, 4 1/8 x 6 7/8 (10.5 x 17.5)
Signed in monogram & dated *26.VI.1923* (lr)

Exhibited: Aldeburgh, 1981 (30)

Study for front left figure, see cat.no.19.

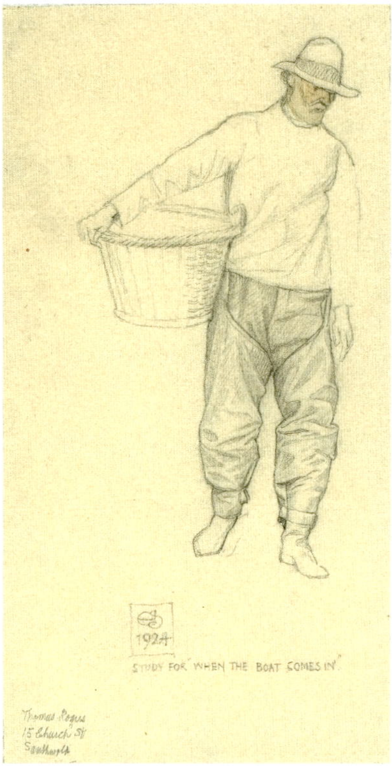

51. Study for When the Boat Comes In, 1924

Pencil, touched with watercolour, on buff paper, 9 x 4 7/8 (23 x 12.5)
Signed in monogram, dated *1924* & inscribed *STUDY FOR "WHEN THE BOAT COMES IN"* (lc) and *Thomas Rogers / 15 Church St / Southwold* (bl)

Provenance: A Morrison: The Fine Art Society: Mr & Mrs Alan Fortunoff

Southall was very observant of the typical stance and posture of the Southwold fishermen as they went about their daily tasks; an almost identical figure, though with the basket under the left arm, appears in the background of *Fishermen and Boat* (cat.no.19).

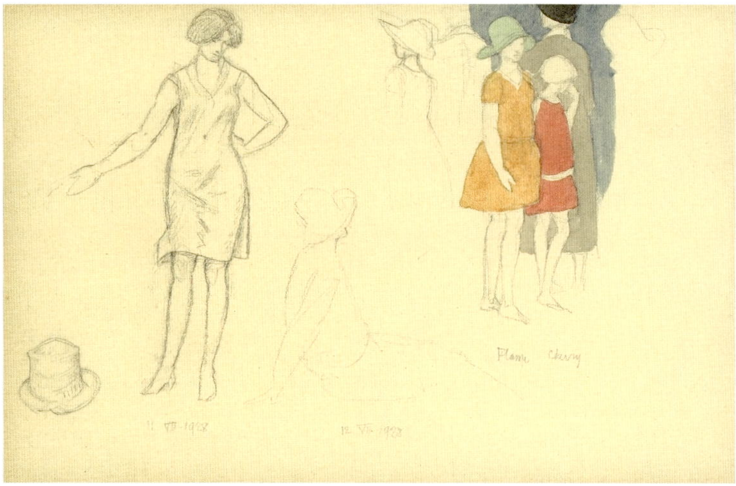

52.* Figure Studies, Southwold, 1928

Pencil & watercolour, 6 x 9 1/4 (15.2 x 25.7)
Dated (twice) *11.VII.1928* and *12.VII.1928* and annotated *Flame / Cherry*

Exhibited: Aldeburgh, 1981 (65)

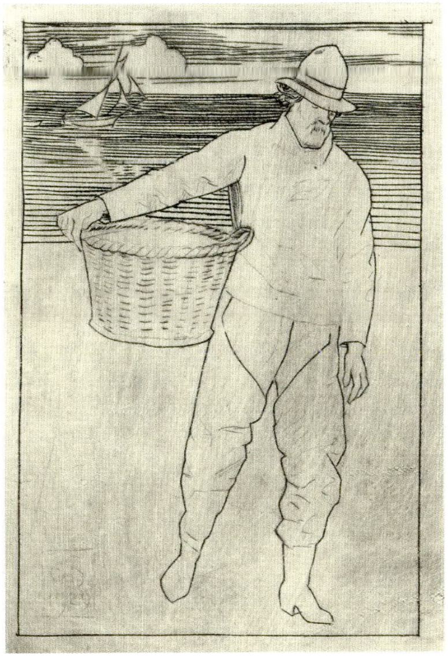

53. Fisherman and Basket, Southwold, 1929

Etching, 4 3/4 x 3 1/2 (12.2 x 8.8.)
Signed in monogram & dated *1929* in the plate (bl) & inscribed in pencil *Drawn, engraved and printed by Joseph Southall XII.1929*

Provenance: John Gere: The Fine Art Society: Mr & Mrs Alan Fortunoff

Southall was in the habit of making small etchings to send to friends at Christmas. They were never editioned and do not seem to have been either exhibited or sold commercially.

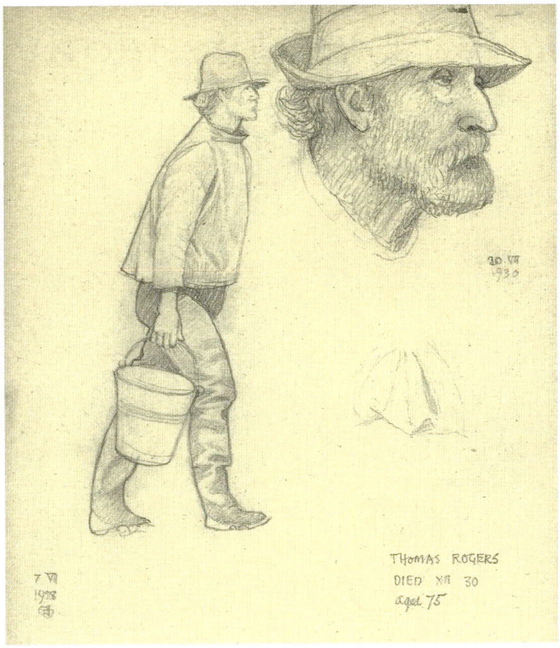

54.* Two Studies of Thomas Rogers, Southwold, 1928–30

Pencil, 9 1/4 x 6 (23.5 x 15)
The full length sketch to the left signed in monogram & dated *7.VII.1928*. The head (top right) dated *20.VII.1930* and the sheet annotated *THOMAS ROGERS / DIED XII 30 / aged 75*

Exhibited: Aldeburgh, 1981 (50)

Thomas Rogers is the left hand figure in *Fishermen and Visitors*, 1931 (Russell-Cotes Art Gallery & Museum, Bournemouth)

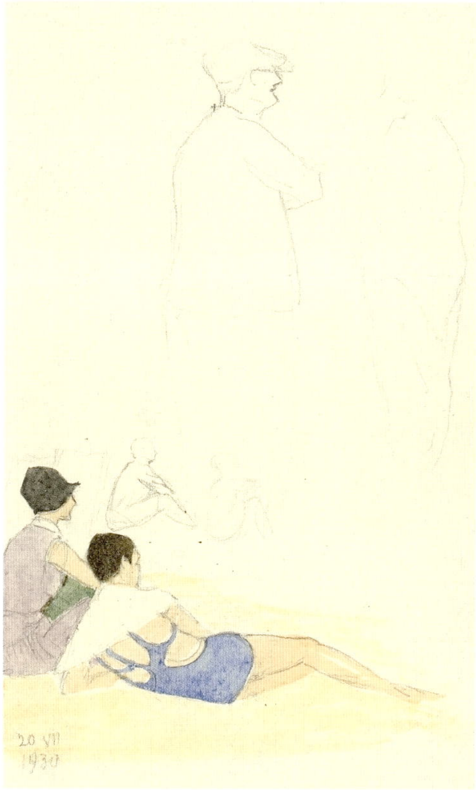

55.* Beach Studies, Southwold, 1930

Pencil & watercolour, 6 3/4 x 3 7/8 (17.3 x 9.8)
Dated *20.VII.1930,* (bl)

Exhibited: Aldeburgh, 1981 (9)

56.* Figures on the Beach, Southwold, 1929

Pencil & watercolour, 6 x 9 1/4 (15.2 x 25.7)
Signed in monogram & dated *13.VII.1929* (ll)

Exhibited: Aldeburgh, 1981 (64)

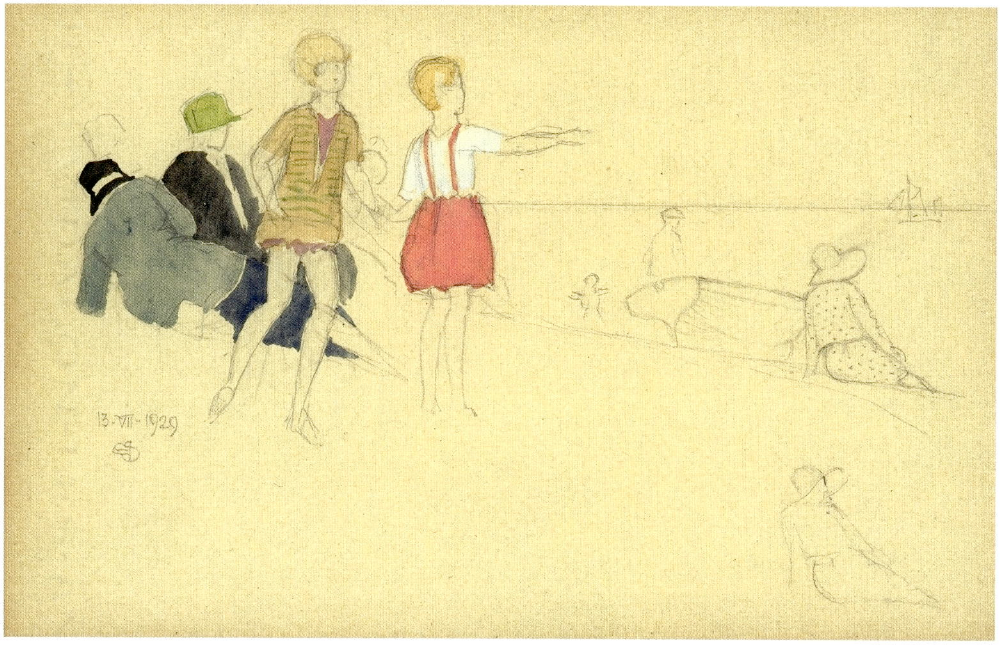

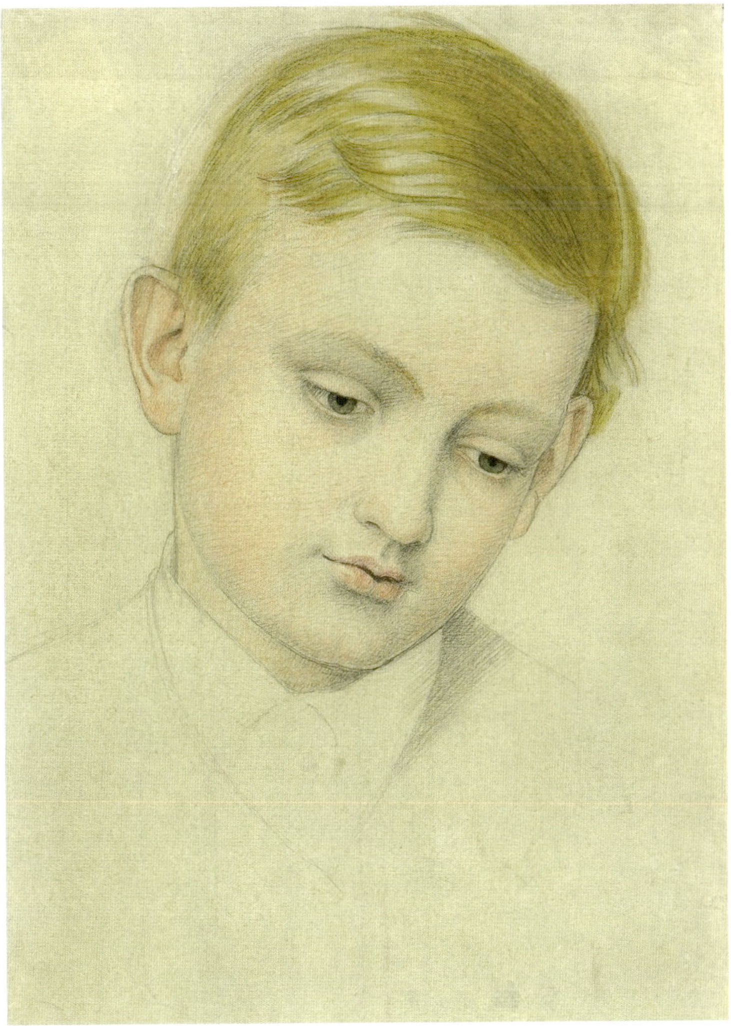

57. Head of a Boy, 1934
Pencil & chalks on tinted paper, 14 1/8 x 9 1/4 (36.4 x 23.8)
Signed in monogram & dated *1934* (bl) and inscribed *Finished 2.VI.34*

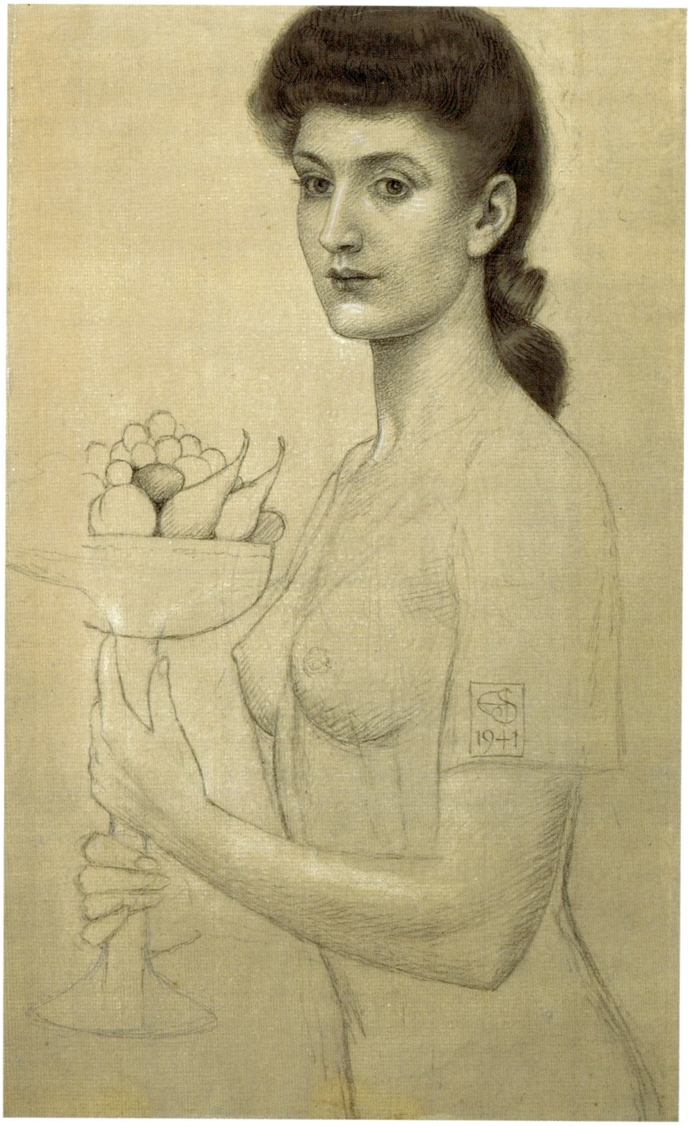

58. Study for *A Dish of Fruit*, 1940–41
Pencil & gouache over an opaque buff ground, 11 3/4 x 7 (30 x 17.5)
Signed in monogram & dated *11.IX.1940*, (ll margin beneath mount), and signed again in monogram & dated *1941* on the model's sleeve

Provenance: J S Maas & Son: Mr & Mrs Alan Fortunoff

Although dated 1940–1, it is unclear whether this is a fresh study done at that date, or whether, like the finished watercolour (cat.no.26), it was an earlier drawing worked up.

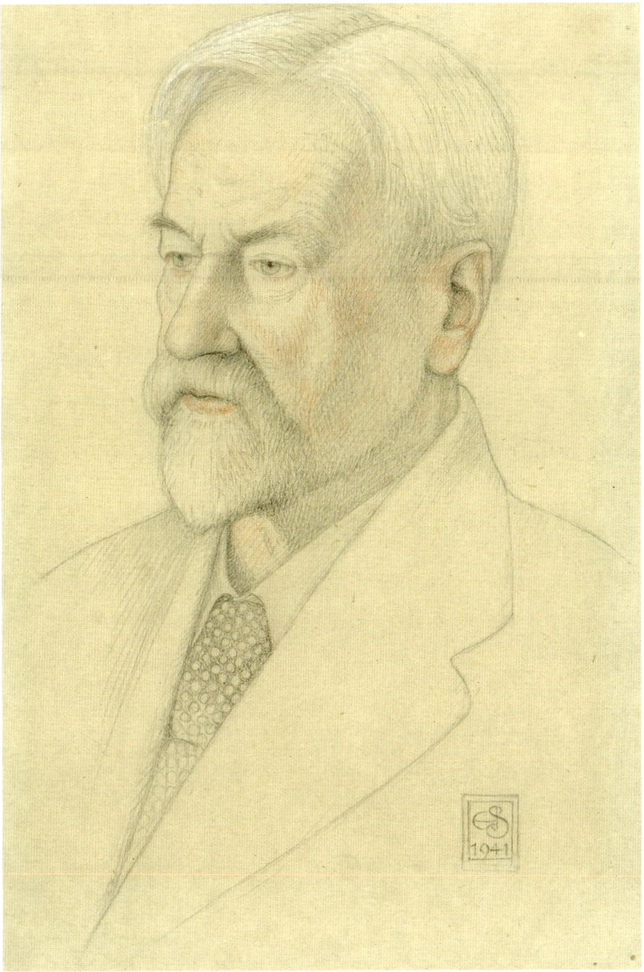

59. Study for Portrait of Henry W Nevinson LLD, LittD, 1941
Chalks, 15 1/4 x 10 1/4 (38.7 x 26.1)
Signed in monogram & dated *1941* (br)

Provenance: Mrs I.L. Nevinson: The Fine Art Society: Mr & Mrs Alan Fortunoff

Henry Woodd Nevinson (1856–1941) advocated conscription in his youth though he later came to hate war. As a war correspondent for many years he pricked the consciences of his readers. In 1939 he was elected to an honorary studentship of his old college, Christ Church, Oxford. Southall executed two portraits of Nevinson, one, in tempera, with which this study is probably associated, being given by the sitter's second wife, Evelyn Sharp Nevinson, to the college in 1946. Henry Nevinson was also the father of the painter CRW Nevinson, who shared a two-man exhibition with Southall at the Leicester Galleries in March 1926.

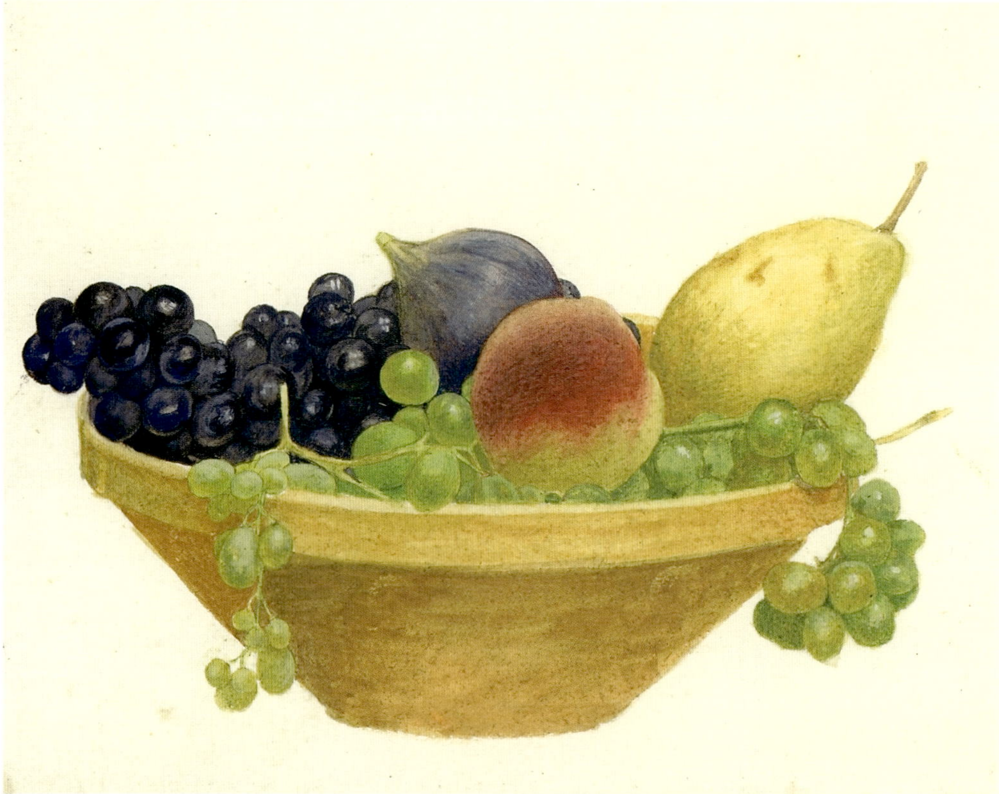

60. Study of a Bowl of Fruit

Watercolour, 5 1/2 x 7 (14 x 17.9)

Southall executed a number of similar studies, nearly always depicting Mediterranean fruits – grapes, peaches, figs, pears, etc. – associated with early Italian or Renaissance painting, probably used when preparing such works as *New Lamps for Old* (1900–1), *Ariadne in Naxos* (1925–6) and *A Dish of Fruit* (1941) (cat.no.26).

Select Bibliography

Armfield, Maxwell, introductory notes, *Memorial Exhibition of Works by the late Joseph Southall*. Exhibition catalogue, Birmingham City Museum & Art Gallery, Birmingham, 1945, pp. 1–8.

Armfield, Maxwell, 'The Work of Joseph Southall', *Old Water-Colour Society's Club, Annual Volume*. 1946, pp. 34–41

Breeze, George, *Joseph Southall, 1861 – 1944: artist-craftsman* (includes technical notes by Jill Dunkerton). Exhibition catalogue, Birmingham City Museum & Art Gallery and The Fine Art Society, London, 1980.

Crawford, Alan, ed., *By Hammer and Hand: the Arts and Crafts Movement in Birmingham*, Birmingham, 1984

Gere, Charlotte, *The Earthly Paradise*. Exhibition catalogue, The Fine Art Society, London, 1969

Harvey, M. M., "A Quaker Artist and Rebel" in *The Friends' Quarterly*, vol. xiv, October 1963, pp. 353–361

Hill, J. & Midgley W., *A History of the Royal Birmingham Society of Artists*, RBSA & Cornish Bros.,1928

Massey, V., *A Testimony to the Life of Joseph Edward Southall*, Warwickshire Monthly Meeting of the Society of Friends, Birmingham, June, 1945

Napier-Clavering, C., "Birmingham painters and craftsmen at the Fine Art Society's galleries", *The Studio*, vol. xlii, 1907–08, pp. 215–222

Outhwaite, R. L., *The Ghosts of the Slain: A Vision of the Future*, with drawings by Joseph Southall, The National Labour Press, Manchester, 1915

Quaker Faith & Practice (the book of Christian discipline of the Yearly Meeting of the Religious Society of Friends (Quakers) in Britain), 2nd edition, London, 1999, particularly chapter 24 "Our peace testimony"

Skipwith, Peyton, "Peace, Politics and Painting". *Country Life*, January 30, 1992, p.65

Skipwith, Peyton, "Southall in Suffolk", Aldeburgh Festival, 1981

Southall, Joseph, "Grounds suitable for tempera", *Papers of the Society of Painters in Tempera*, vol. 1 (1901–1907), 2nd edition, Brighton,1928, pp. 1–7

Southall, Joseph, *Fables and Illustrations*, The National Labour Press, London, 1918

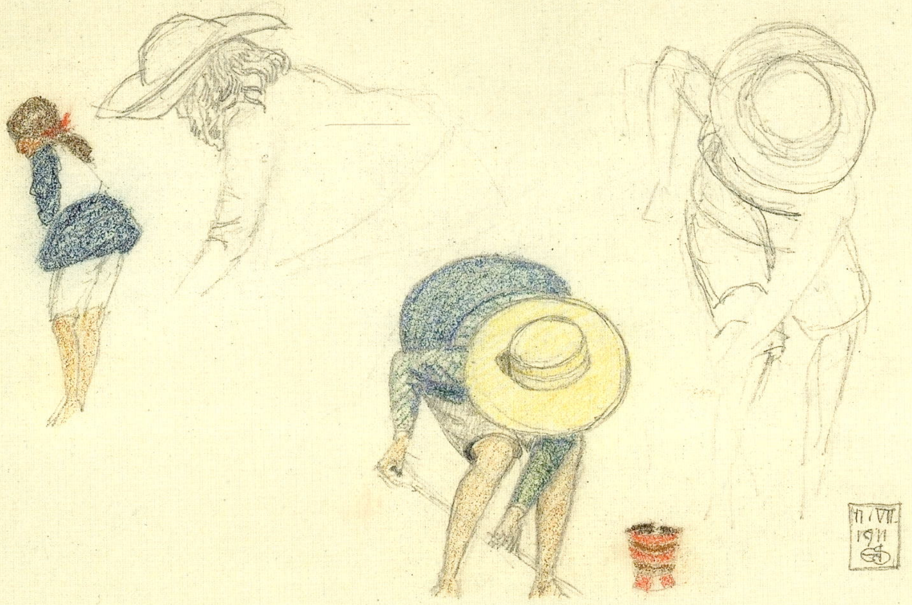
11/VII
1911

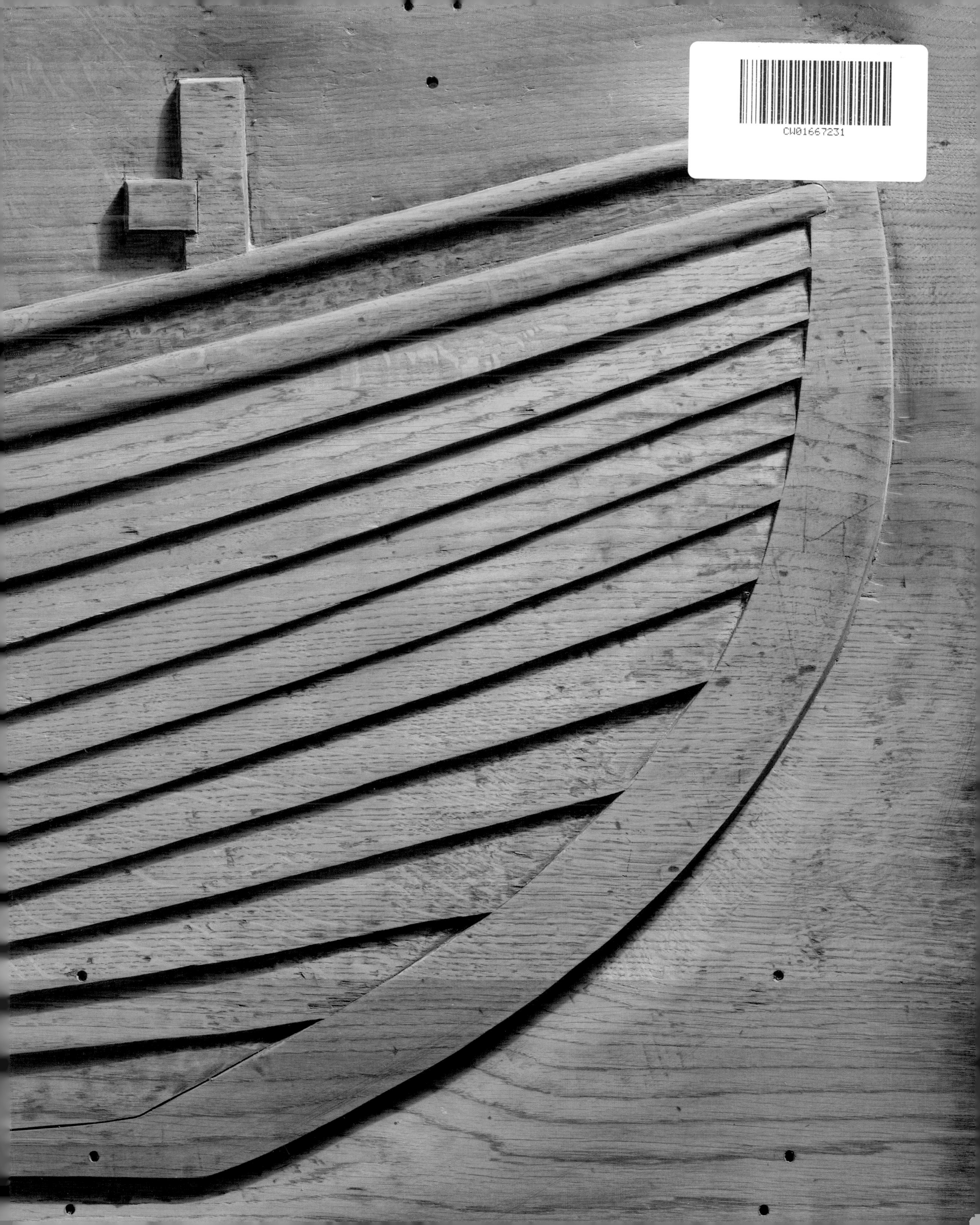

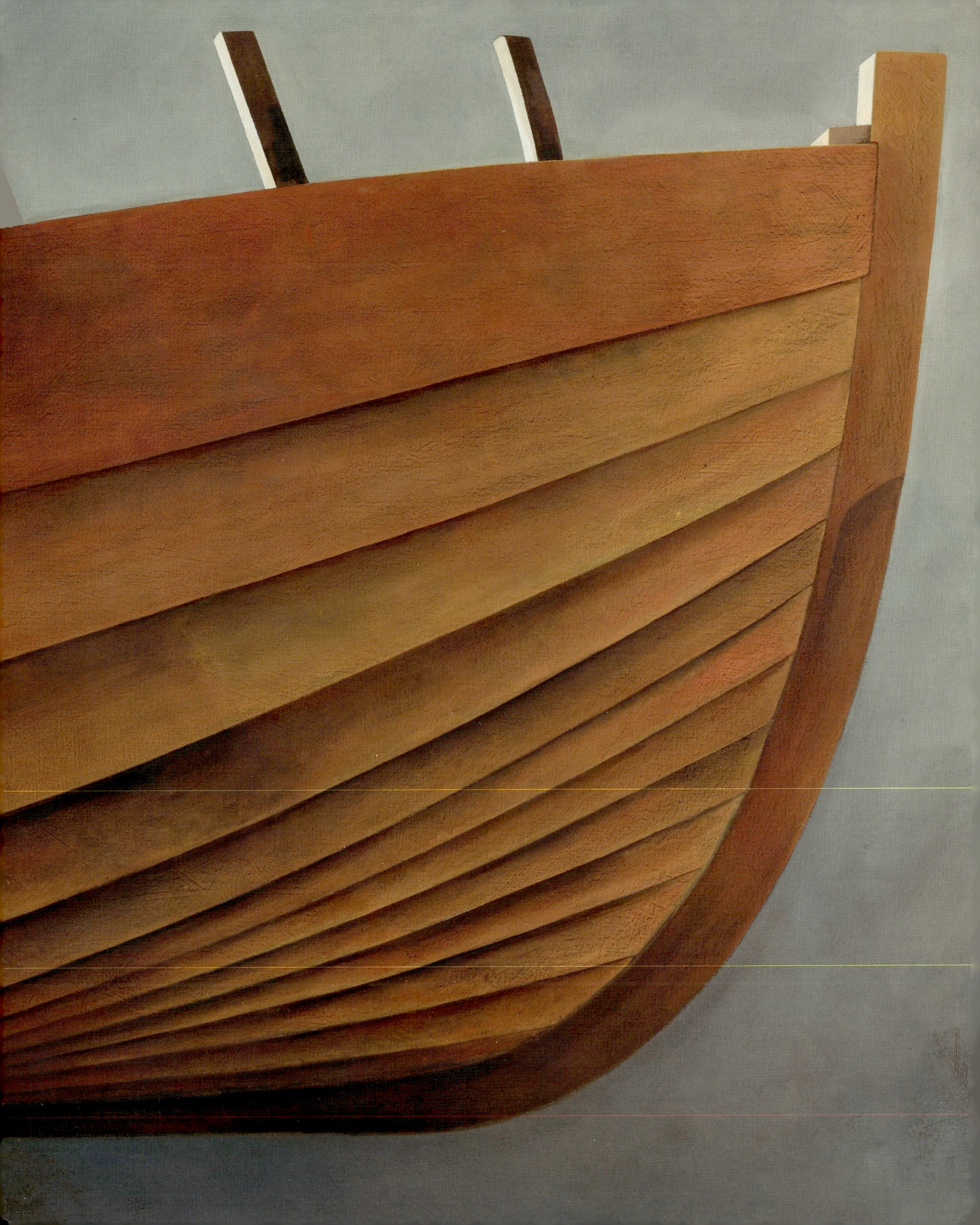

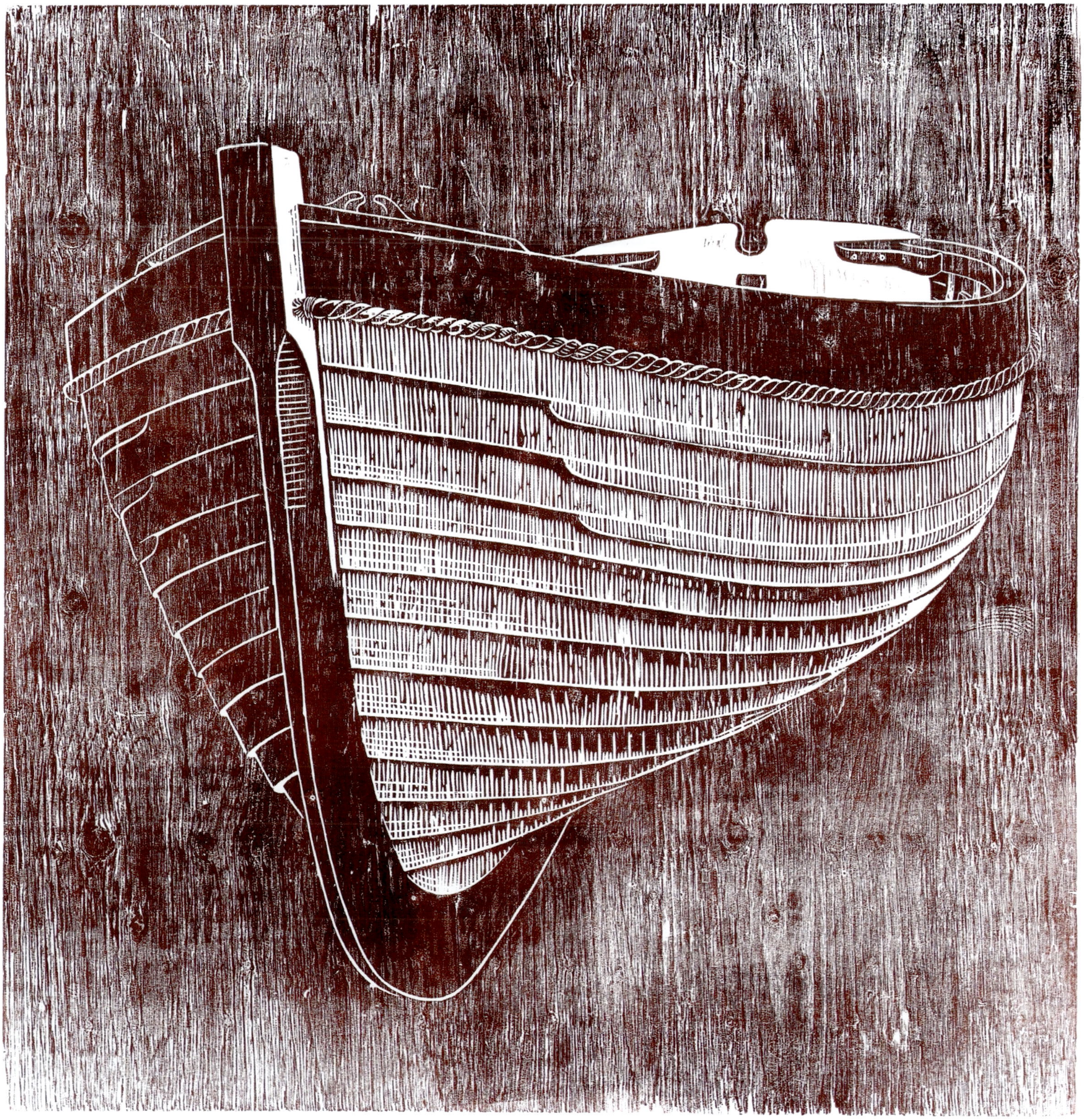

1. Red Boat
woodcut - edition of 50
107 x 107 cms 42⅛ x 42⅛ in

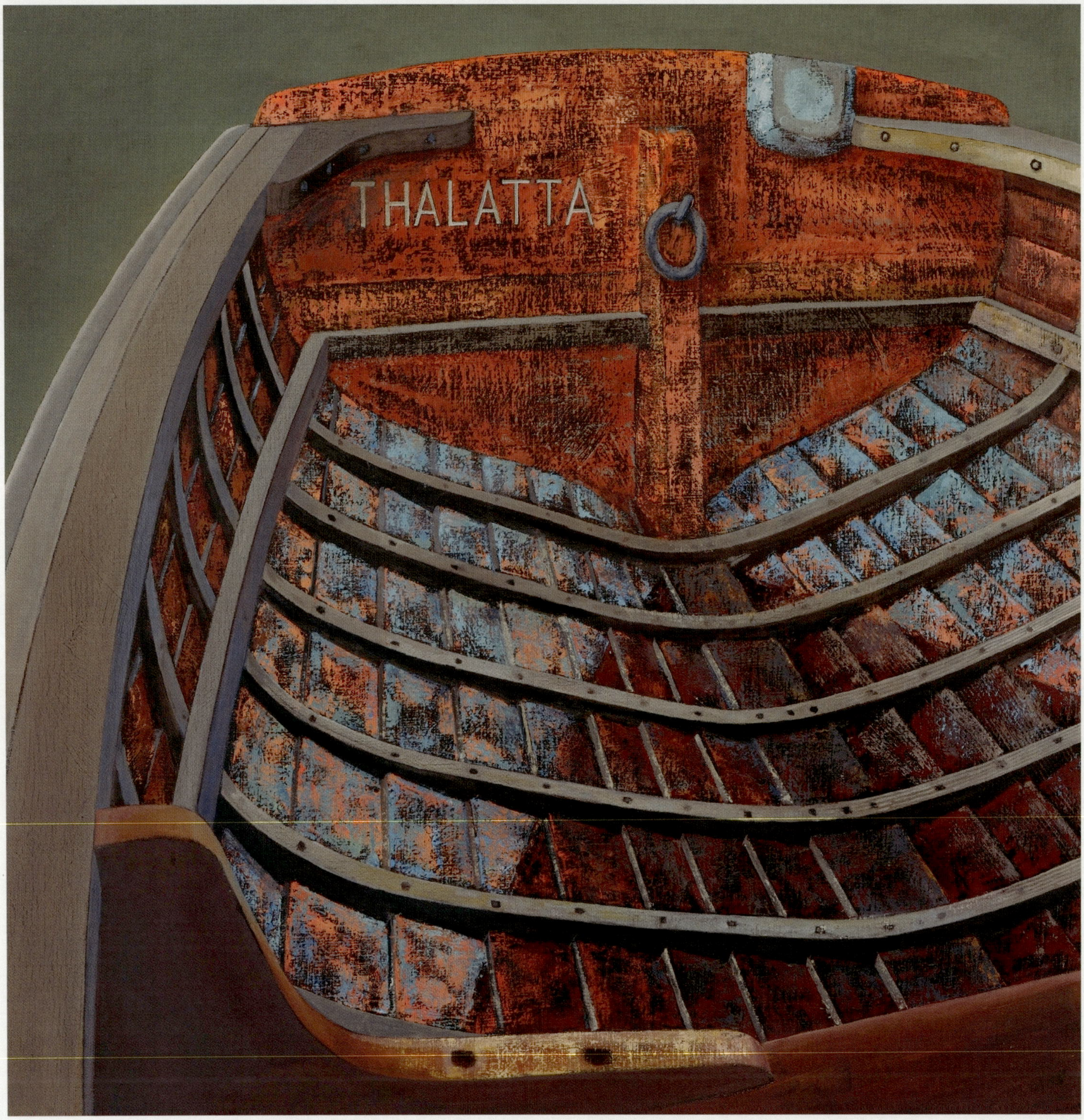

2. "Thalatta" Barge Boat
oil on linen
90 x 90 cms 35⅜ x 35⅜ ins

JAMES DODDS

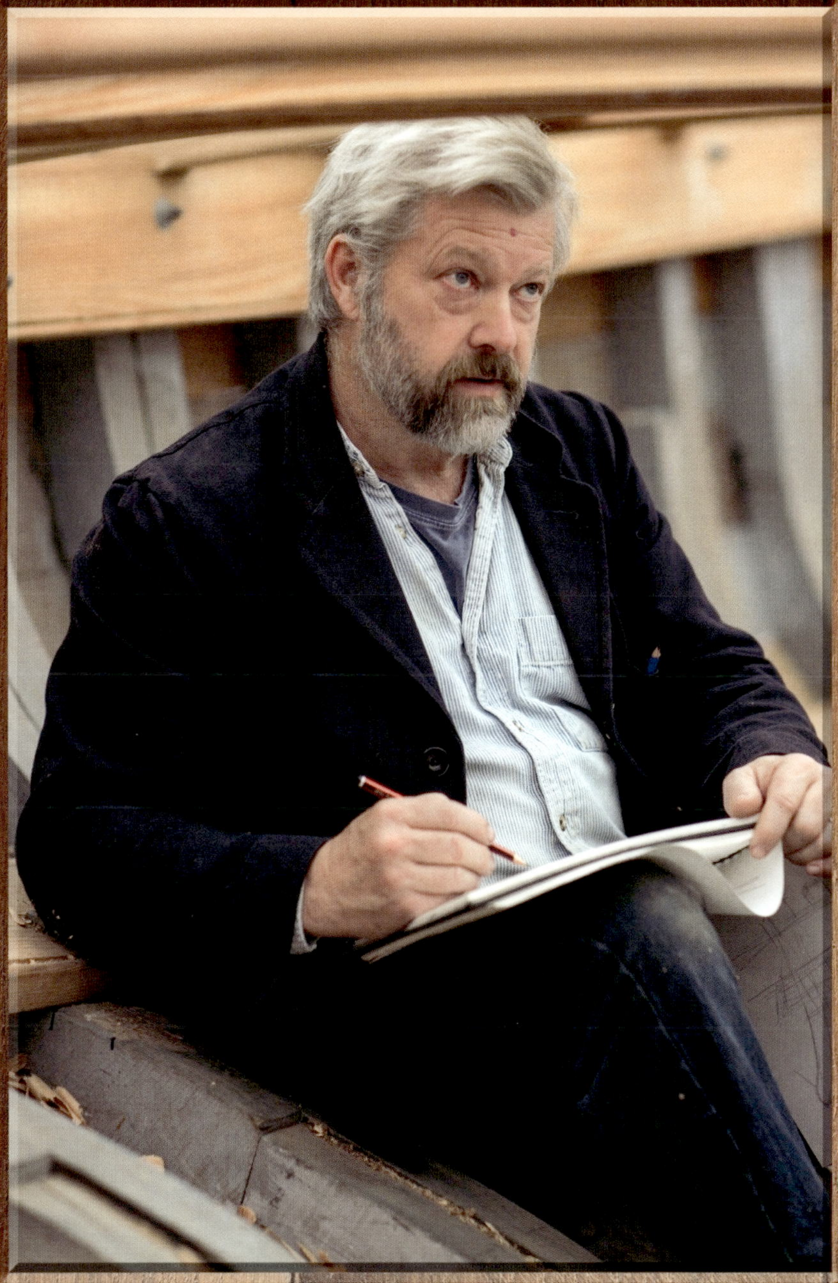

2015

Messum's

www.messums.com
28 Cork Street, London W1S 3NG
Telephone: +44 (0)20 7437 5545

Foreword

James Dodds is happily at work in his new studio, with walls of glass giving a sweeping view over mud and water and sky. Essex in its barest glory – an artist in his element.

The prospect up and down and across the River Colne, from the site of a once-great boatyard, takes in remnants of manual and mechanical labour: a gravel works whose barges shipped load after load for the London Olympics; glimpses of Wivenhoe's last four working fishing boats; tractors trailing seagulls.

A descendant of doughty Scottish farmers, and of enterprising Essex men who built sea walls around the Walton Backwaters – as well as in his native port of Brightlingsea, at the Colne's mouth – James adds to the surrounding scene. He has lately dug a deep channel into the river to aid the launch of his prized and much-painted winklebrig and a more recently acquired double canoe. Retrieved mud has been blended into the backgrounds of a new line in shallow-relief images on salvaged boards. Famously a shipwright who then turned his hand to the depiction of boats, he continues to build his pictures and his story in singular style.

James works slowly and with quiet deliberation and painstaking experimentation amid a constantly shifting drama of sky and water. Here a reflected sunset can flood over everything. And although a barrier is now in place to keep tidal surges at bay, the river can still reach almost level with the studio floor. He has even looked up to see a seal's head rising above a high tide, with jaws clamped on a flatfish. His home, a couple of hundred metres distant, is next to the base of Wivenhoe's last boat-builder. This artist's life and work are forever immersed in the spirit and spectacle of the sea.

With a reputation now enhanced by exhibitions on both sides of the Atlantic, James has won fresh acclaim since his last Messum's show in London. He was one of the few living artists to feature in the blockbuster exhibition Masterpieces: Art and East Anglia, which charted the saga of the eastern region in nearly 300 pictures and objects drawn from the dawn of time to date. His triptych painting of a Cromer crabber floated comfortably between a Turner storm scene at Great Yarmouth and modernist marvels of constructivism and abstraction. The celebratory Norwich display won rave reviews and more than 46,000 visitors and resulted in the Sainsbury Centre for Visual Arts being short-listed for 2014 Museum of the Year.

And now James is the subject of a new film by Emily Harris of Classic Yacht TV. The profile documentary Shaped by the Sea –

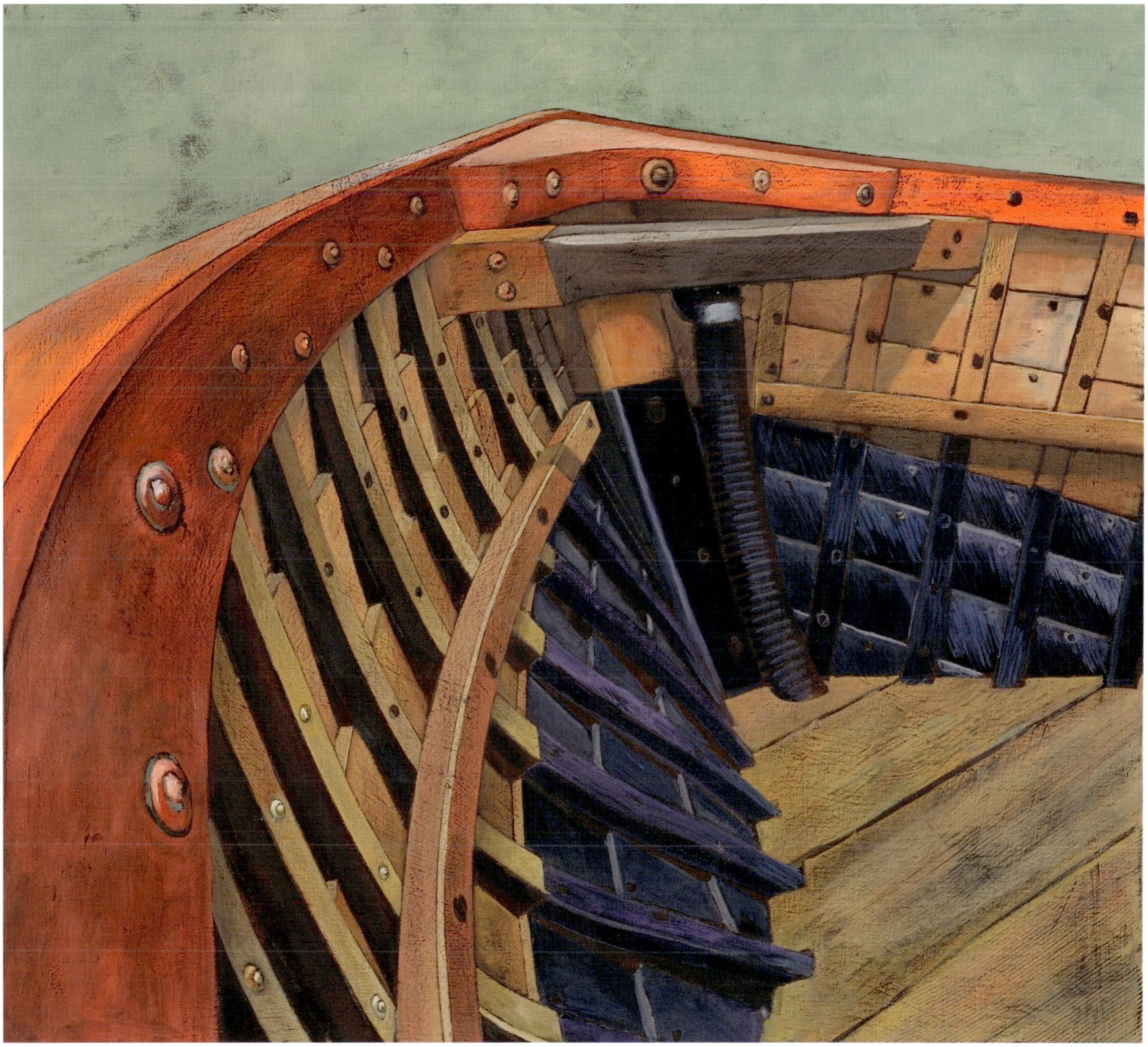

3. Stern of a Crabber
oil on linen
80 x 90 cms 31½ x 35⅜ ins

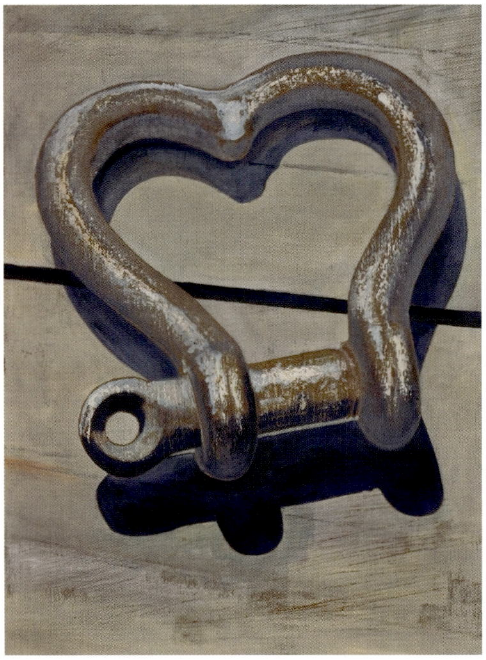

4. Heart-shaped Shackle
oil on linen
61 x 46 cms 24 x 18 ins

viewable on YouTube – draws many parallels between the art of the boat-builder and the evolving painter of boats. Both vessel and image are plotted by rule of thumb and manual dexterity. And what emerges in both cases is a voyage of discovery – a crafted journey between history and destiny.

James is firmly anchored in his origins and adrift in a creative process which keeps his imagination and our keen interest alive. Here are new perspectives on familiar Wivenhoe One and Brightlinsea One boat designs. And images of the Thames sailing barge Thalatta recall his roots as an apprentice boat-builder at Maldon, where this restored vessel is now the pride of the East Coast Sail Trust fleet. The Edwardian survivor, built in Harwich in 1906 and rebuilt in nearby St Osyth in 2012, saw a century of toil along the east coast and across the North Sea, and now hosts educational and recreational adventures for youngsters – helping to free the seafarer still lurking deep inside most of us within our island nation.

While the young James Dodds was struggling at school with undiagnosed dyslexia he swiftly mastered the art of sailing on a smack called Shamrock and a small winklebrig much like the one he owns today and which shares his studio space (also being represented in the sole print, and paradoxically the most monumental exhibit, in this show). There were many explorations of the creek-rife Essex marshes before, at 14, he gained his dream weekend job as a trainee mate on a Baltic trader. School holidays allowed longer voyages to France and Holland. For this 2015 exhibition he has taken a fresh look at historic North Sea crossings. Now he contends, after recent trips to Norfolk and Denmark, that all clinker-built boats around our shores derive from Viking vessels.

James Dodds has long championed boat-building traditions around the British coastline, via many productive partnerships – with makers, poets and campaigners. His latest alliance is with Rescue Wooden Boats on the North Norfolk coast at Stiffkey – a classic Dodds triptych image of a Cromer crabber now graces the trust's website. The rescue team revealed to James the difference between a crabber and a whelker. Although constructed along similar lines, the latter is heavier and berths in harbours, while the lighter crabber can be hauled on to the beach. Both vernacular vessels prompted pictures in this exhibition, but the most exhilarating tale concerns Auk – the first wooden crab boat to be built in Norfolk for a quarter of a century.

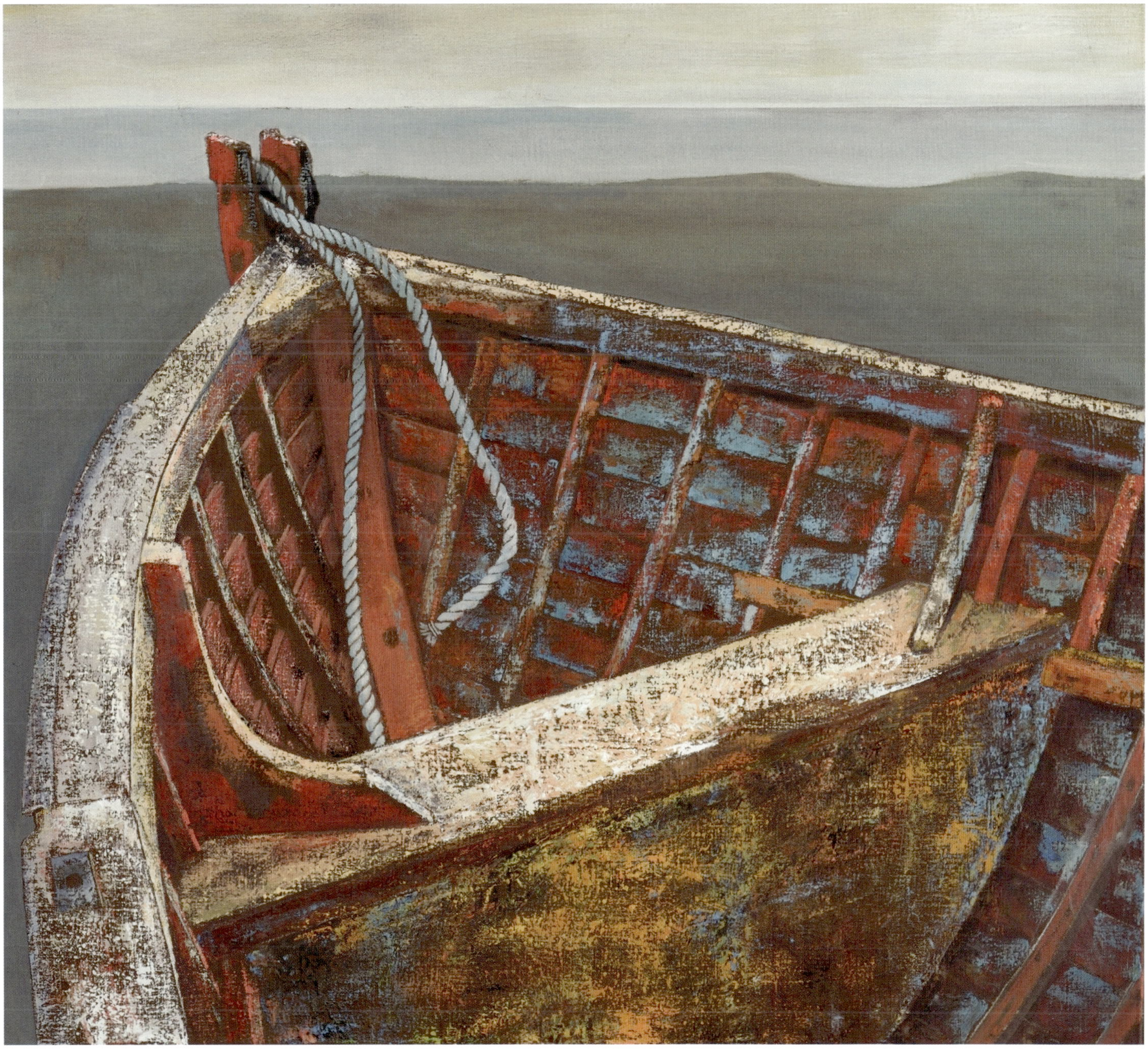

5. Old Aldeburgh Beach Boat
oil on linen
81 x 92 cms   32 x 36 ins

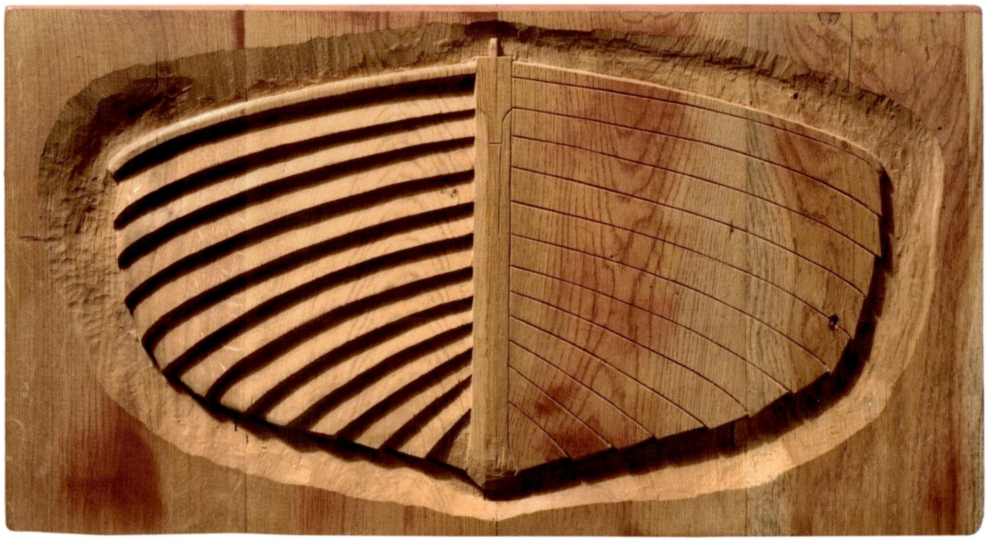

6. Brightlingsea One Design
carved oak panel
34 x 64 cms 13¼ x 25 ins

7. Crabber Bow Detail
oil on linen canvas
90 x 60 cms 35⅜ x 23⅝ ins

David Hewitt and 17-year-old apprentice Tom Gathercole spent nearly 1,500 hours constructing Auk without plans or diagrams. Components comprised one oak tree, two larches (one straight grown and one "swept" for the curved parts), 2,000 copper nails and 10 metres of copper rod for hand-made bolts, 1,200 larch wedges, 400 silicon bronze woodscrews and gripfast nails, 22 litres of paint, two litres of glue and 12 tubes of sealer. Commissioner Henry Faire says: "She's absolutely beautiful, the most wonderful piece of craftsmanship I've ever seen – a Stradivarius of boats. I will use her for mackerel and bass fishing and maybe the odd bit of crab potting. Just messing about in boats which is what I like doing."

Leaving the yard and following the present trickle that is the River Stiffkey a few miles inland leads to the Danish Camp at Warham. Norfolk's best-preserved Iron Age fort was built by Celts when this little river was navigable from the sea, but named by our Angle ancestors after the last invaders to occupy it. The same marauders who killed King Edmund of East Anglia in 869 and beat combined Anglo-Saxon forces at the Battle of Maldon in 991. They left settlements ending in –by and more mysteriously inspired the eastern region's peculiar congregation of round-towered churches. But perhaps the Norse inheritance remains strongest in locally adopted and adapted boat designs.

Last summer James made a pilgrimage to Denmark and in a futurist museum to the sea, created from a disused dry dock beside Hamlet's castle at Elsinore, he felt instantly at home. His Danish journey produced images of eel drifters and pleasure dingies – all with Viking origins. He was less moved by the awesome remains of dragon-prowed longboats carrying raiders and invaders than by later trading boats – smaller craft but with far stronger an influence in the evolution of Britain's fishing and haulage vessels. The link is clearest in the most northerly Orkneys, but evident all down the east coast.

A human presence haunts all these pictures, even when figures are unseen. Boats are made by and for people. Back in the 1980s James created a triptych tribute to the striking Solidarnosc shipyard workers of Gdansk who helped to bring down the Iron Curtain – a work hanging in the University of Essex ever since. Now he has produced a partner picture in a three-part salute to Upper Clyde shipbuilders – the central panel marking the 1971 sit-in led by Jimmy Reid when the yard was facing closure. Even the director called the peaceful occupation "an understandable

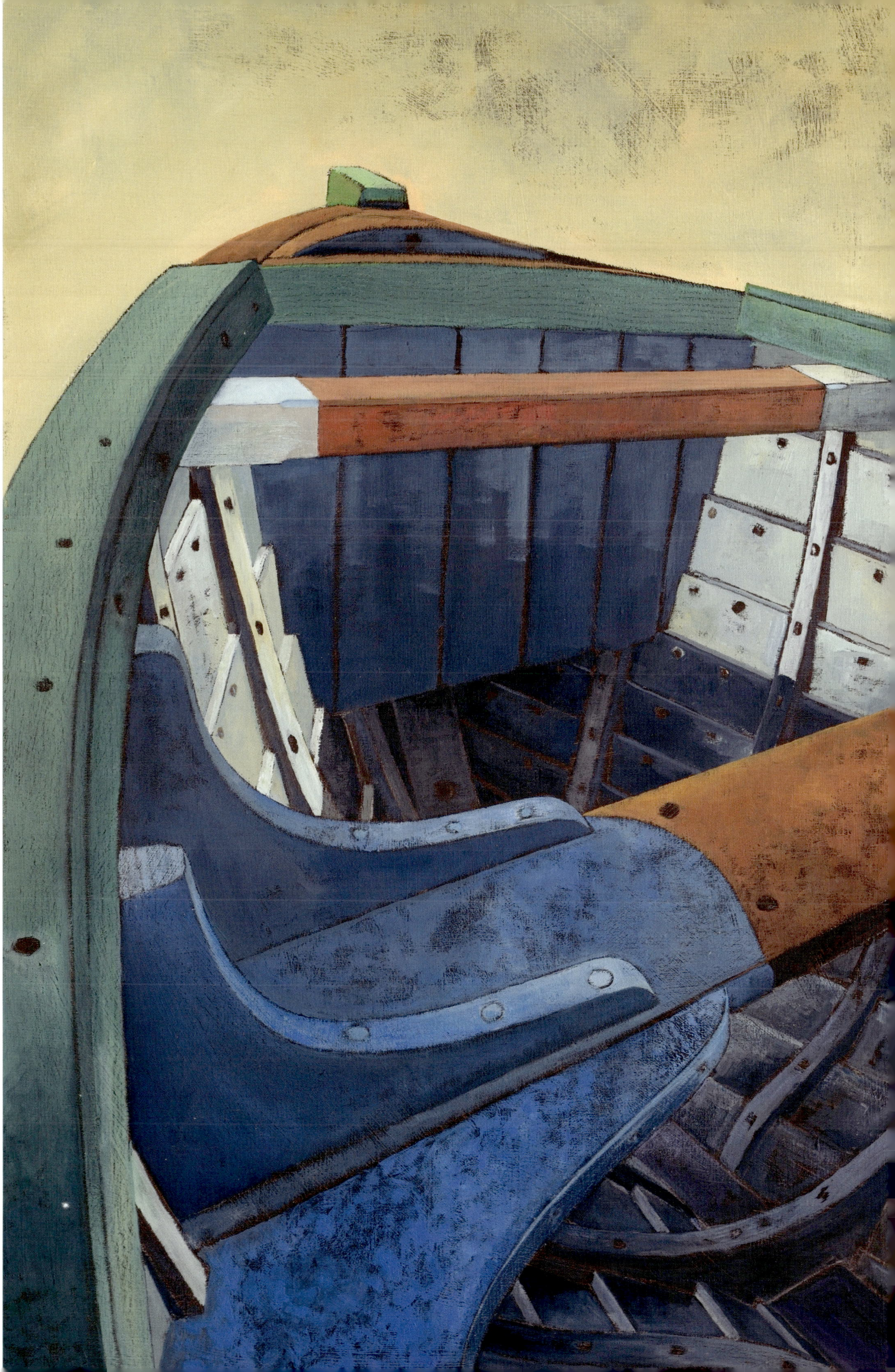

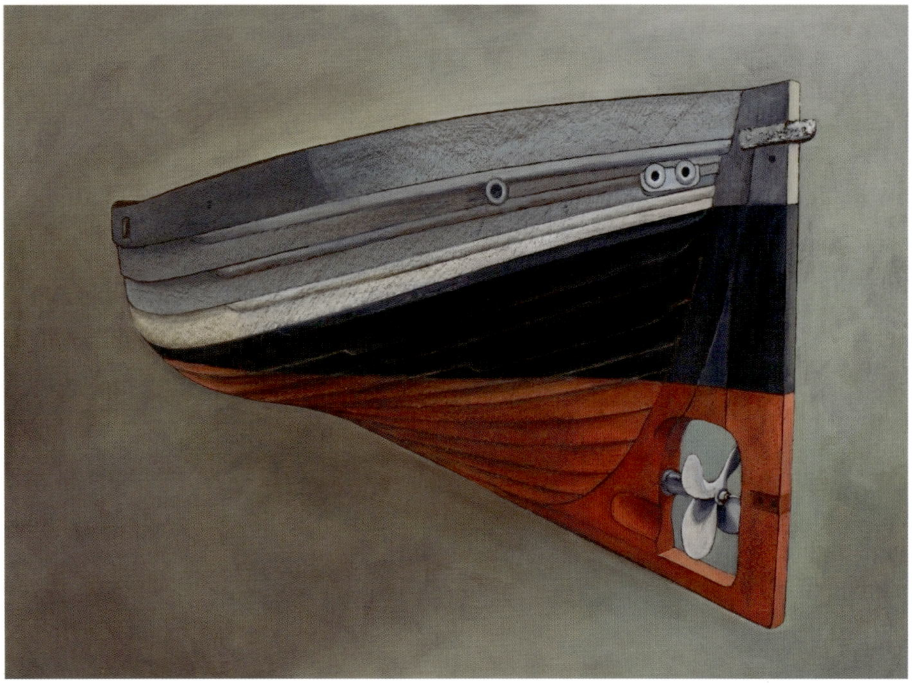

8. Norfolk Whelker Study
oil on board
40 x 50 cms   15¾ x 19⅝ ins

9. Stern of a Crabber
oil on linen
90 x 60 cms   35⅜ x 23⅝ ins

expression of legitimate grievances". Flanked by images of the liner Empress of Britain under construction around 1930, and the aircraft carrier Queen Elizabeth taking final shape in 2014, the message is that action to save our heritage and secure our dreams can really work. The roses at the heart of the design recall a floral gift to the Clydesiders (along with a cheque for £5,000) from John Lennon.

When James Dodds moved from boat builder to boat painter his images were chiefly concerned with structure. Gradually he has changed towards a preoccupation with colour, tone and texture – moving away from the literal and towards the symbolic and mythic. His most beautiful pictures now have a luminous quality and an inner light suggesting a sturdy optimism. When those sunsets wash over his studio he can certainly echo Turner's last words that "The sun is God."

But human continuity is the key here, even though this artist seems to be working at the very end of an age-old line – saying: "My sources for now are museums and charities and the occasional enthusiast who builds a boat in the traditional way. I think there is one working wooden fishing boat on Aldeburgh beach and the rest are plastic. In my childhood nearly all were wooden."

And yet, unbalanced Britain sorely needs to look beyond a superficial service economy to recover its manufacturing base and all the myriad skills of making things – indeed this is surely our key economic challenge in the 21st century. For the moment our coast and waterways retain small but vital skill pools – East Anglia, for instance, has an International Boatbuilding Training College at Oulton Broad as well as the localist stalwarts of Stiffkey.

Worked boats are the perfect symbol of our history and destiny. Lose them and we're all at sea.

IAN COLLINS
Southwold,
February 2015.
(Art critic and writer. Author of Tide Lines: The Life and Art of James Dodds)

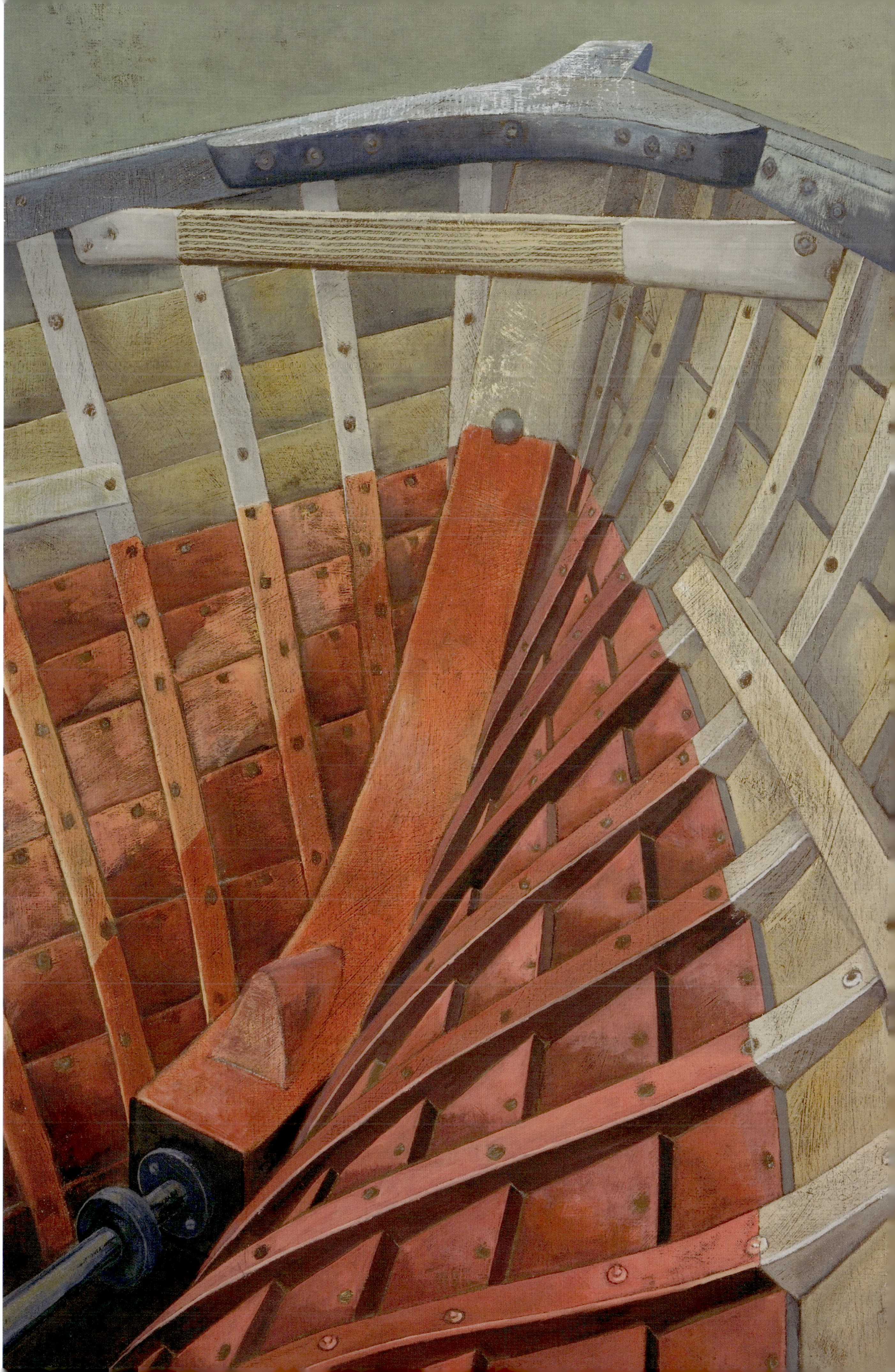

10. Crabber Stern
oil on linen
90 x 60 cms   35⅜ x 23⅝ ins

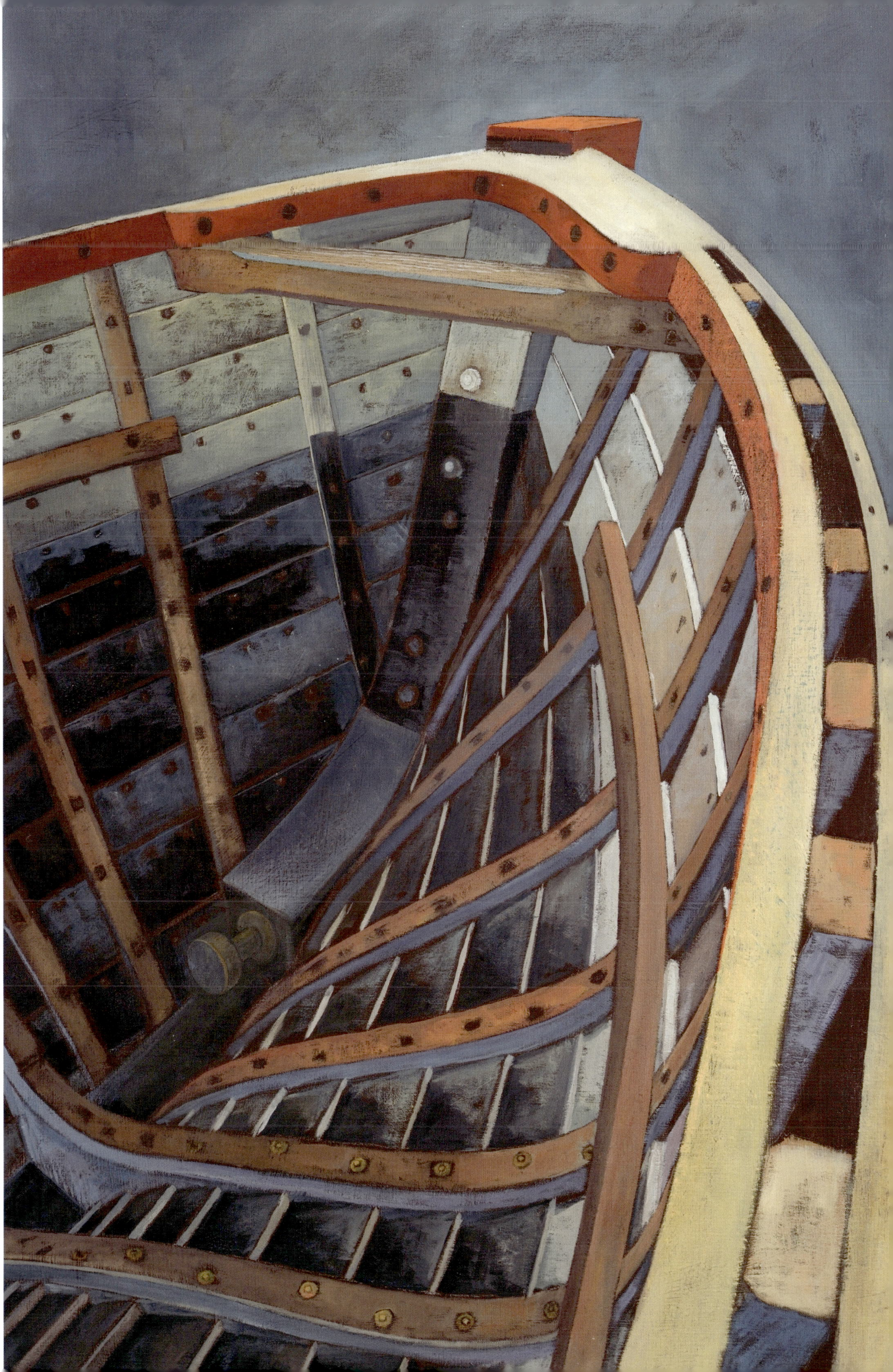

Upper Clyde Shipbuilders

James Dodds' triptych oil of the Clyde's shipbuilding heritage is a welcome addition to this artistic canon. Intended to be read chronologically from left to right, the left panel depicts the RMS Empress of Britain near to completion. Built between 1928 and 1931 by John Brown & Company, the Empress of Britain left Southampton on her maiden voyage to Quebec on 27 May 1931. She would remain in commercial service until 1939, during which

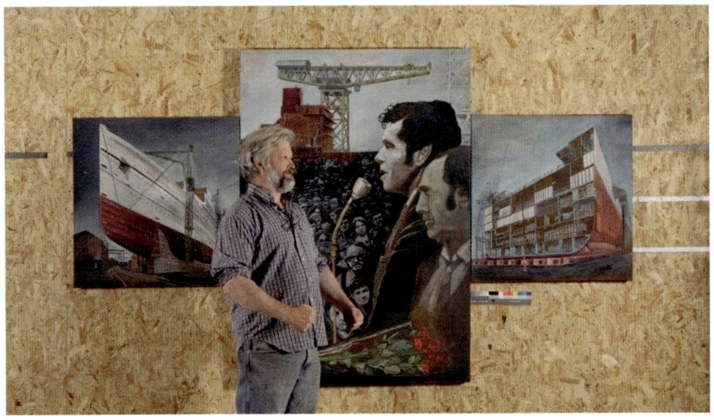

she made 100 transatlantic voyages and several world cruises. The 42,348 tonne liner was commissioned and owned by the Canadian Pacific Steamship Company, which hoped that North American and European passengers would travel to and from Canada, rather than the traditional Southampton – New York crossing. Unfortunately, in spite of being the most luxurious cruiser to ever operate between England and Canada, there were not so many people that could afford the Empress of Britain's exorbitant prices, thus making her one of the least commercially successful liners of the interwar years. On 26 October 1940, not long after she was requisitioned as a troop transport, the Empress of Britain was bombed by a German long-range Focke-Wulf Condor aircraft off the northwest coast of Ireland. She was taken in tow by the Polish destroyer Burza and two British tugs, however, two days later a German submarine torpedoed and sank her, making the Empress of Britain the largest liner ship to be sunk during World War II.

The centre panel illustrates the first day of the UCS campaign on which Jimmy Reid (with Bob Dickie stood at his side) delivered his famous 'no bevvying' speech to several thousand workers, the press and television crews. Reid's announcement was to set the tone for the fifteen month work-in, which was peaceful, disciplined, and sanguine. Even the managing director of UCS praised the conduct of the workers 'as an acceptable and understandable expression of their legitimate grievances'. Based on an iconic photograph taken at the time, Dodds' painting captures the miscellaneous drama of this historic occasion: the workers gathered at John Brown's, the same shipyard that had built the Empress of Britain forty years previously, and which was the largest employer of labour in Clydeside at the time; the then ubiquitous and towering presence of shipyard cranes along the Clyde; the union's vehement insistence on 'Not a man down the road – the right to work – not a yard will close'; the self-loading Clyde Class cargo ship, Sam John Pioneer, being fitted out in the yard's basin (one of only seven such vessels to be built); actually existing working-class collectivism and a spirit of social hope, even though many of the workforce and shop stewards didn't fully comprehend the novelty of what was being proposed; above all, Reid's powerful oratory, and his unerring faith in the goodness of humanity, commitment to labourism and socialist ideals, and celebrated status as a working-class hero.

Of the many messages of encouragement and donations that had been forthcoming during the work-in, one of the most meaningful was a £5,000 contribution and a bunch of red roses given from another influential household name, John Lennon. (On hearing of the donations, one comrade allegedly remarked, "I thought Vladimir Lenin was deid!") Dodds' foregrounding of Lennon's gift of red roses is significant, not only because it serves as a subtle reminder of the widespread support for the UCS work-in, but because it also represents an (albeit implicit) articulation with other kinds of fraternity. Although commonly associated with romance and desire, the blood-red rose has long been a symbol of solidarity and of an enduring belief in redemption: as seen, for example, in early Christian mythology, such as the Immaculate Conception, Catholicism's devotion to the rosary, the Passion of Christ, the Cleansing Blood of Christ, and Christian martyrdom; or through the rituals of certain mythical, heretical and esoteric circles, which established sub rosa iconography (the Rosy Cross in particular) as a sign of secret fellowship, mystical enlightenment, a chastened generative organ, and, most importantly, the Christic rose line; yet more recently, the red rose has been adopted by socialists, trade unionists and Social Democratic parties, as a gender-neutral icon that signifies cooperation and universality, and political opposition to free market economics, conservatism, and social inequality.

Insofar as the UCS campaign roughly coincided with him beginning a four year apprenticeship at Walter Cook & Son boatyard in Maldon, North Essex, when barely 15, Dodds' triptych is essentially a semi-autobiographical work of retrospective comradeship. And though he left for London aged 19 to study at the Chelsea School of Art, and then the Royal College of Art, Dodds continued to work in local yards on a part-time basis up until becoming a fully professional artist in 1993. Indeed, Dodds' years as a shipwright were to profoundly influence his love for documenting maritime heritage and sea mythologies through his many paintings, original

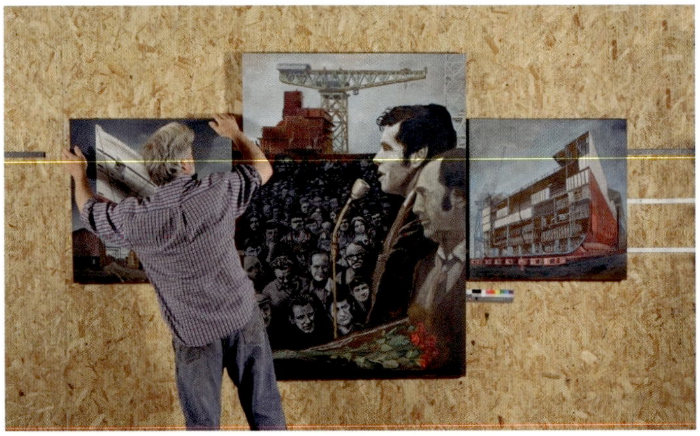

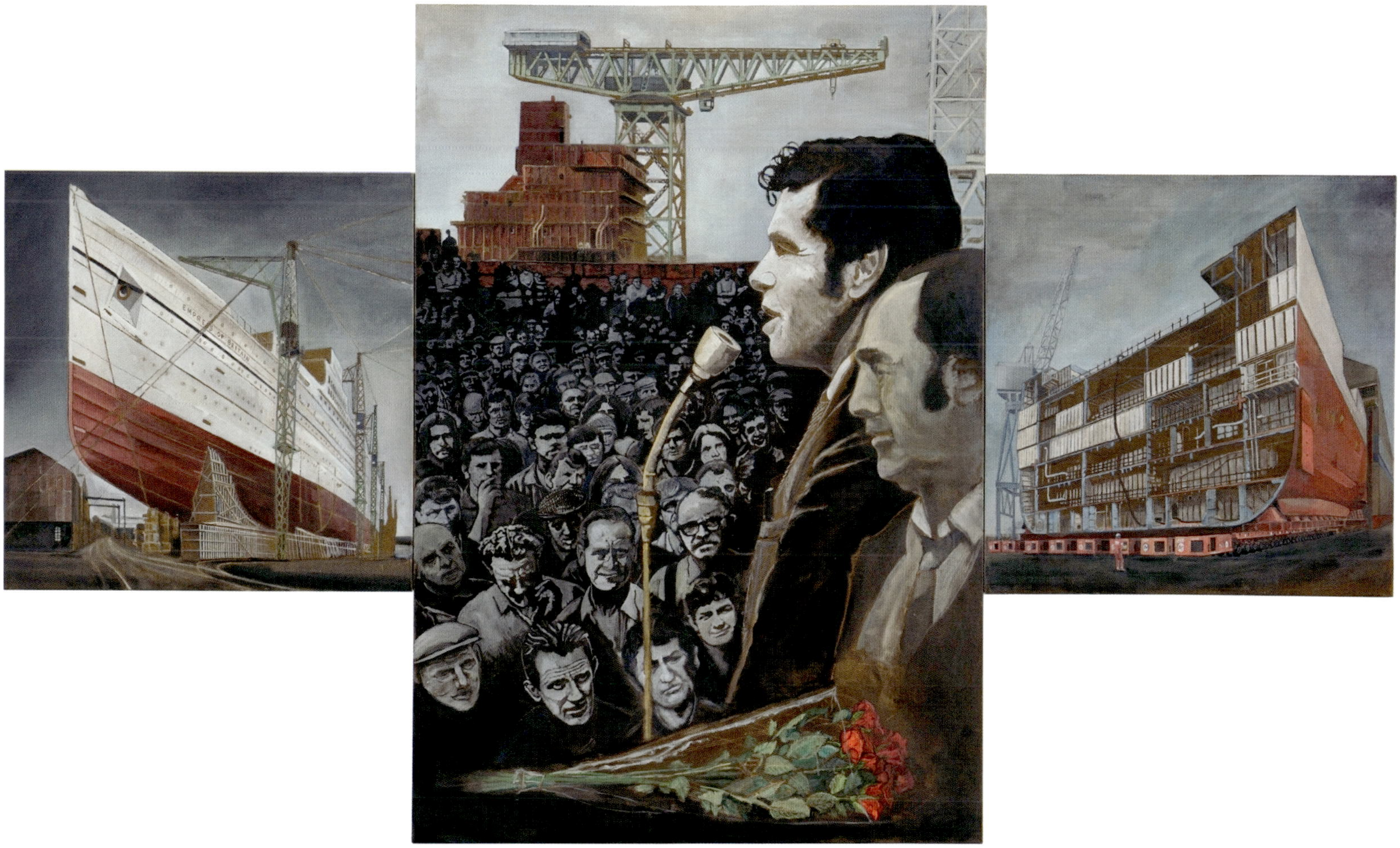

11. Upper Clyde Shipbuilders
oil on three linen canvas panels
153 x 260 cm   60¼ x 102⅜ ins

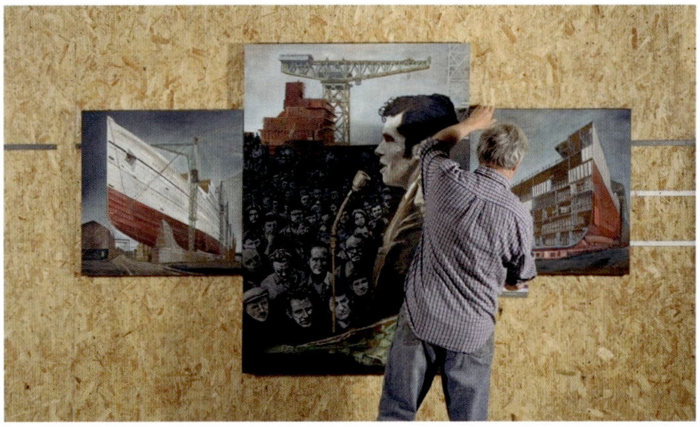

prints and publications (including a 314 page history of shipbuilding on the River Colne, 1786-1988). But what comes across most strongly in Dodds' work is his deep-rooted emotional attachment to the ebb and flow of shipping communities. For instance, following the closure of Cook's Yard at Wivenhoe in 1986 and James & Stone at Brightlingsea in 1988, he was one of a handful of activists who organised a campaign for the sites to be regenerated by and for local people. And though the sites were eventually sold for residential development, the collective action was to be an epiphany moment in Dodds' career, an experience he was to reflect upon to his close friend and biographer, Ian Collins.

To sum it up, I feel as an artist the importance of expressing the community I come from. The boat building community is as singular as the artistic community and I love doing linocuts of the people I used to work with. Sadly, it's all vanishing. Shipyards are worth more as building plots for houses than as places of work where skills and communal spirits are kept alive … The feeling of belonging to a place is the same as being part of the rhythm of the tide and the sea. This, and the spiritual contemplation of making things, is what really matters. It's something you can't own but which is part of you. This is the sense of enduring value I try to put in my work.

But Dodds is not only interested in localities along his native East Anglican coast or just in the United Kingdom. As early as 1982, he painted a triptych oil entitled 'Solidarność', a pseudo-religious homage to Andrzej Wajda's films 'Man of Marble' (1976) and 'Man of Iron' (1981), and the striking Solidarity trade unionists in the Lenin Shipyard at Gdansk, who had elected the unemployed electrician and dissident activist, Lech Walesa, as their leader. (Interestingly, Walesa had been greatly impressed by the UCS work-in and he persuaded his co-workers to adopt similar tactics. And Reid wrote several articles criticising the Kremlin's suppression of 'fundamental human freedoms' and Communist Party apologists.) In the painting we see a lifeless, Christ-like figure being stretchered on a door panel by a shipyard worker, a reference to Wajda's controversial portrayal of the 1970 Polish food riots, their brutal suppression by the Polish authorities, and the death of a heroic 18-year-old male protestor, whose deceased body was similarly carried by fellow demonstrators through police and army cordons. Dodds' triptych also depicts the contemporaneous power struggle between the Soviet Union, the Polish workers and the Catholic Church, by means of a metaphorical game of chess in which red's isolated King has been checked by a white Pawn-Bishop combination. Certainly, the Solidarity movement was saturated with religious allegory, which was not only a mark of defiance towards the atheist Communist authorities, but also a messianic symbol of sacrifice and of Poland as the Christ of nations. Indeed, when invited to pose for his first sanctioned portrait after the strike had ended, Walesa chose to stand under a crucifix holding a bouquet of red roses.

The right section of Dodds' triptych shows the 8,000 tonne Lower Block 03 of HMS Queen Elizabeth being moved by one man on a Self-Propelled Module Transport system in Govan shipyard (formerly Kvaerner-Govan and Fairfields before that), whence it was loaded onto a large barge and shipped 600 miles around the northern coast of Scotland to Rosyth dockyard, near Edinburgh, on 16 August 2011. The fabricated section was then assembled with the ship's other blocks, which had been built by a partnership comprising BAE Systems, Babcock, Thales and the Ministry of Defence, across seven shipyards. One of two aircraft carriers presently under construction for the Royal Navy (at an estimated cost of £6.2 billion), the Queen Elizabeth was christened on 4 July 2014 by Elizabeth II with a bottle of Scottish malt whiskey, five years after her first metal was cut. Internal fitting-out will be completed in December 2015, with sea trials due to commence in 2016, and

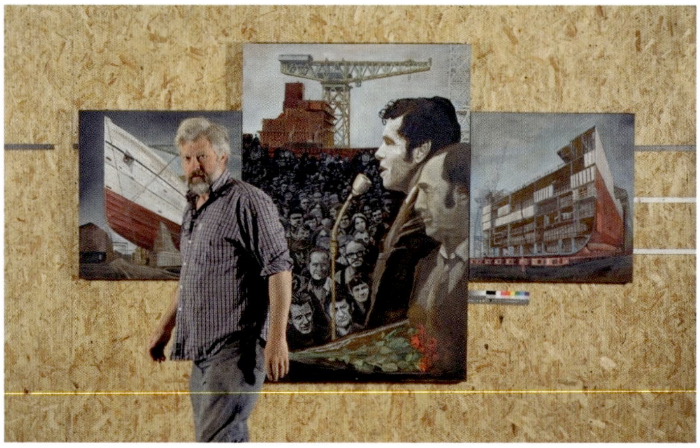

operational capability is planned for 2020. At 280 metres long, with a displacement weight of approximately 65,000 tonnes and four acres of sovereign territory, Queen Elizabeth will be the largest British warship ever constructed, roughly three times the size of the Invincible class aircraft carriers. And with a range of 10,000 miles, a top speed of 25 knots, and a carrying capacity of up to forty aircraft, a streamlined crew of 679 and embarked forces of up to 921, she will be one of the most powerful aircrafts in the world. Her first seagoing Commanding Officer is to be Commodore Jerry Kyd, the former captain of HMS Ark Royal and HMS Illustrious.

An extract from "Changing Tides of Industrial Democracy: Tales from the Shipyard"

By Dr Michael G W Bailey,
Department of Sociology, University of Essex.

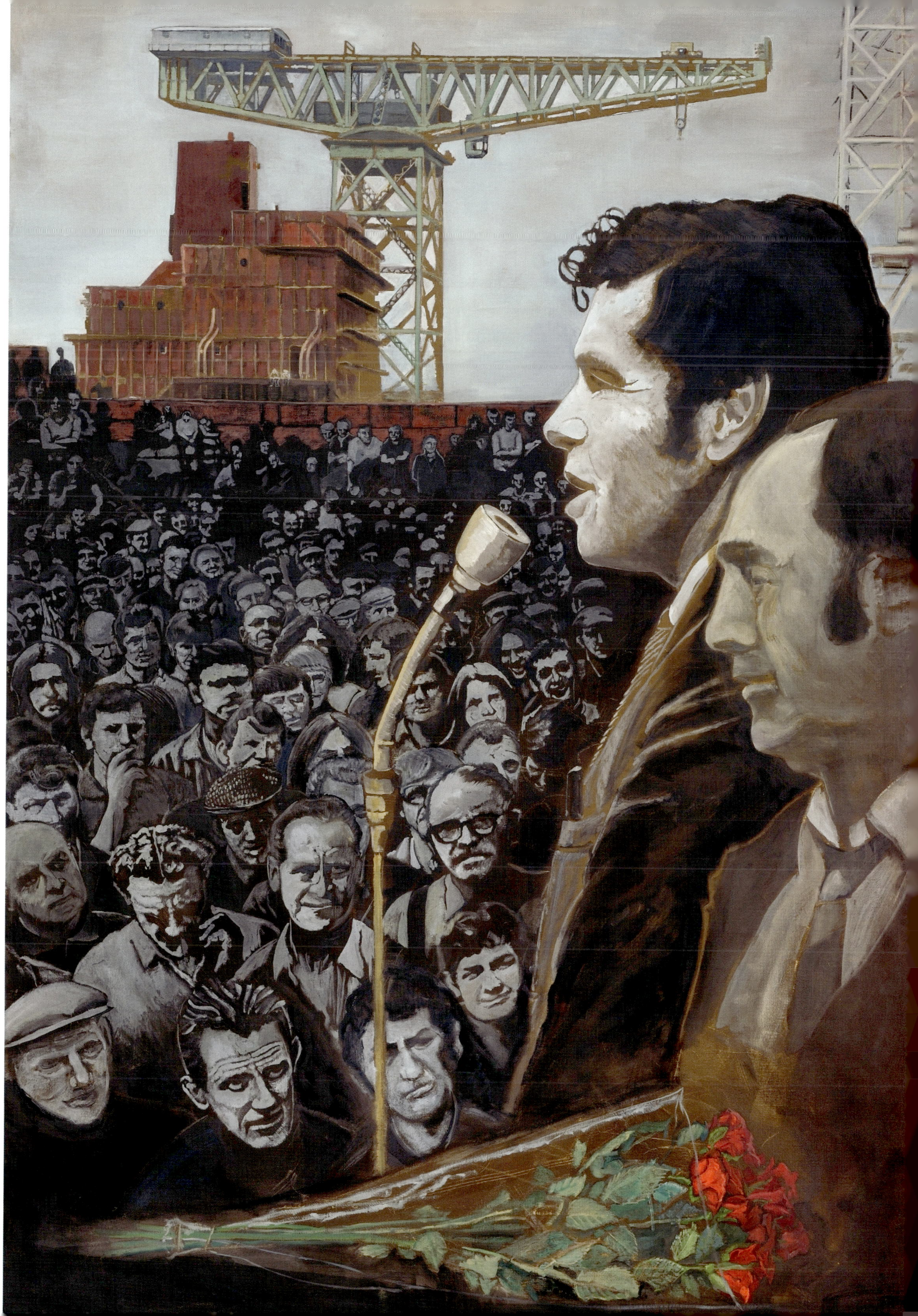

Upper Clyde
Shipbuilders
(detail)

12. Stern Sheets
oil on linen
90 x 60 cms 35⅜ x 23⅝ ins

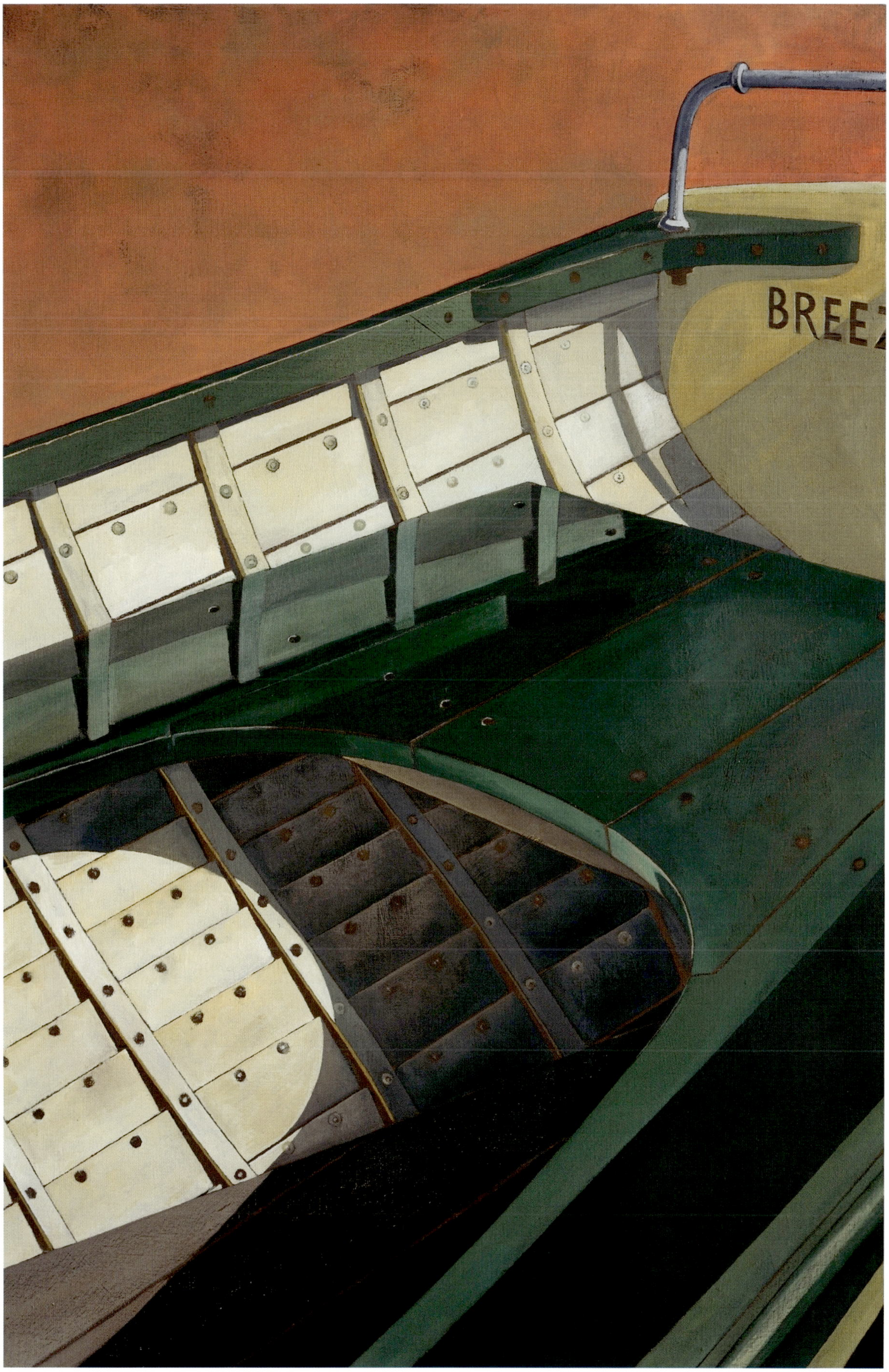
BREEZ

13. Wivenhoe One Design, New Decks

oil on linen

80 x 110 cms   31½ x 43¼ ins

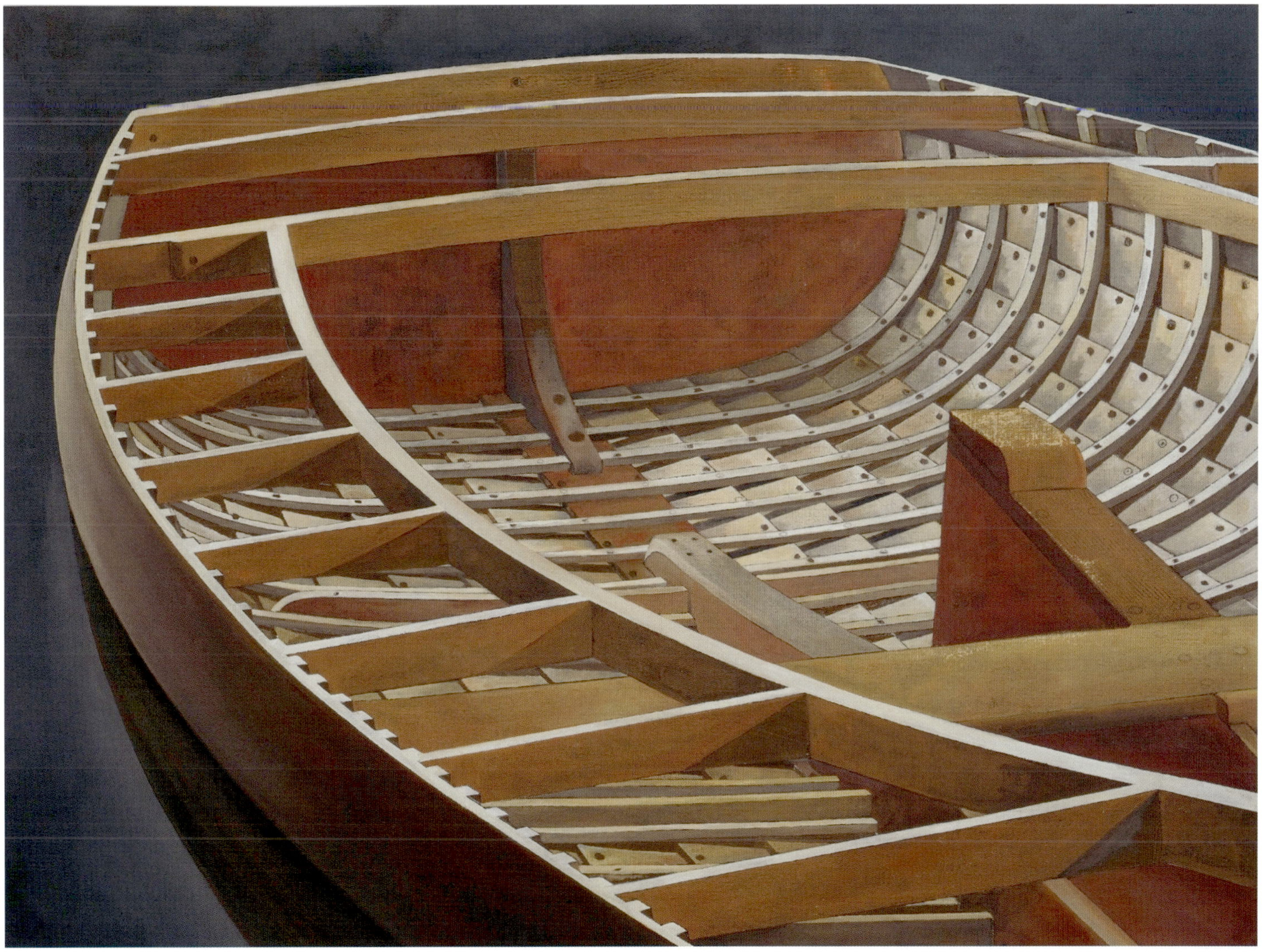

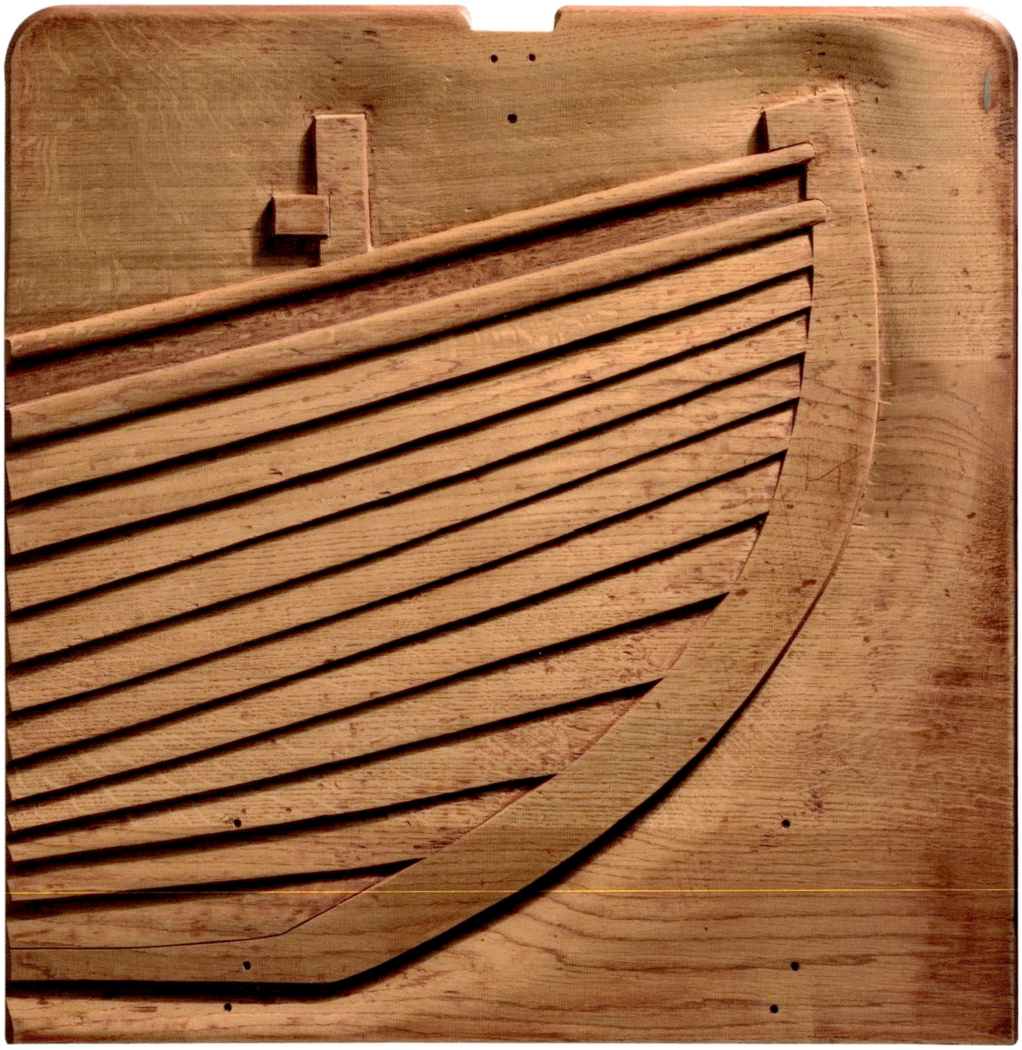

14. Danish Eel Drifter
carved shallow relief on oak wood panel
61 x 61 cms 24 x 24 ins

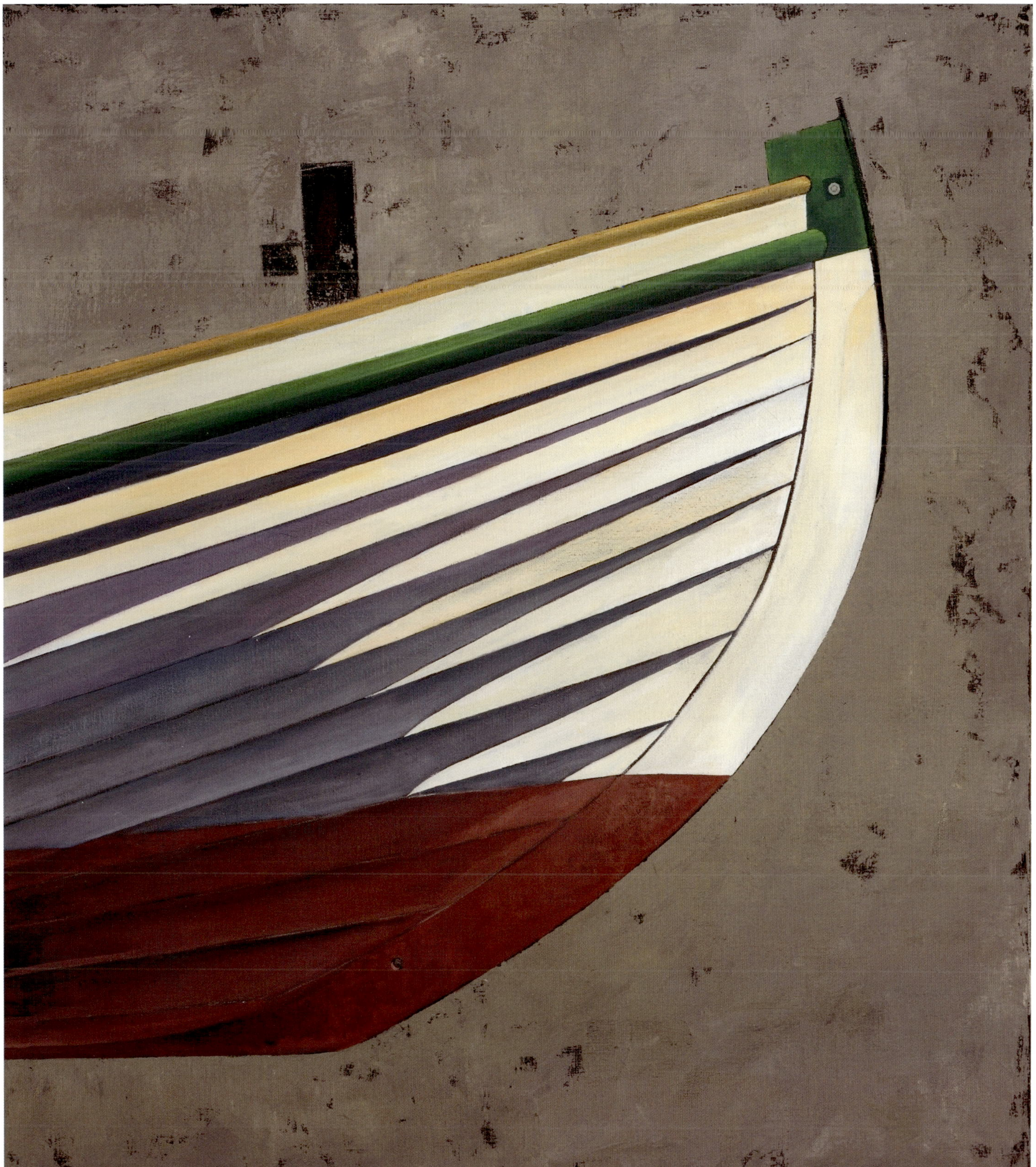

15. Bow of a Danish Eel Drifter
oil on linen canvas
100 x 90 cms   39⅜ x 35⅜ ins

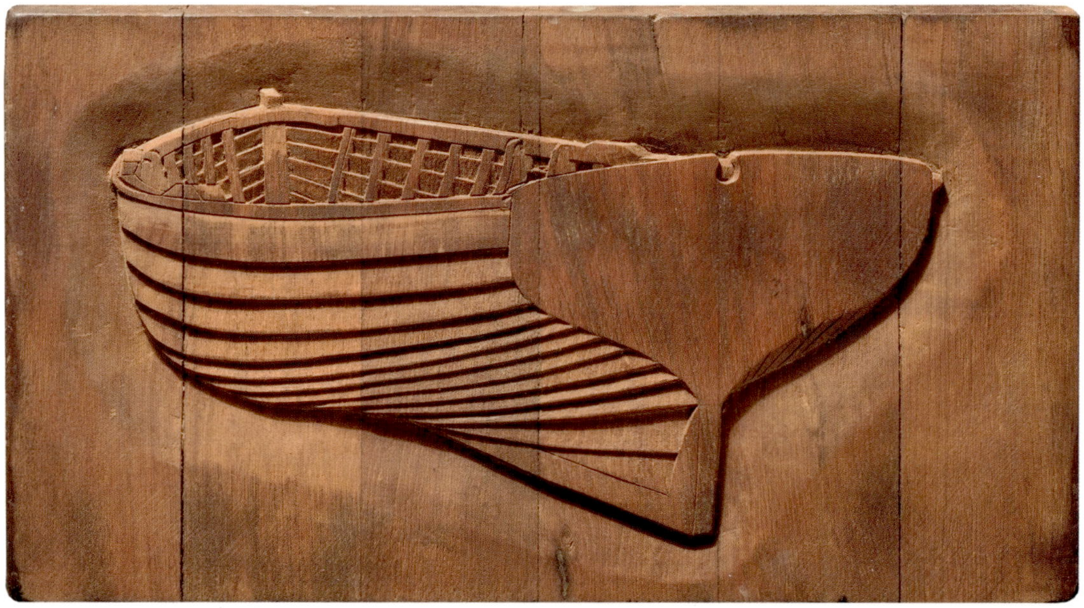

16. Winklebrig, Transom
carved on old hatch board
29 x 52 cms 11⅜ x 20½ ins

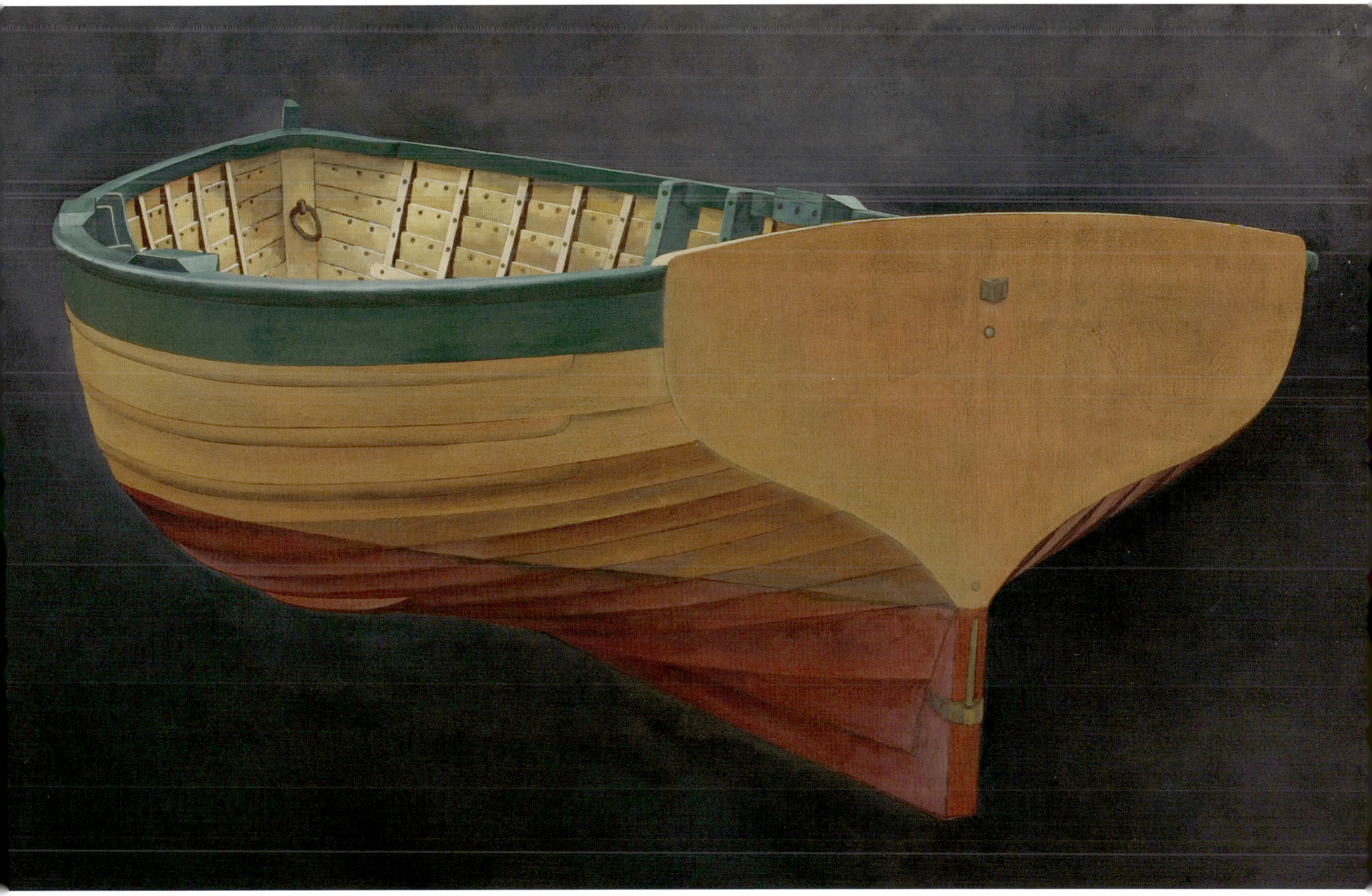

17. Winklebrig 5
oil on linen
90 x 150 cms 35⅜ x 59 ins

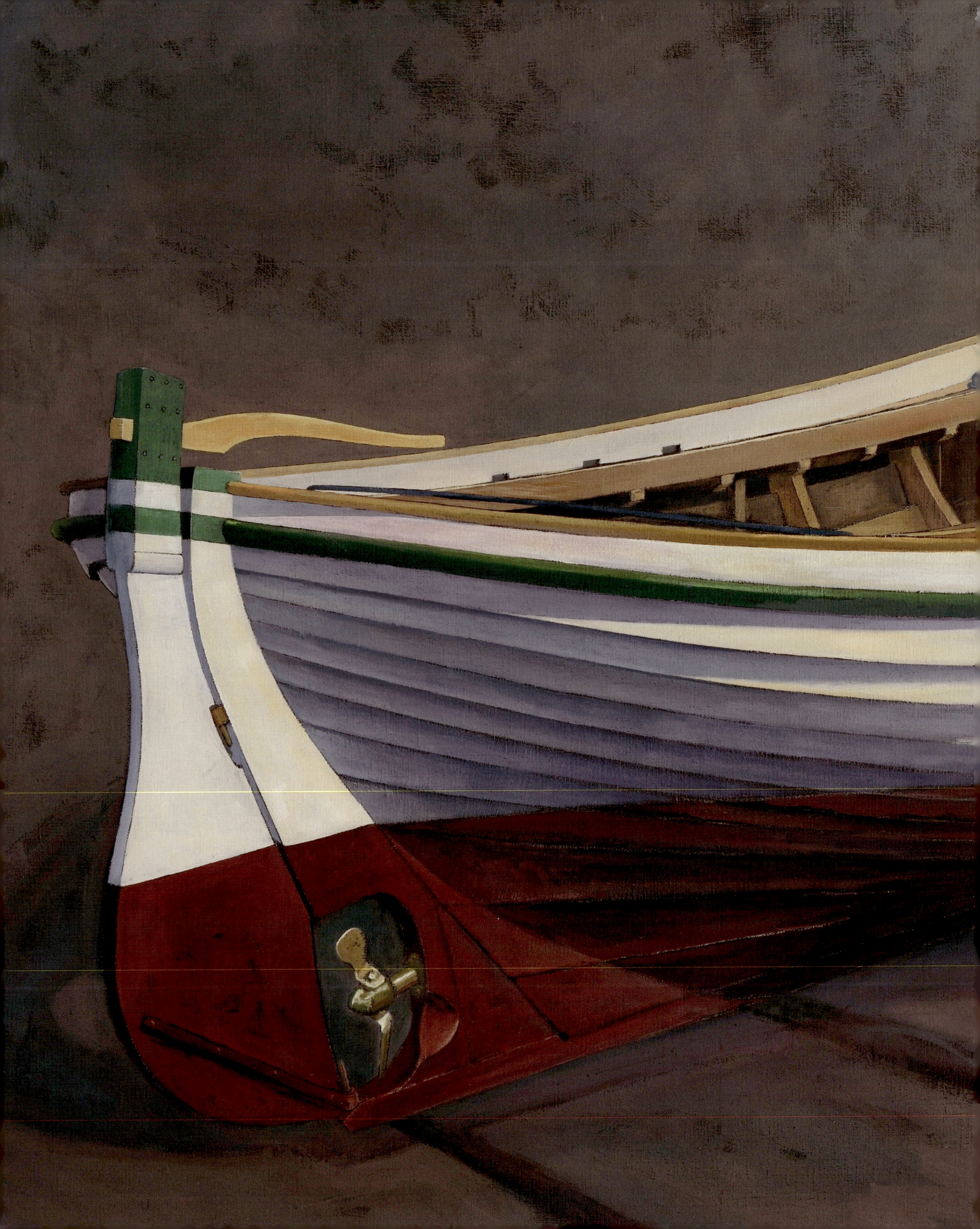

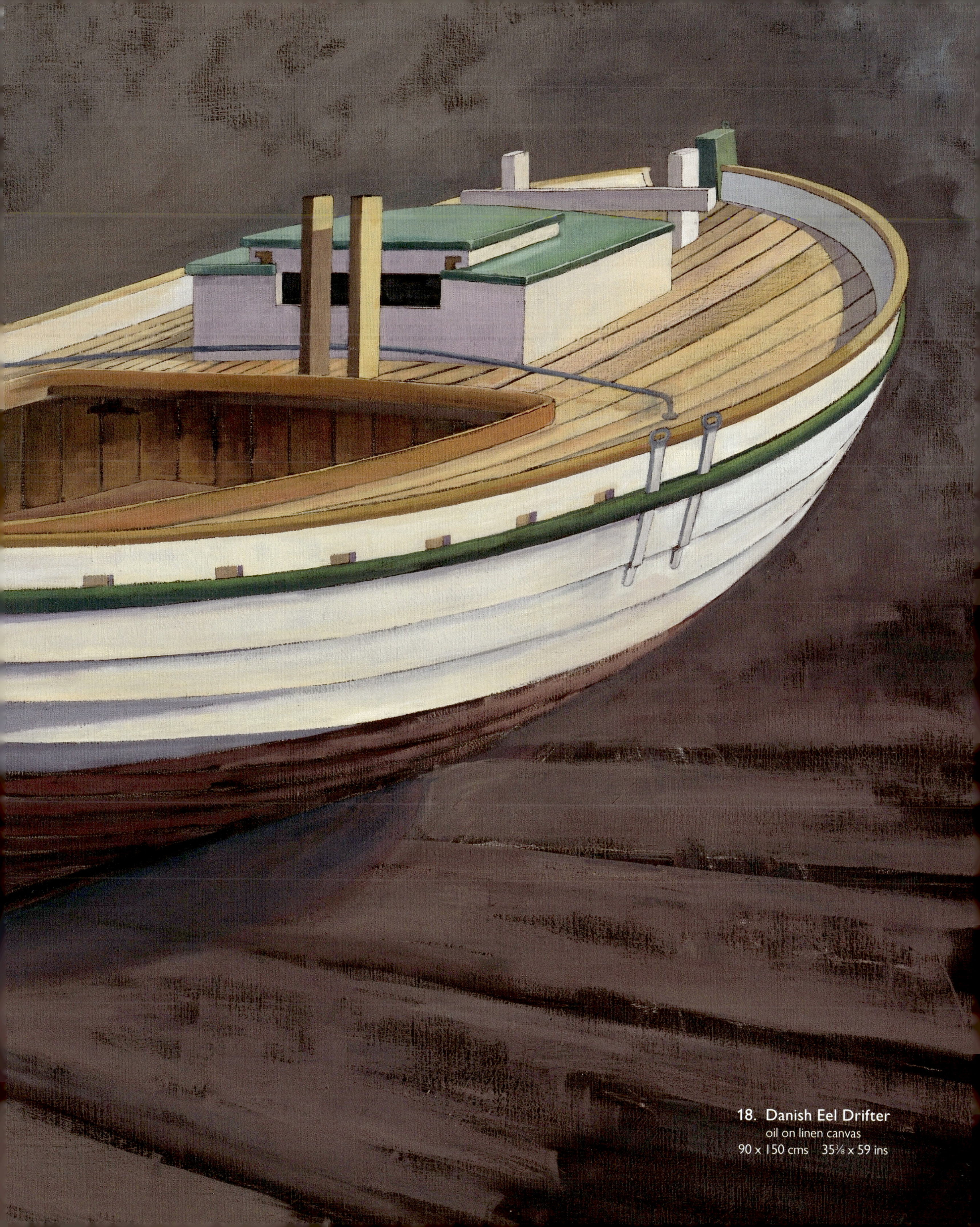

18. Danish Eel Drifter
oil on linen canvas
90 x 150 cms   35⅜ x 59 ins

19. New Timbers on a Norfolk Crabber

oil on linen

111 x 90 cms   43½ x 35½ ins

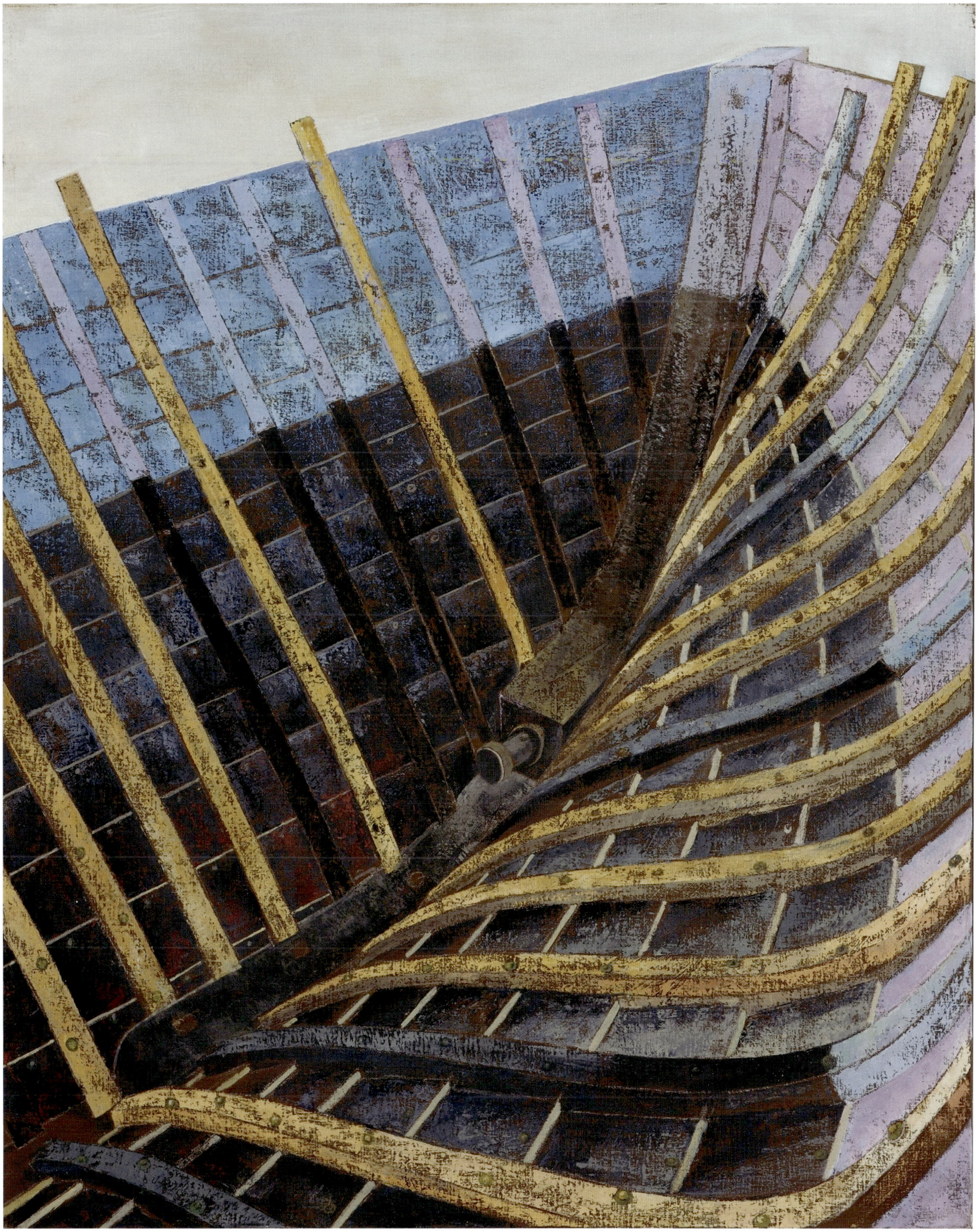

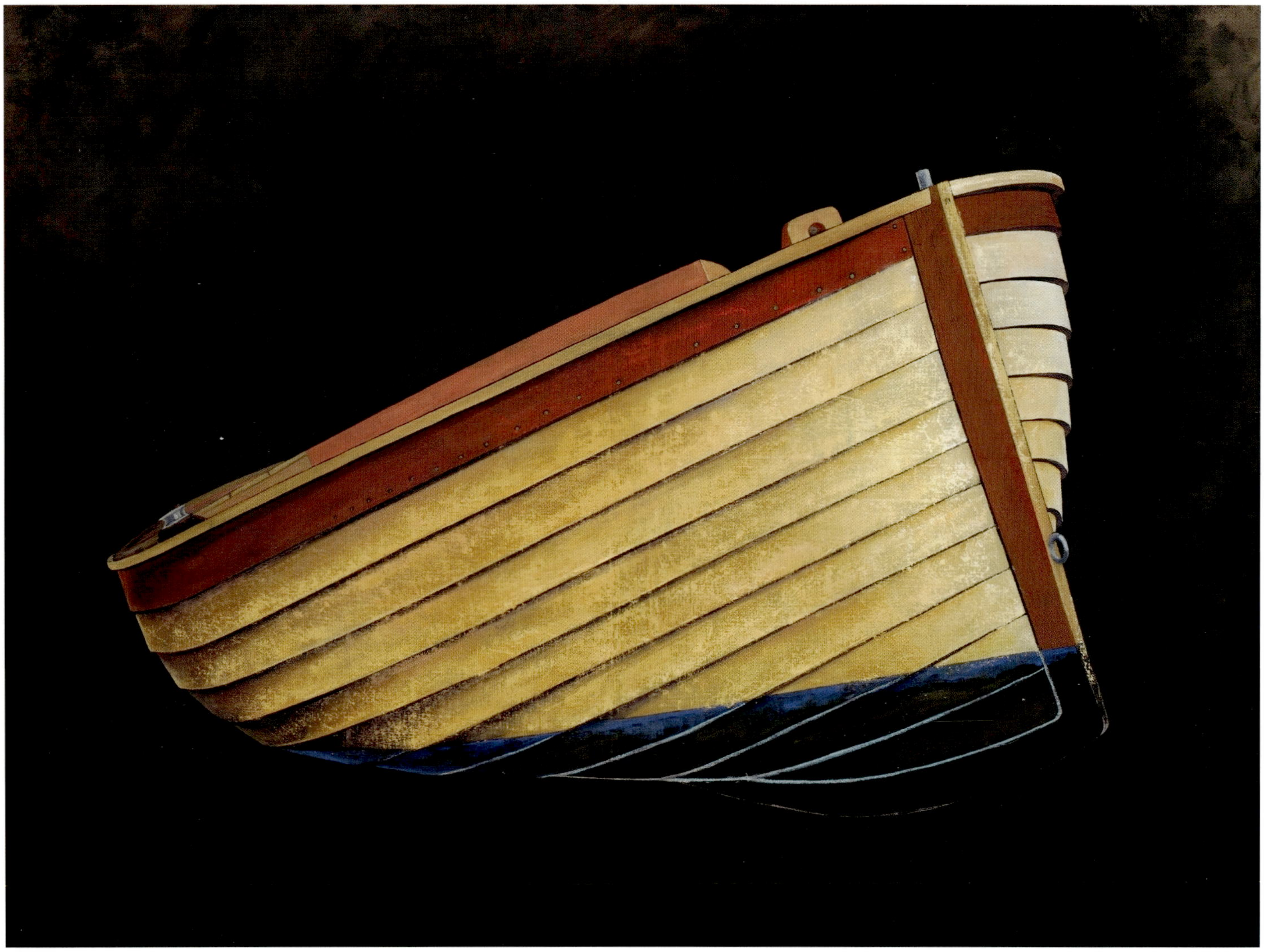

20. Salcombe Yawl
oil on linen
122 x 168 cms 48 x 66⅛ ins

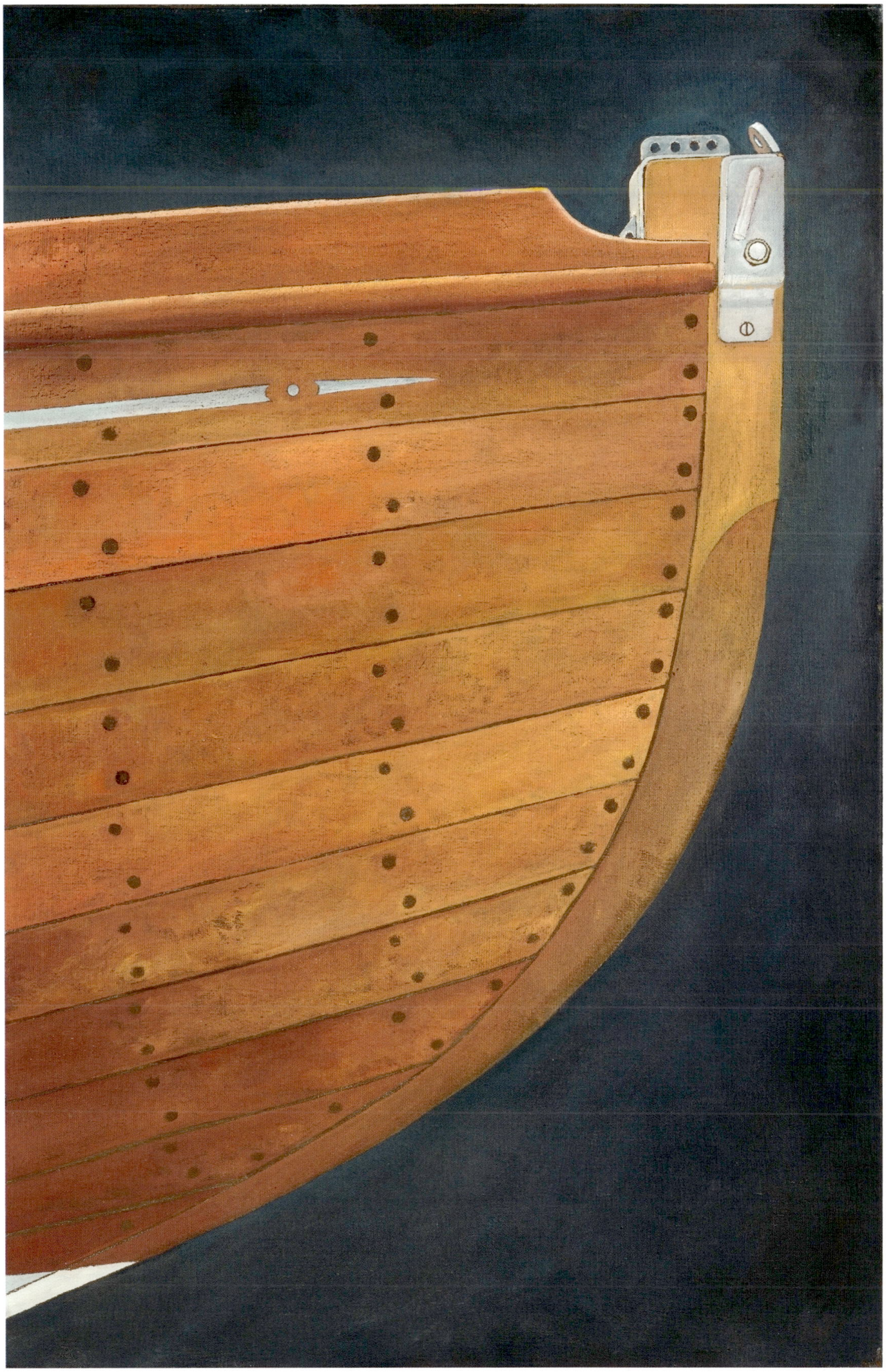

21. Bow of Poole Harbour One Design
oil on linen
92 x 61 cms   36 x 24 ins

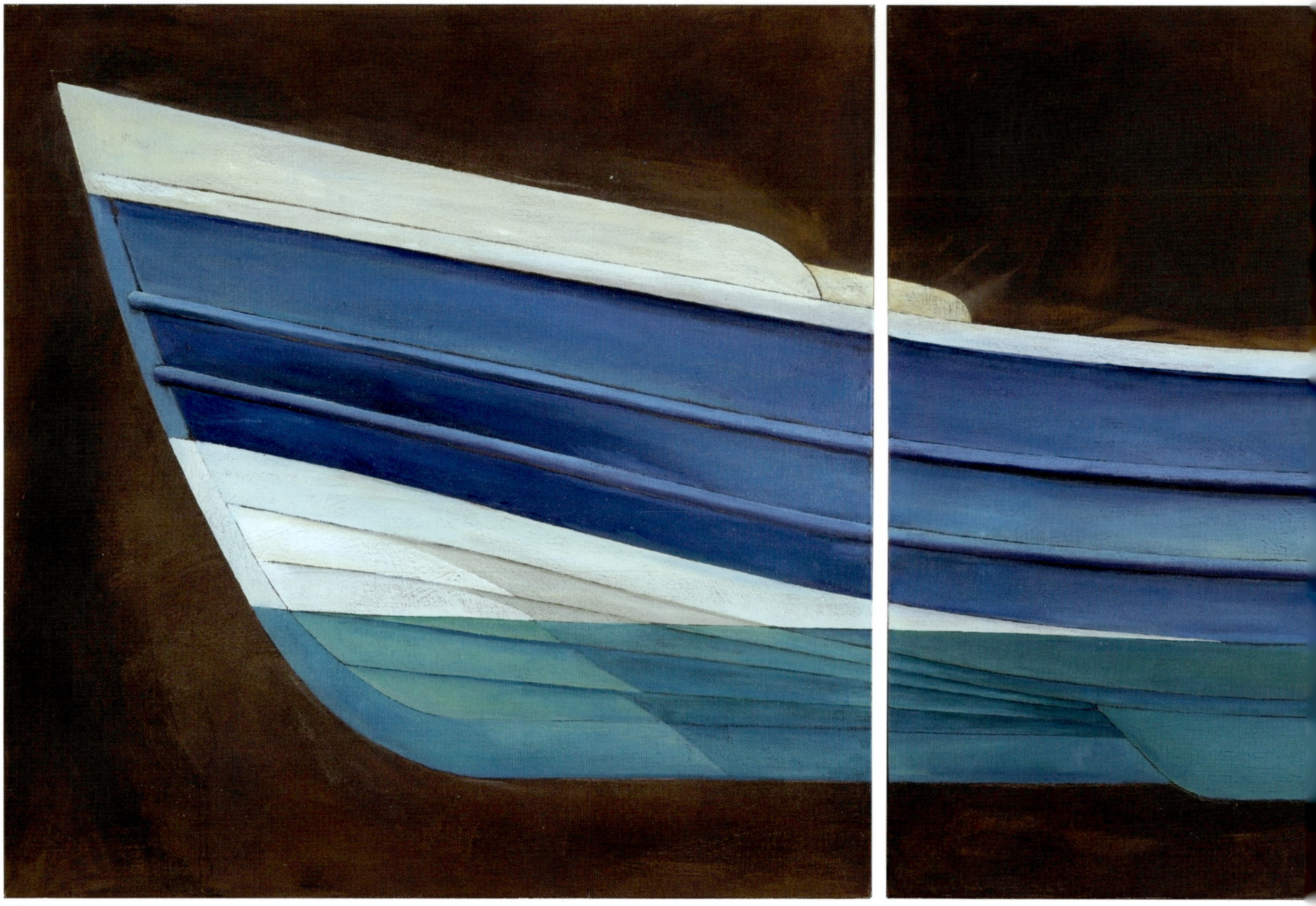

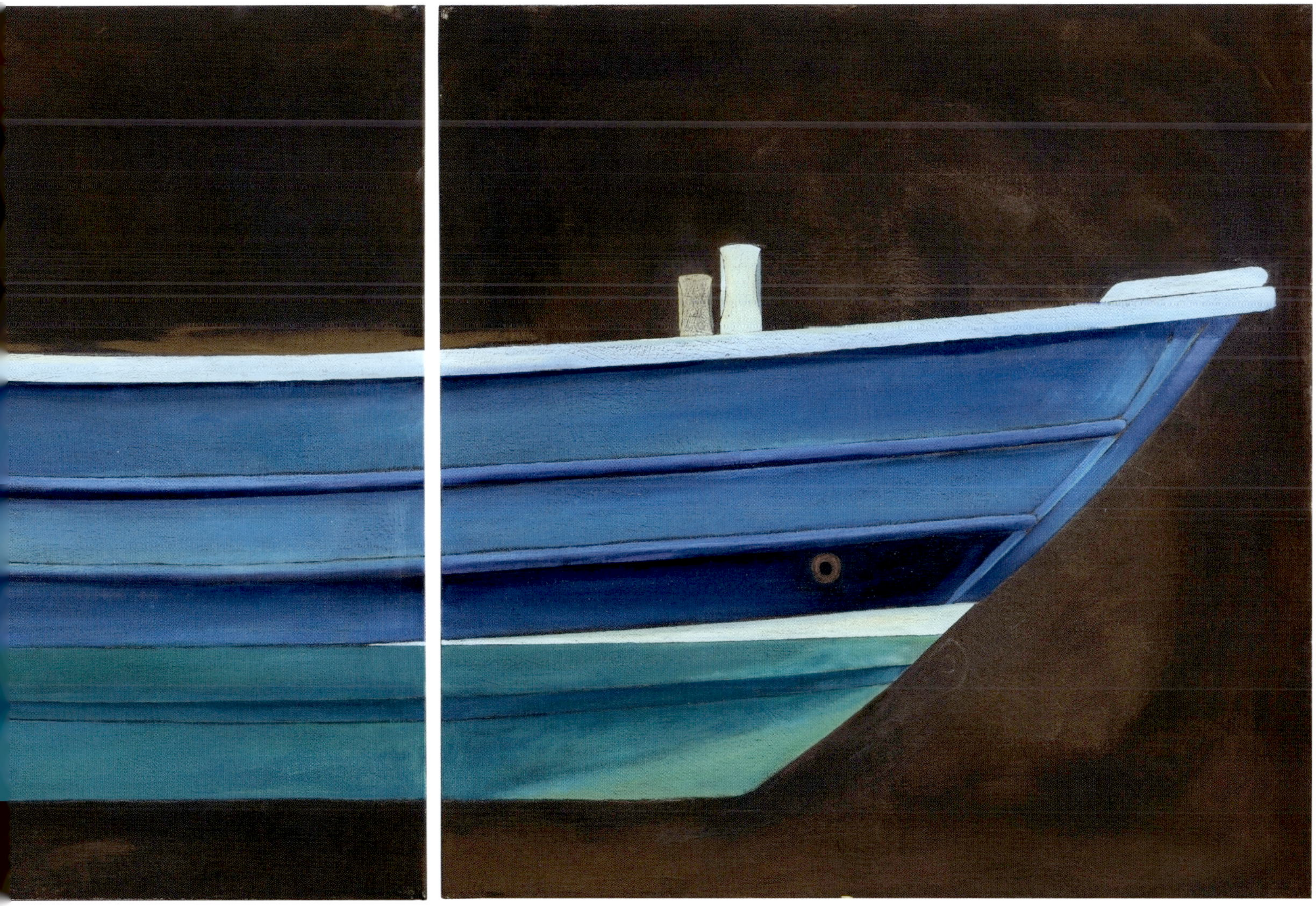

22. Yorkshire Coble (Triptych)
oil on linen on panel
91 x 274 cms 36 x 108 ins

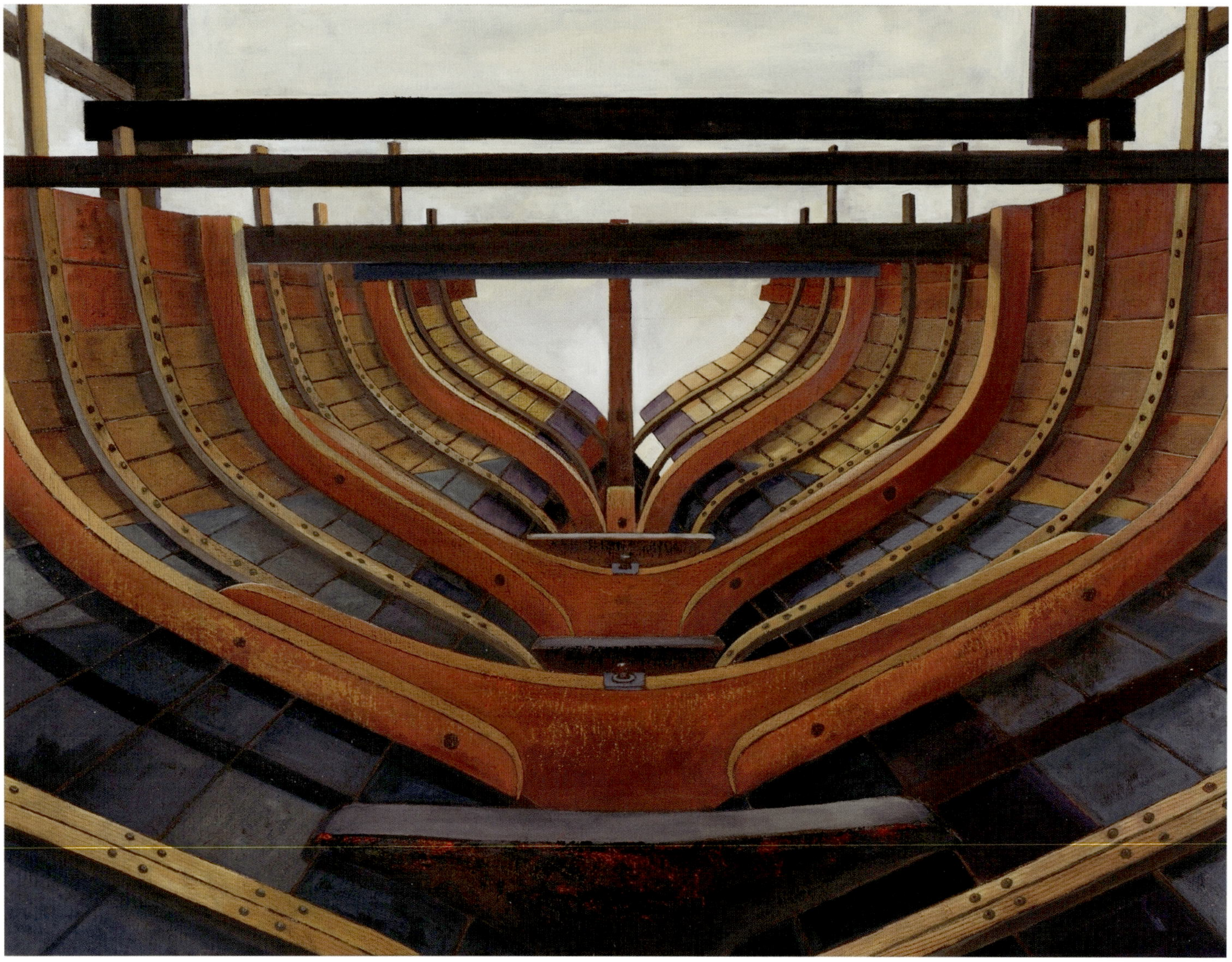

23. Falmouth Workboat, Looking Back
oil on linen
90 x 120 cms 35⅜ x 47¼ ins

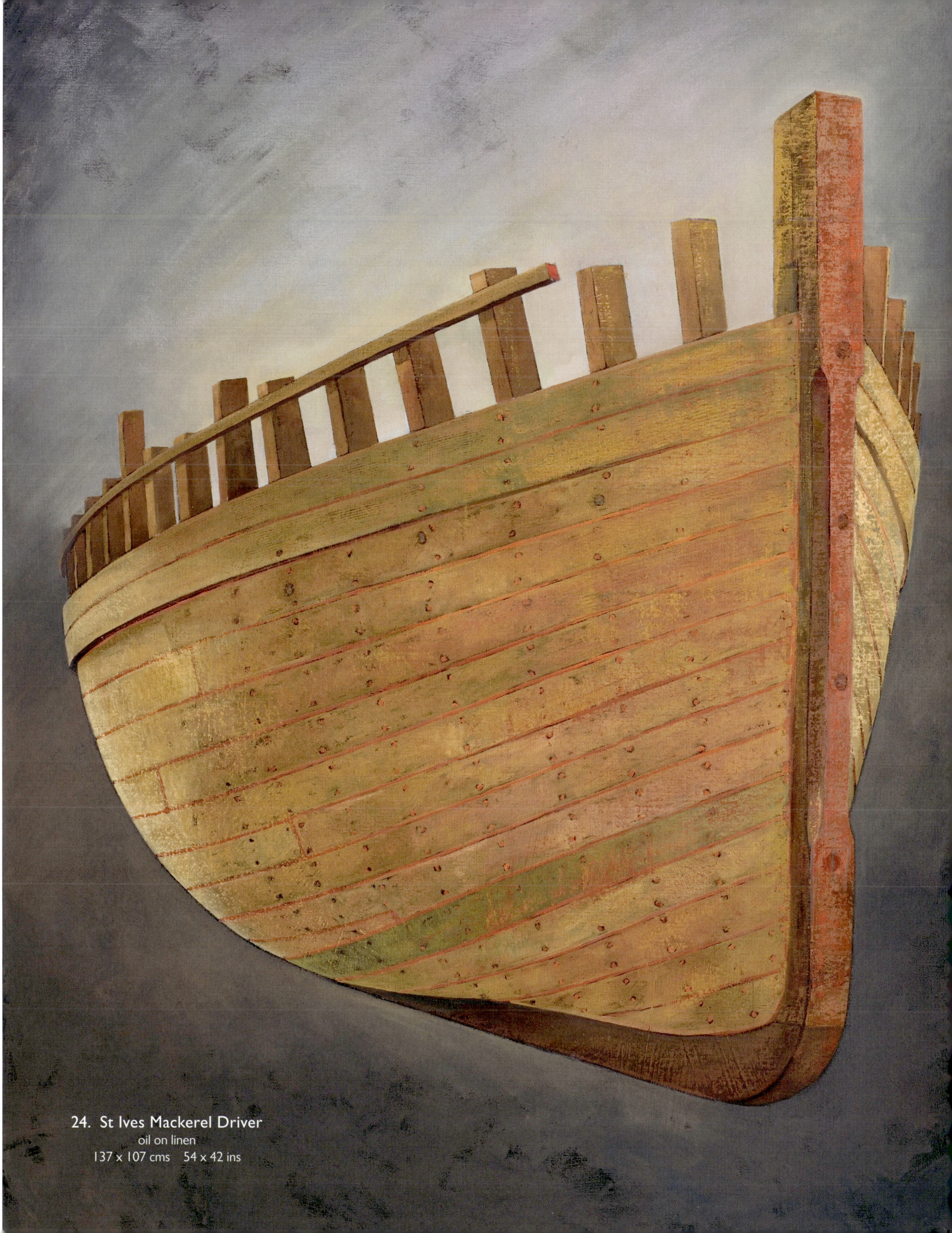

24. St Ives Mackerel Driver
oil on linen
137 x 107 cms 54 x 42 ins

25. Whelker, Stern

oil on linen

100 x 100 cms   39⅜ x 39⅜ ins

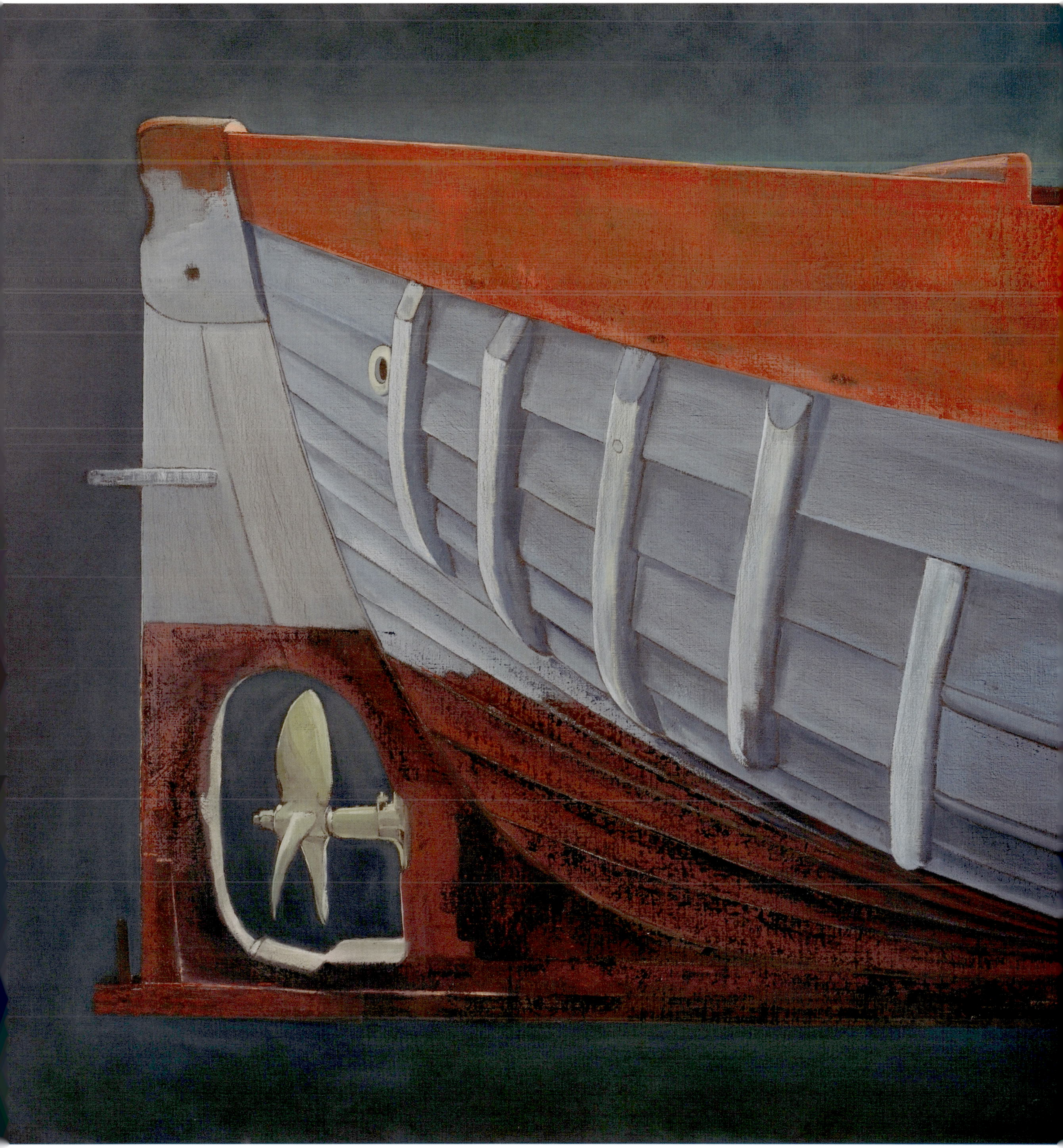

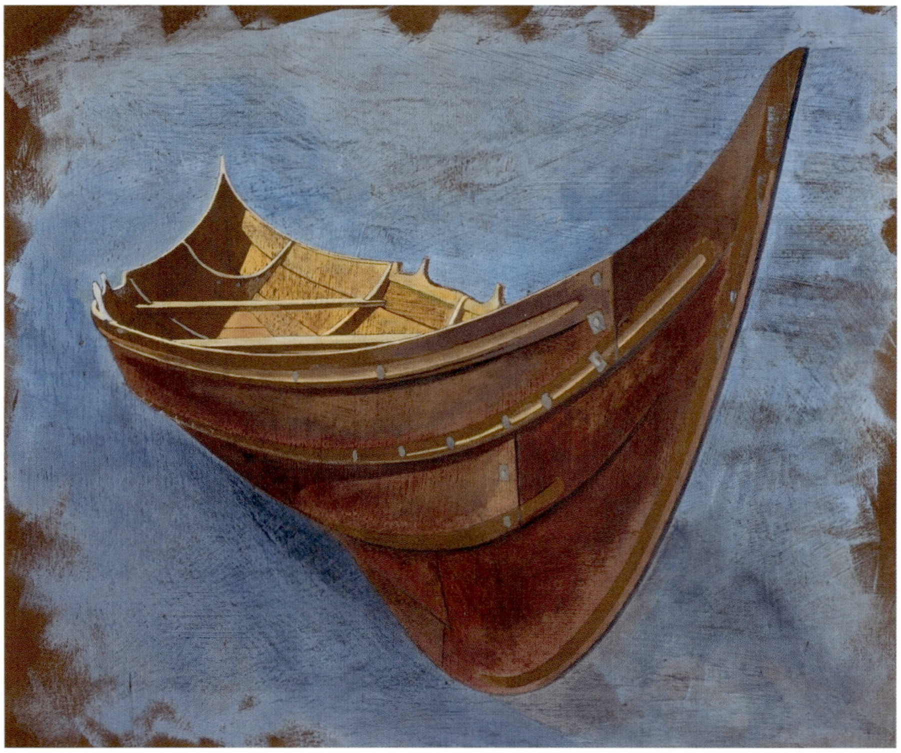

26. Roskilde Boat 1
oil on panel
40 x 49 cms 15¾ x 19¼ ins

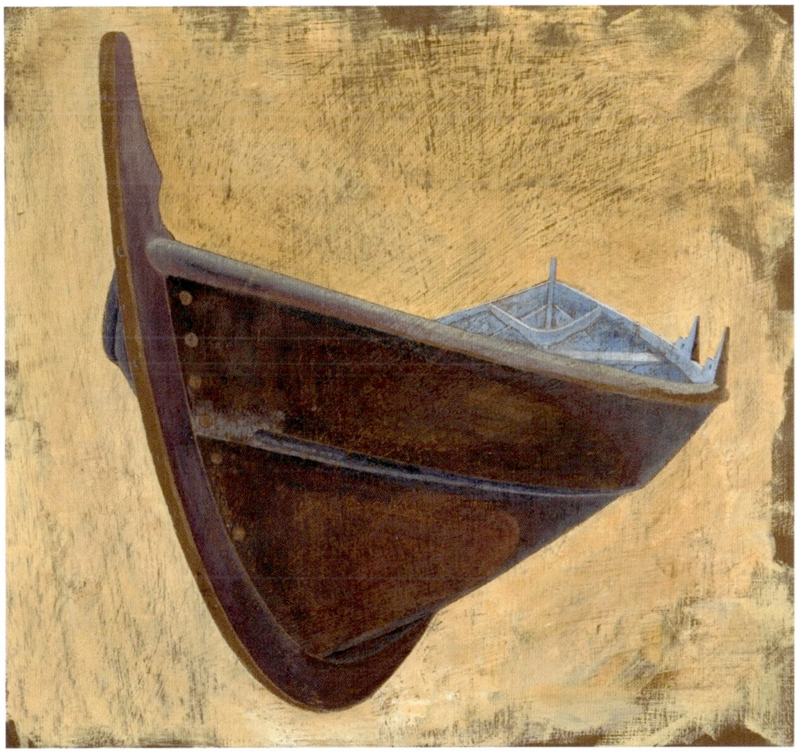

27. Roskilde Boat 2
oil on panel
40 x 44 cms 15¾ x 17⅜ ins

28. Grey Crabber

oil on linen

90 x 120 cms 35⅜ x 47¼ ins

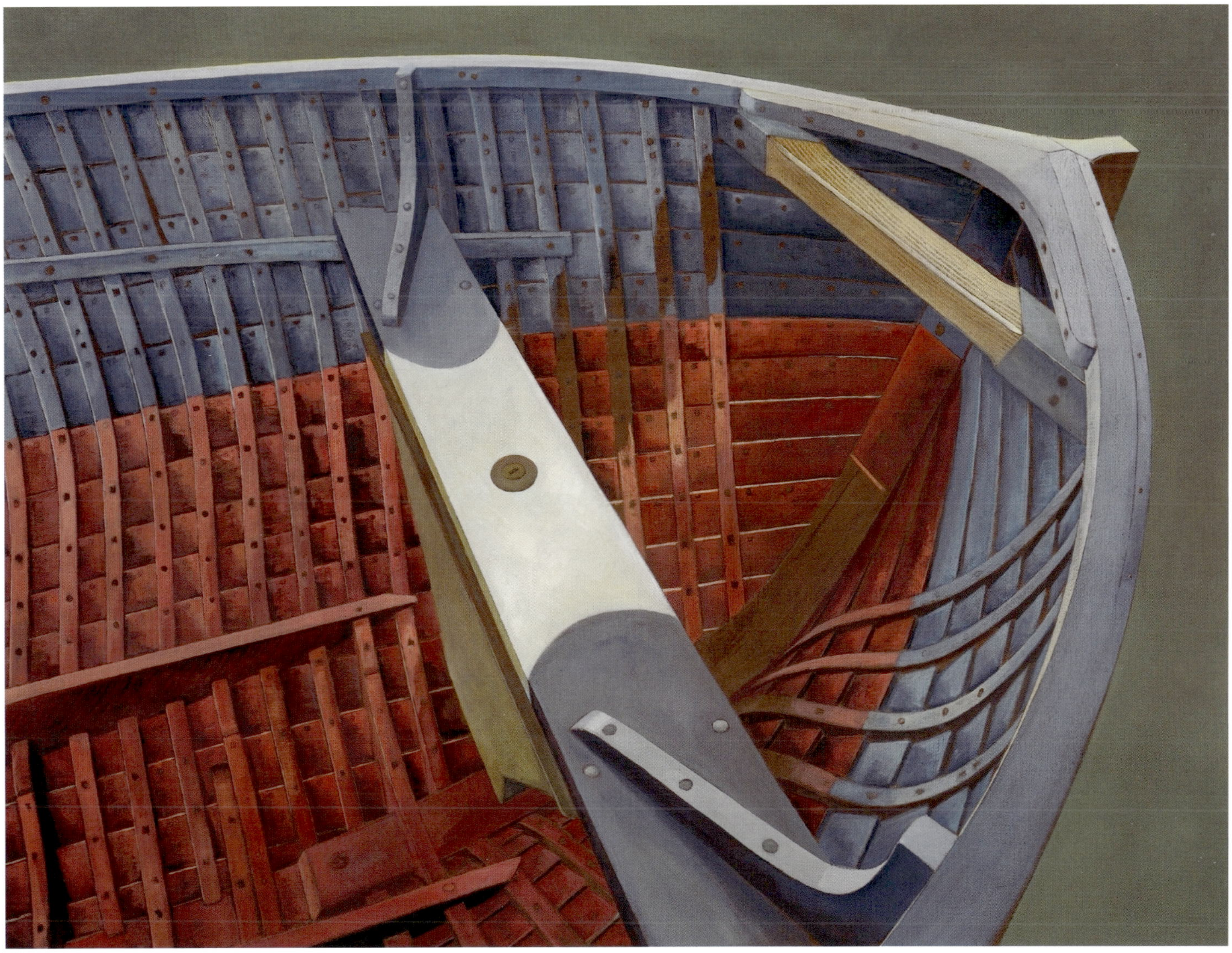

29. Yellow Transom

oil on linen

110 x 100 cms   43¼ x 39⅜ ins

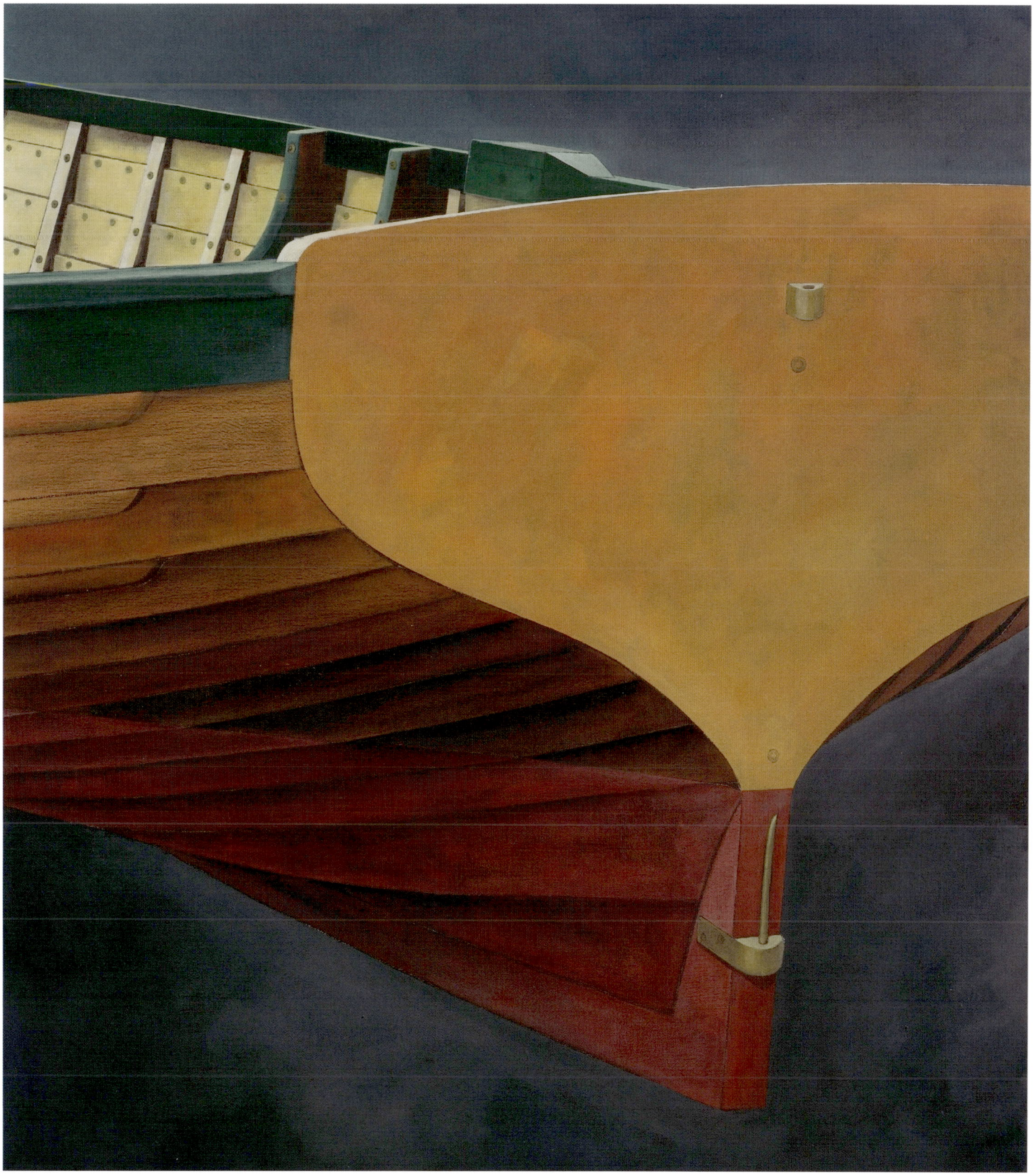

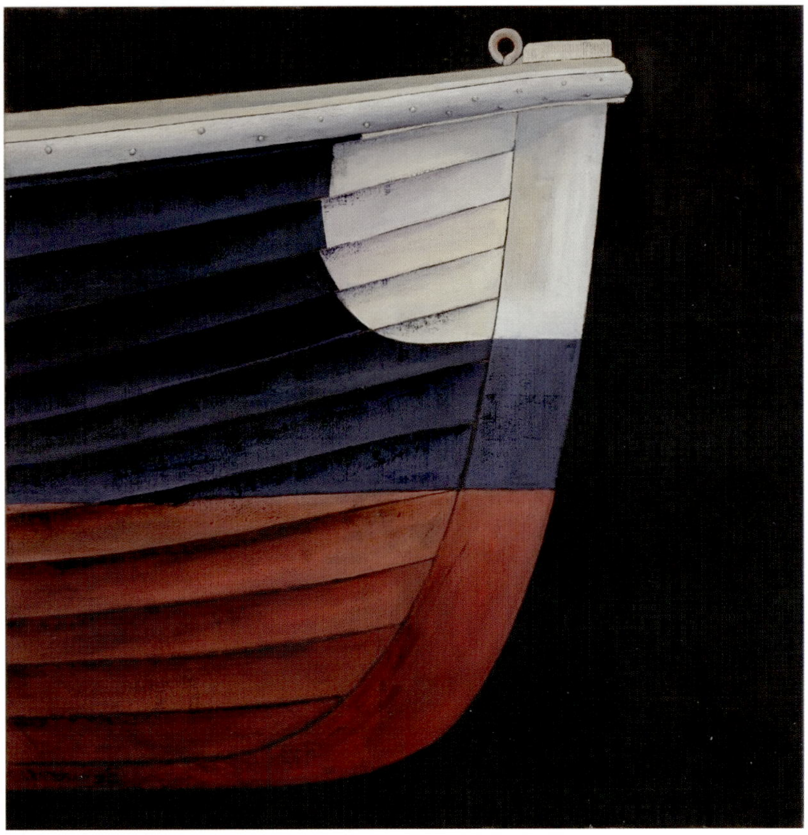

30. Bow of Norfolk Wherry
oil on linen
97 x 97 cms 38 x 38 ins

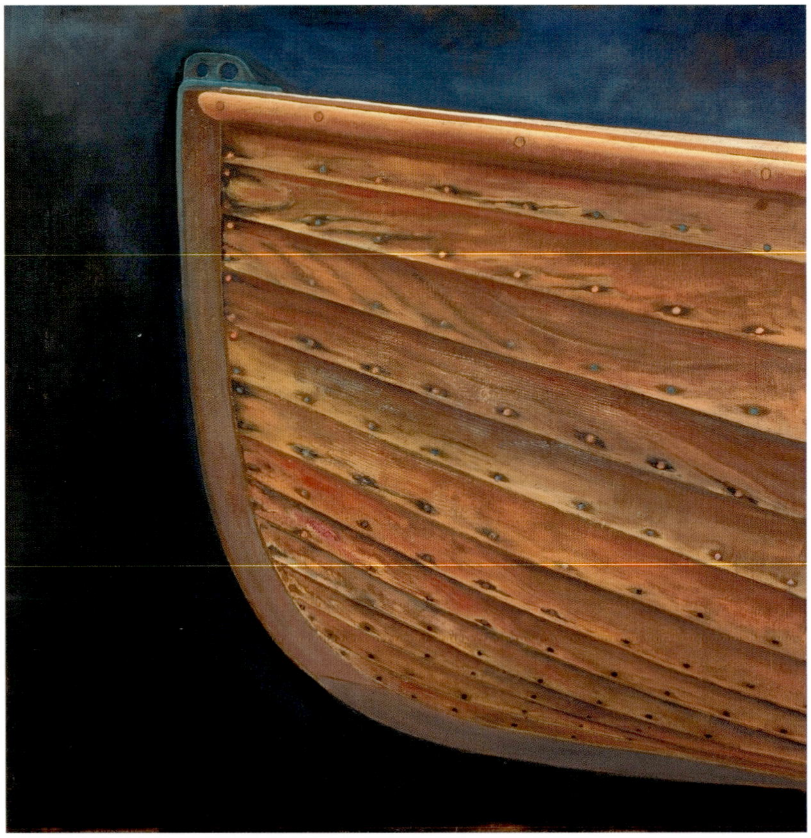

31. Bow of Brightlingsea One Design
oil on linen
97 x 97 cms 38 x 38 ins

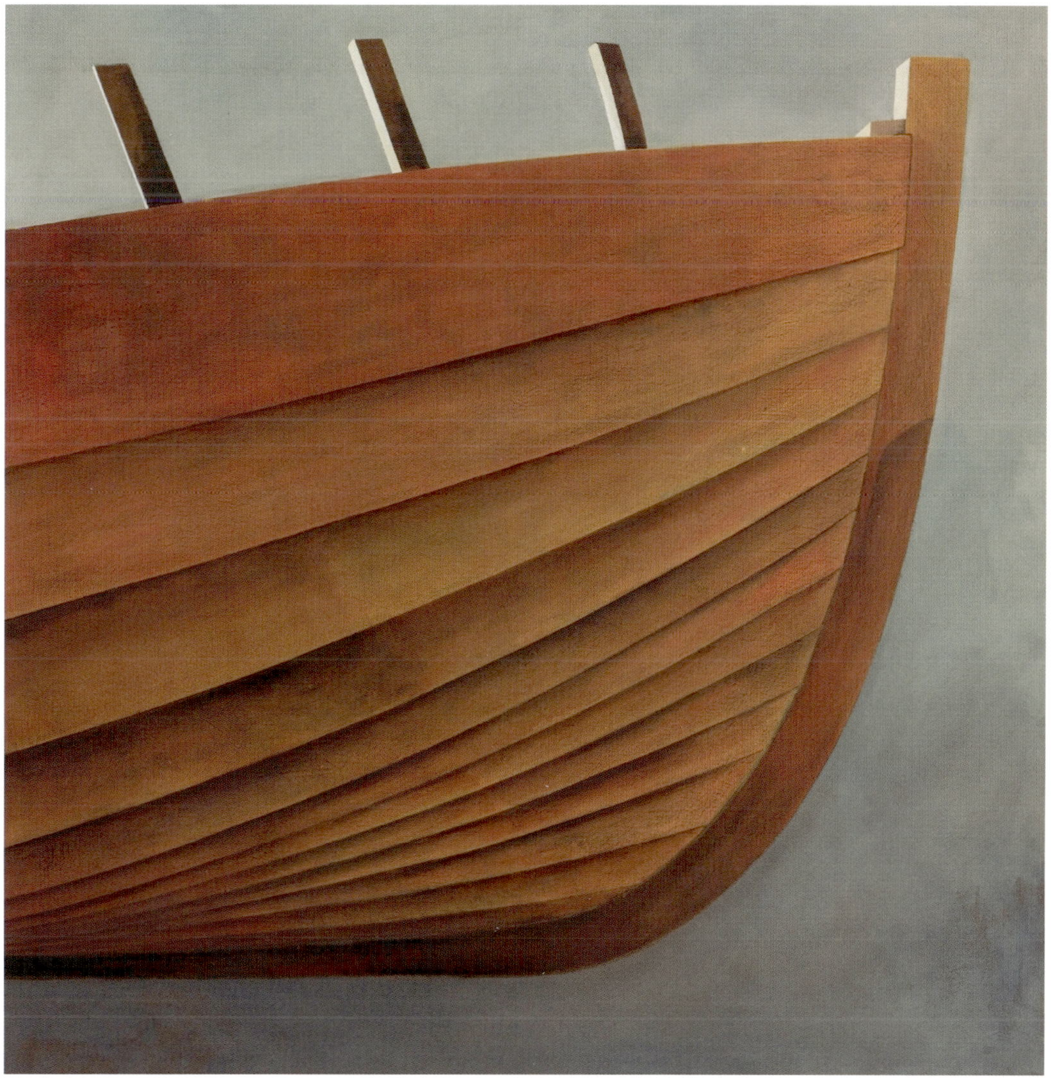

32. Bow of a New Crabber
oil on linen
100 x 100 cms 39⅜ x 39⅜ ins

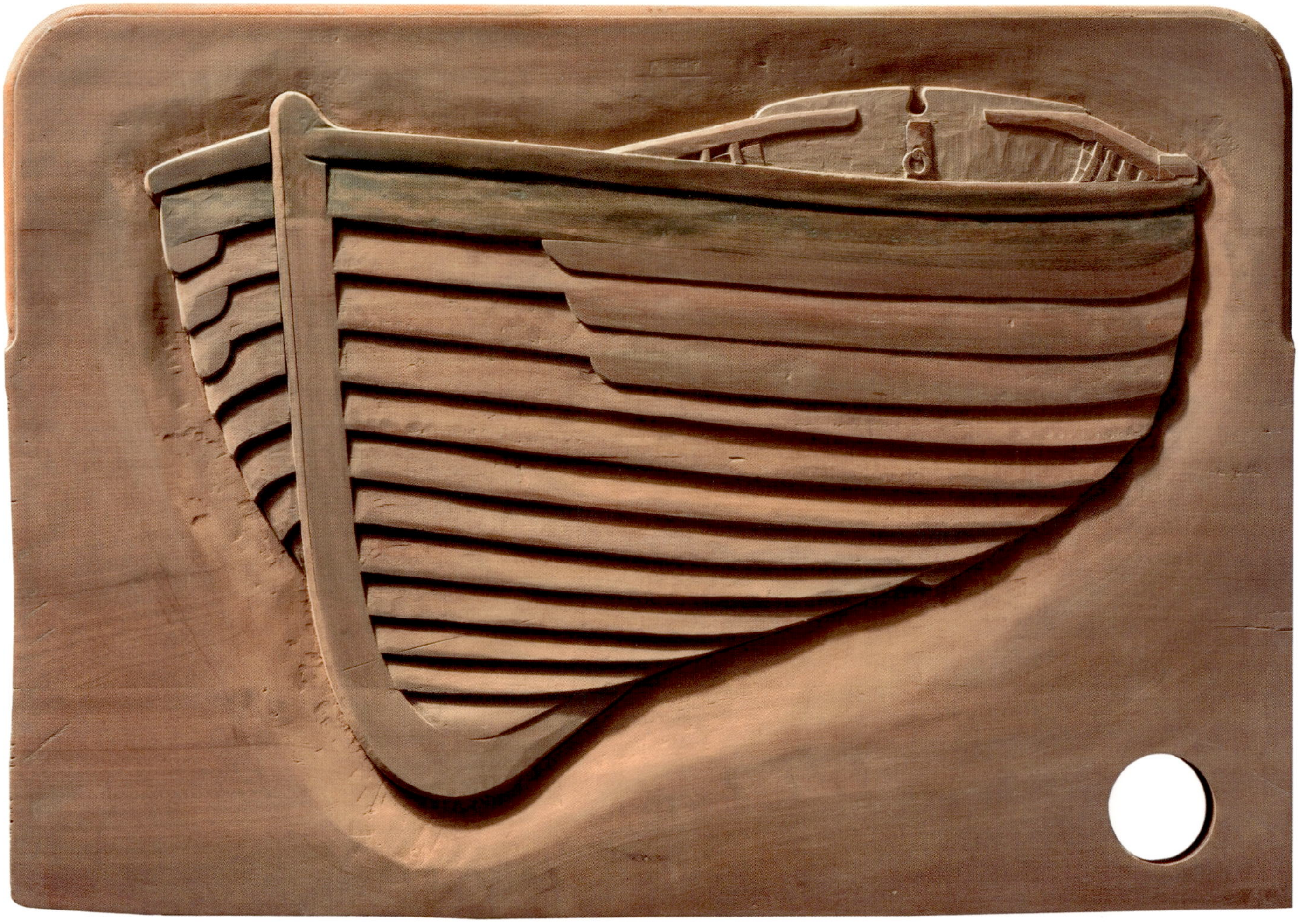

33. Winklebrig, Relief carving
carved shallow relief on mahogany wood panel
58 x 85 cms 22⅝ x 33¼ ins

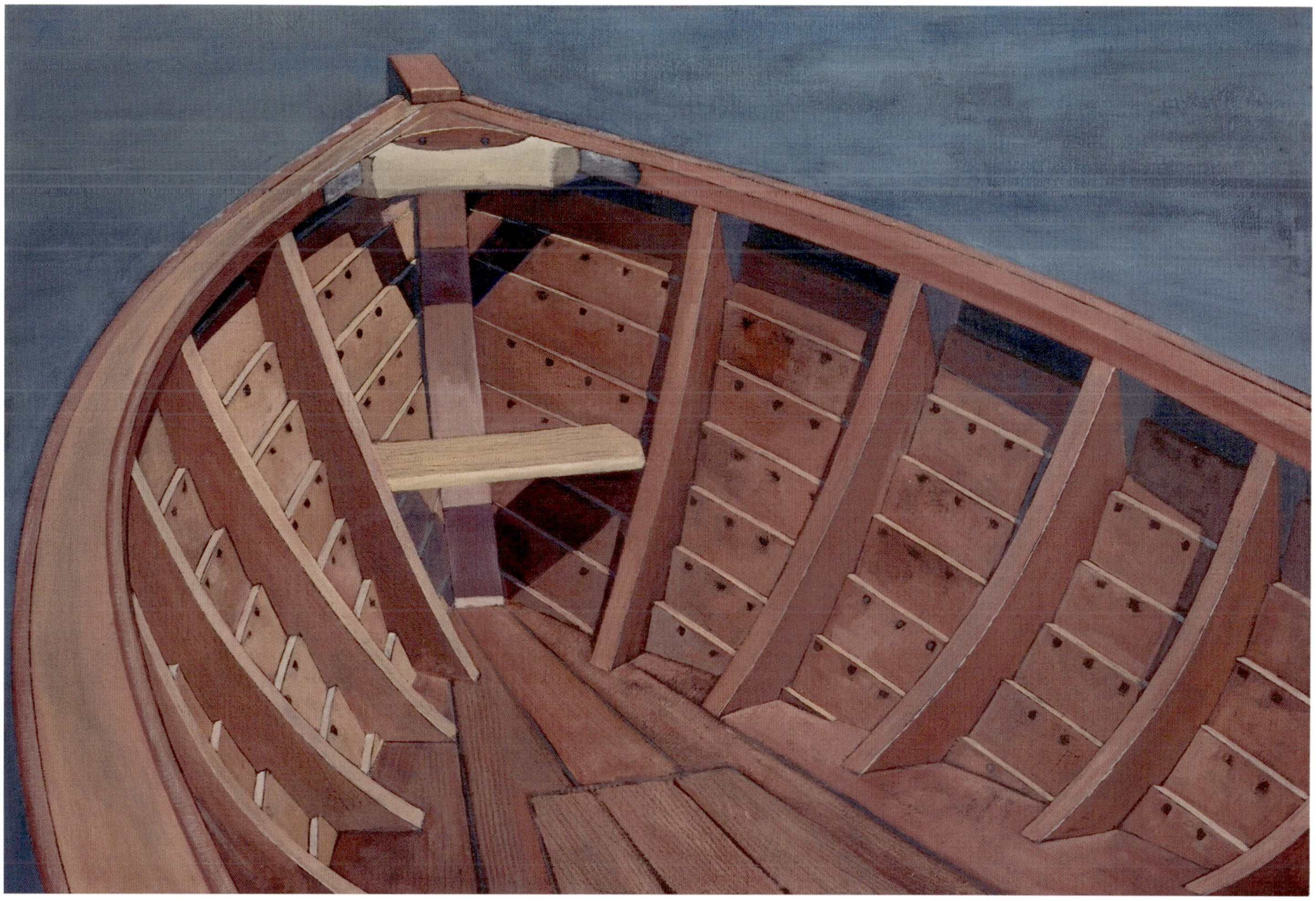

34. Roskilde 19 ft. Eel Boat
oil on linen canvas
60 x 90 cms   23⅝ x 35⅜ ins

35. Golden "Auk"

oil on linen

100 x 130 cms   39⅜ x 51⅛ ins

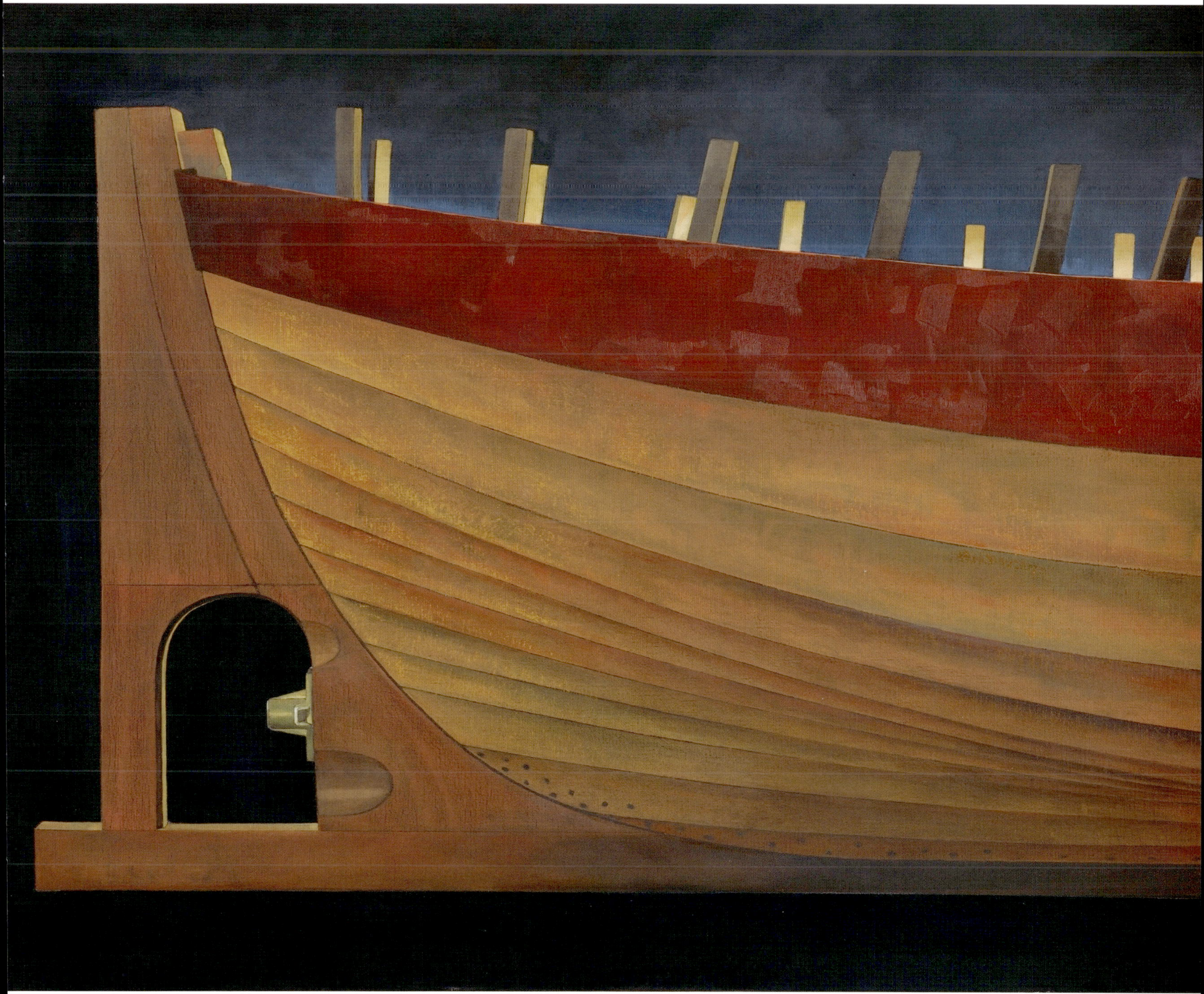

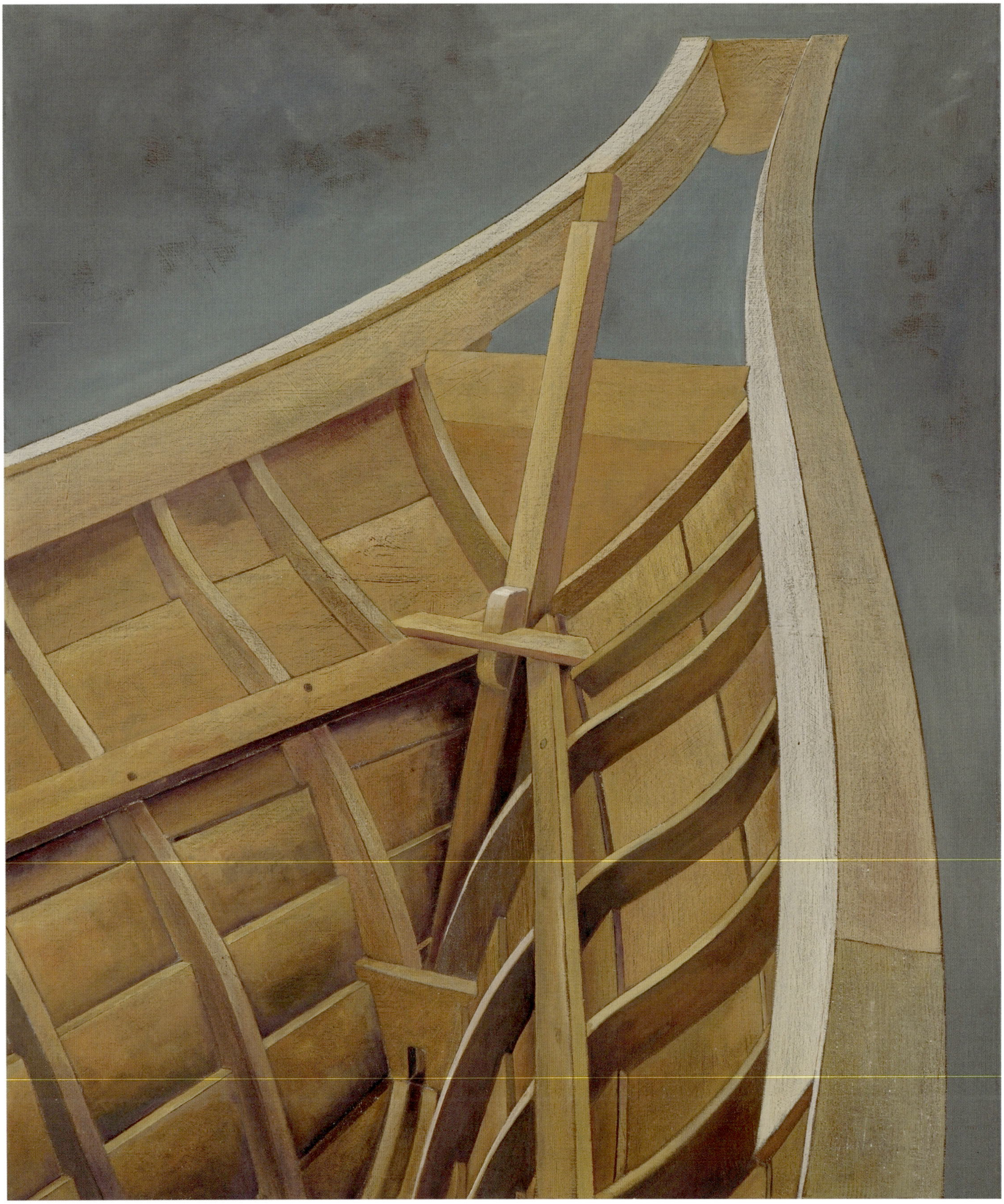

36. Stern of the Royal Barge "Gloriana"
oil on linen
107 x 92 cms 41⅞ x 36¼ ins

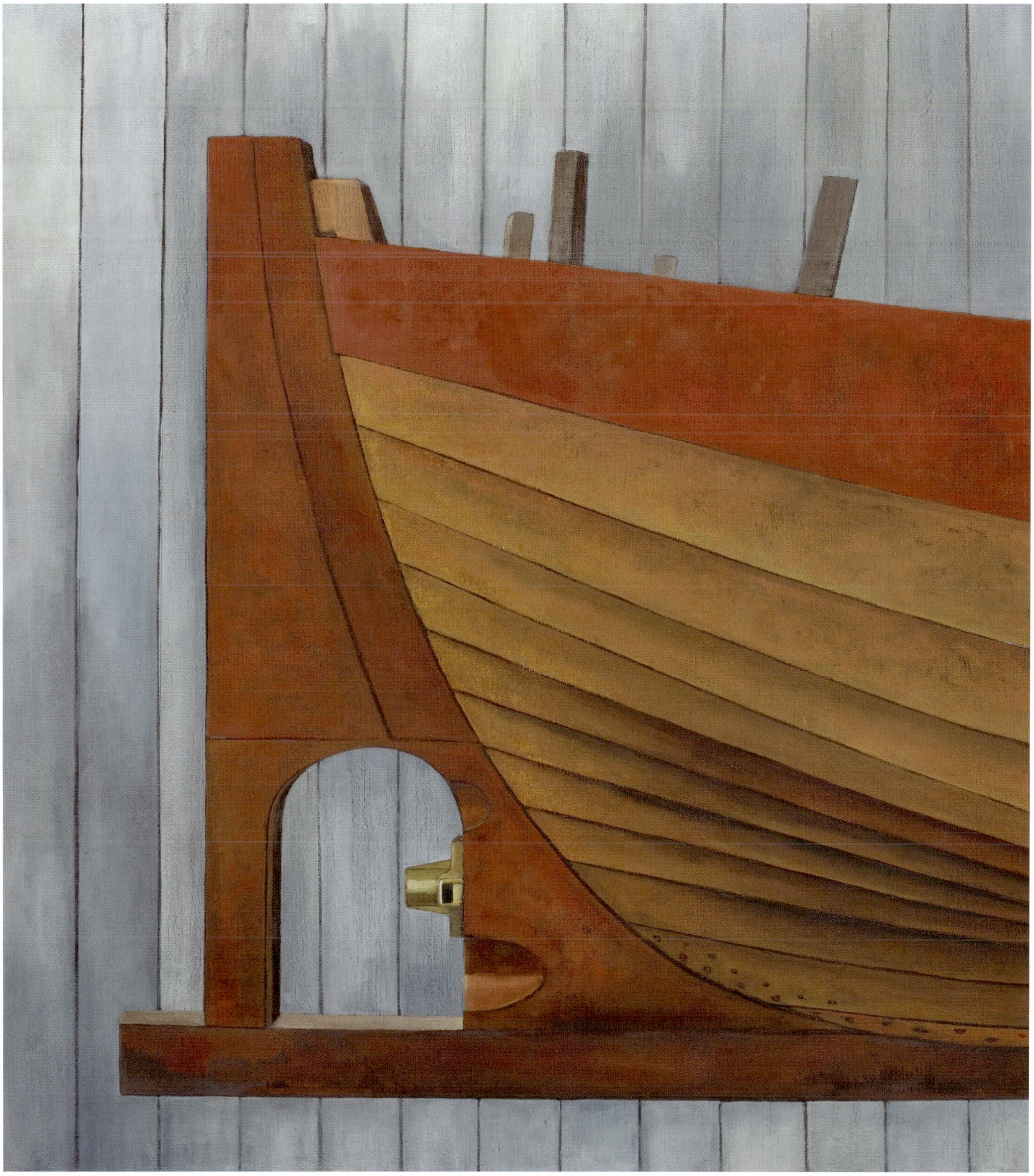

37. New Wooden Crabber

oil on linen

100 x 90 cms 39⅜ x 35⅜ ins

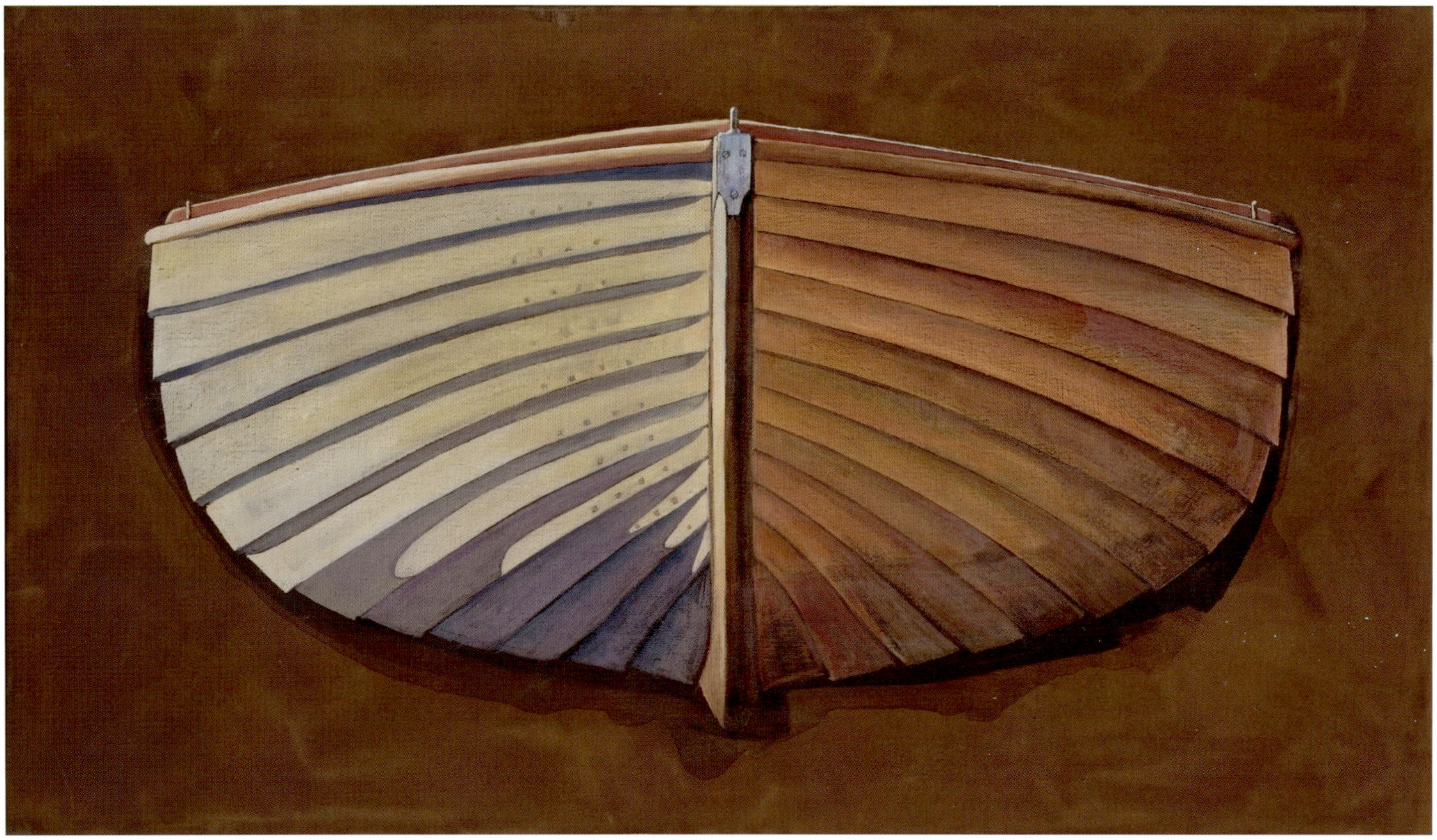

38. B.O.D. Bow
oil on linen canvas
60 x 106 cms 23⅝ x 41¾ ins

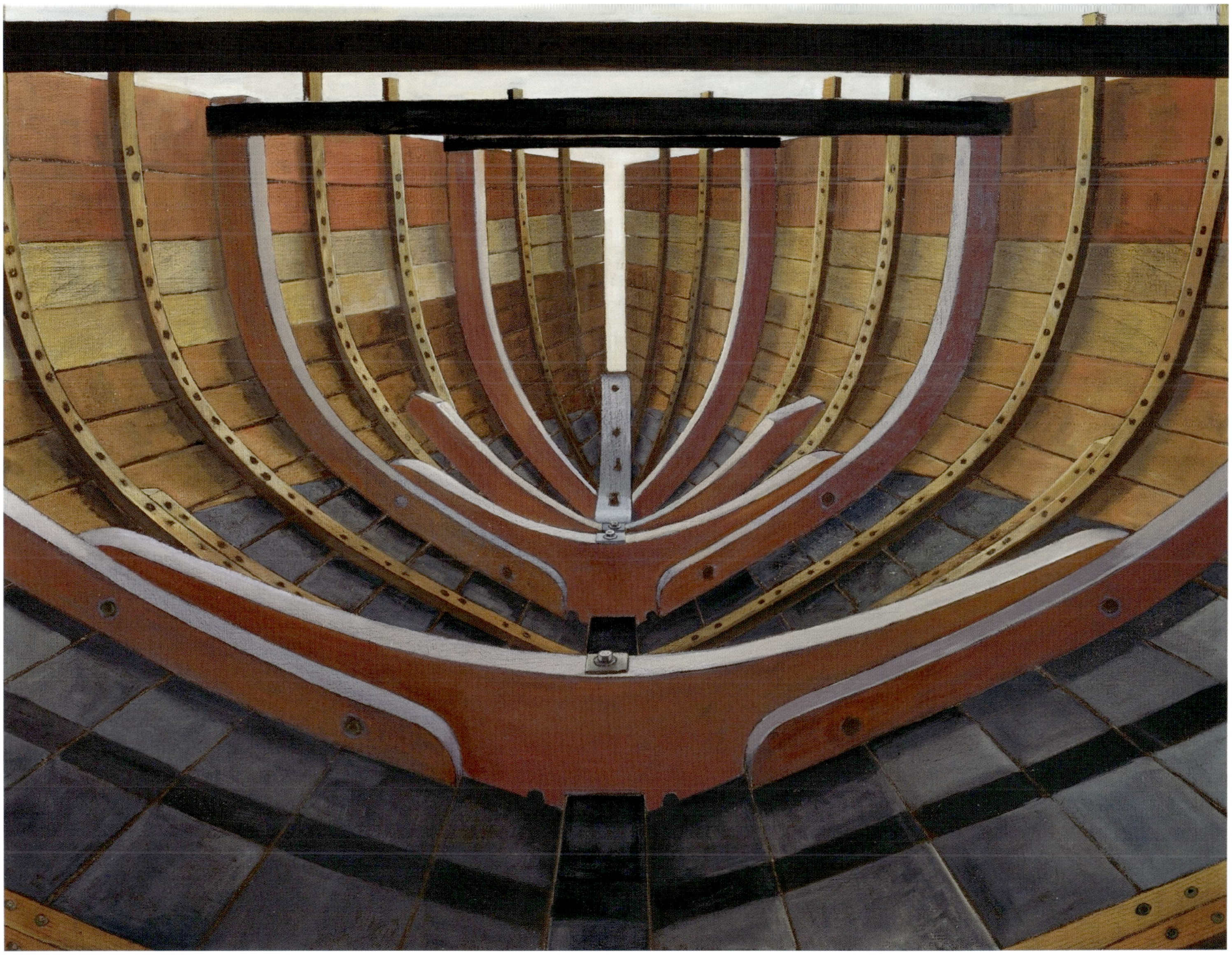

39. Falmouth Workboat, Looking Forward
oil on linen
90 x 120 cms   35⅜ x 47¼ ins

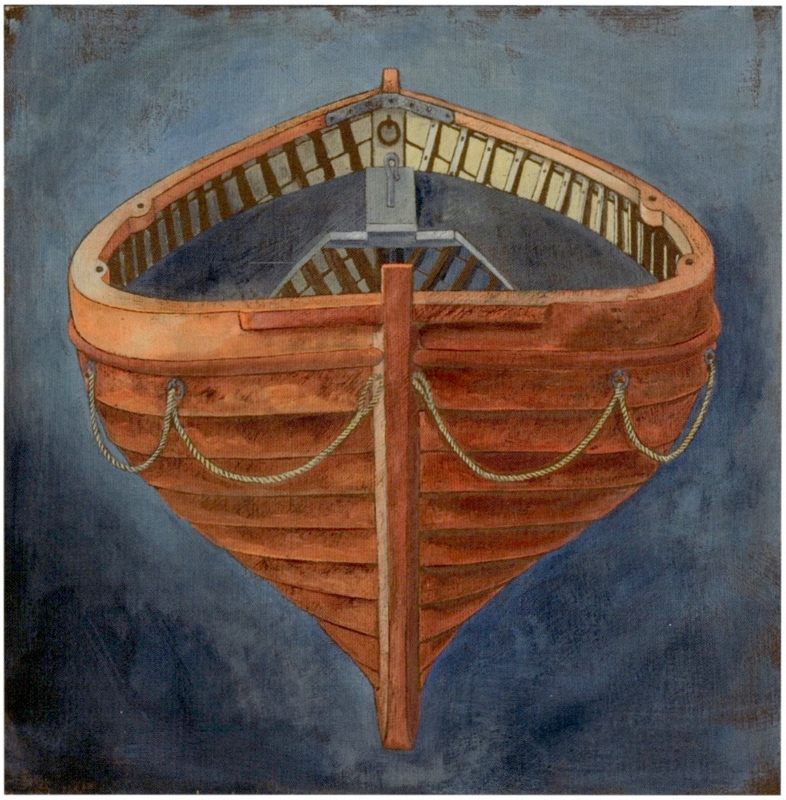

40. Orange Lifeboat Study
oil on board
40 x 40 cms   15¾ x 15¾ ins

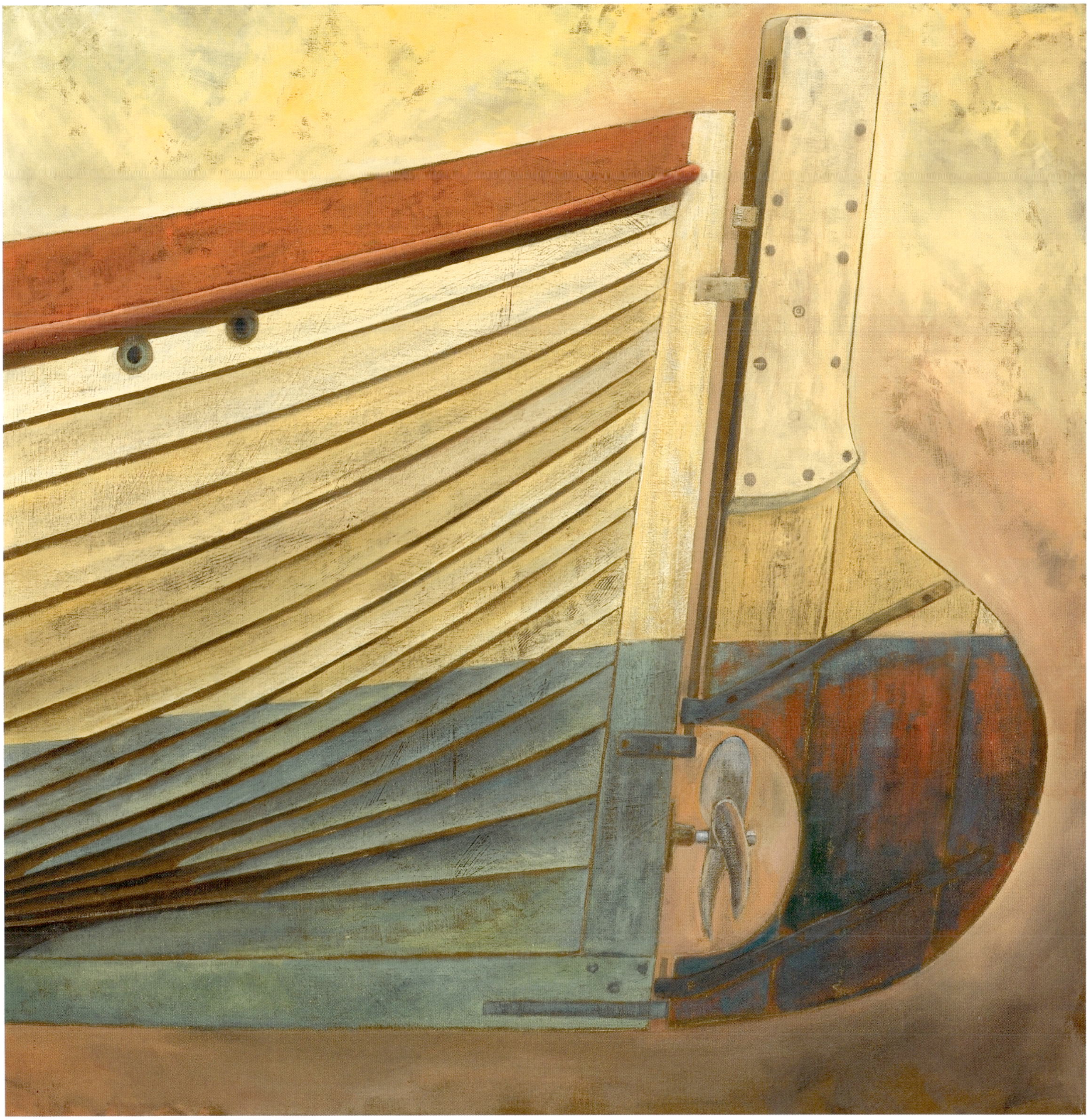

41. Stern of a Ship's Lifeboat
oil on linen
97 x 97 cms   38 x 38¼ ins

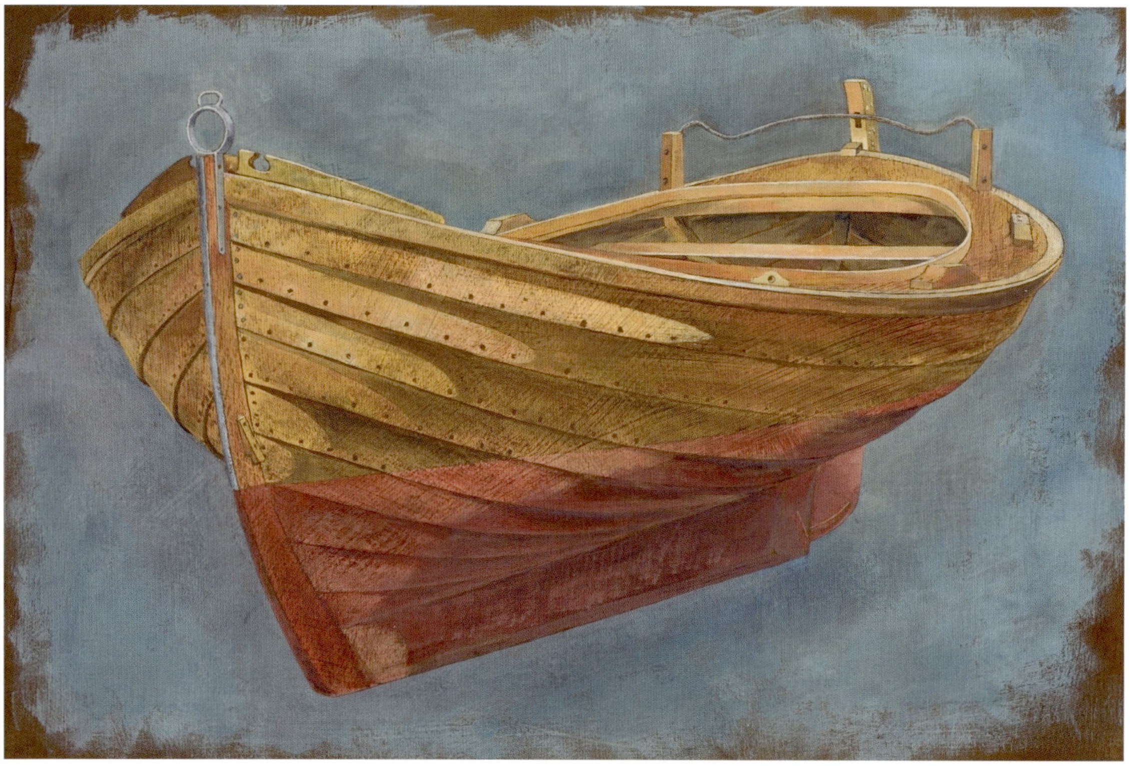

42. Frederikssund Dinghy
oil on linen
40 x 60 cms   15¾ x 23⅝ ins

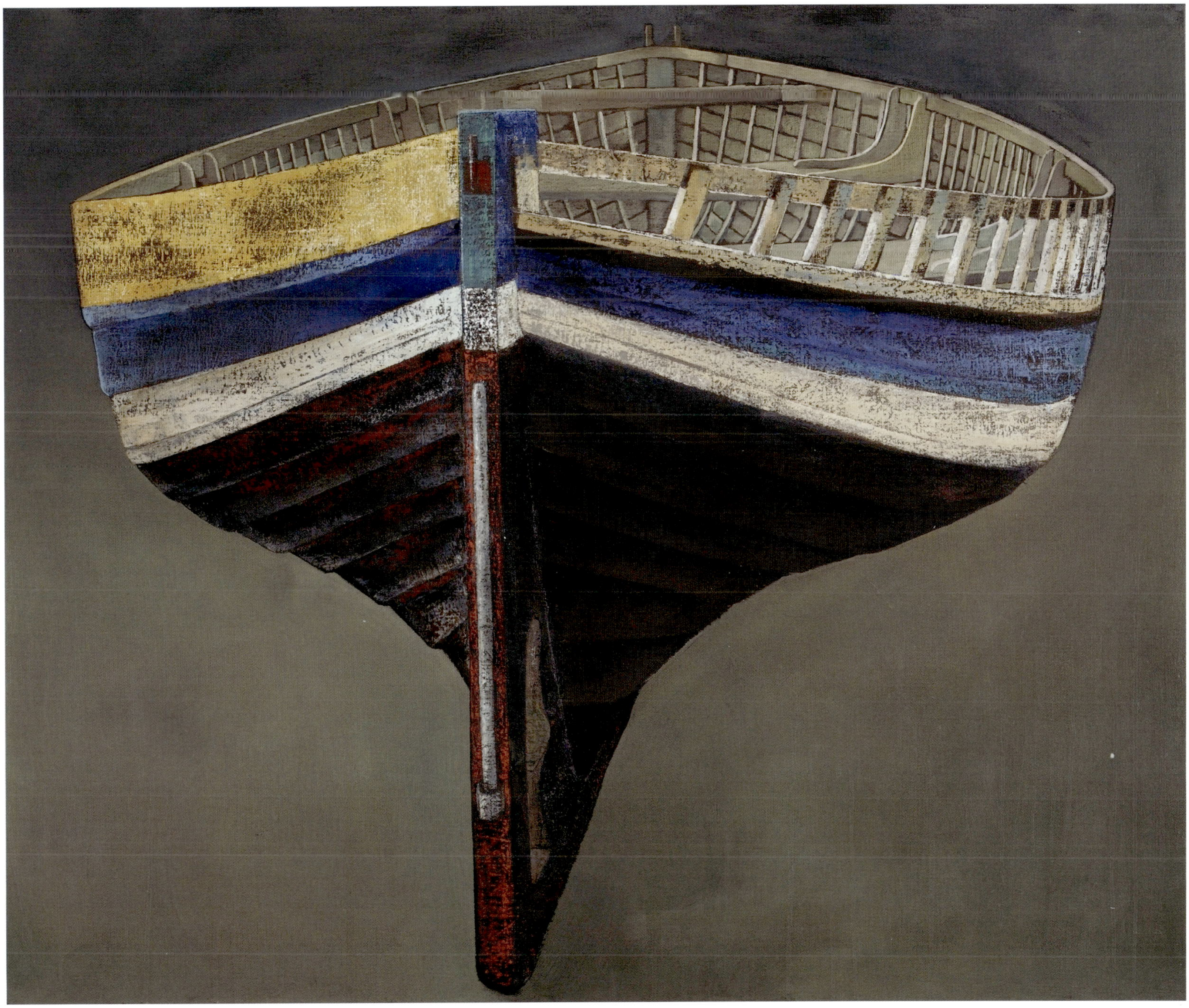

43. A New Plank on a Norfolk Crabber
oil on linen
91 x 109 cms   36 x 42⅞ ins

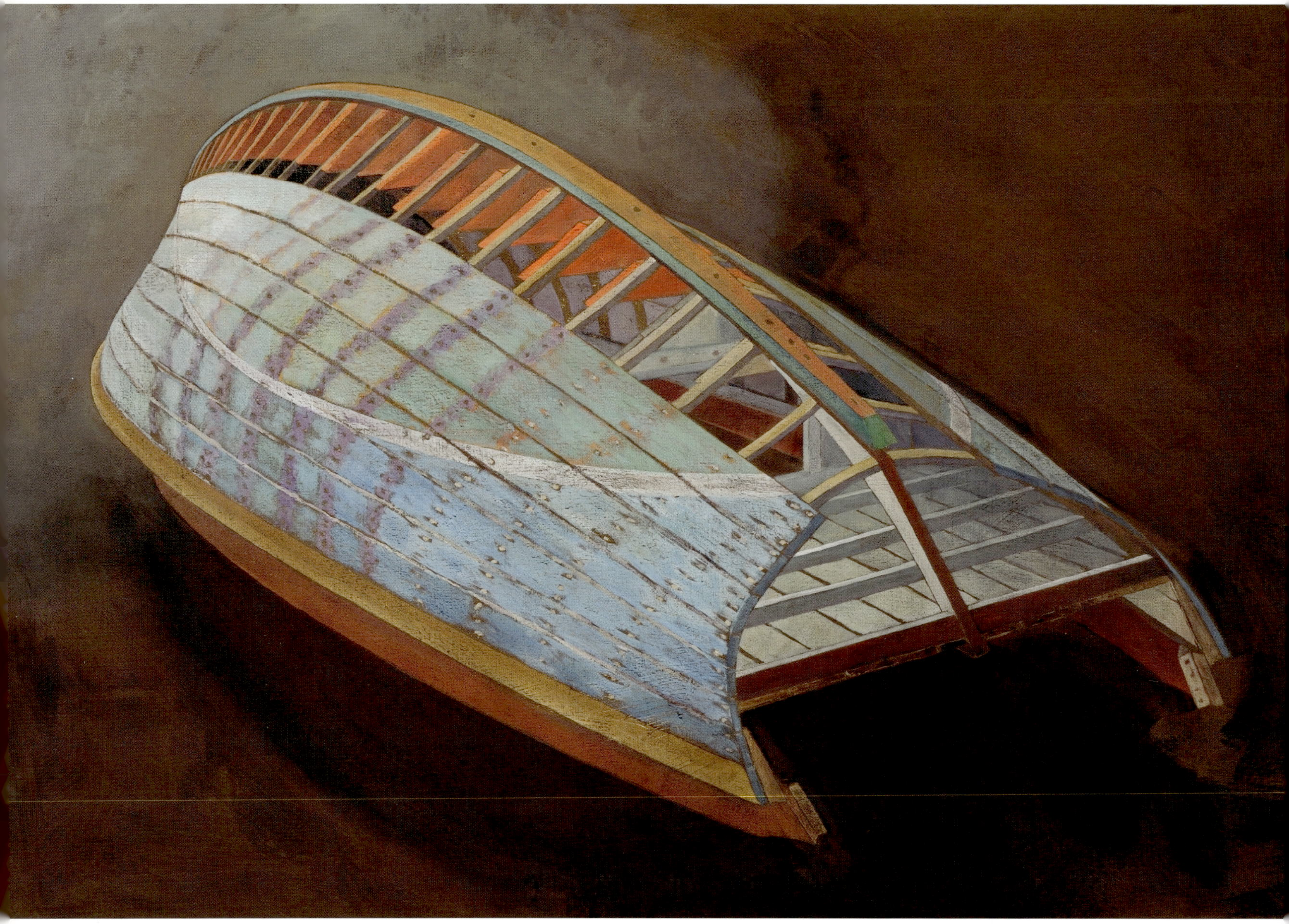

44. "Shadow" Re-build
oil on linen
91 x 137 cms   36 x 53⅞ ins

45. "Peapod" Under Construction
oil on linen
97 x 76 cms   38 x 29⅞ ins

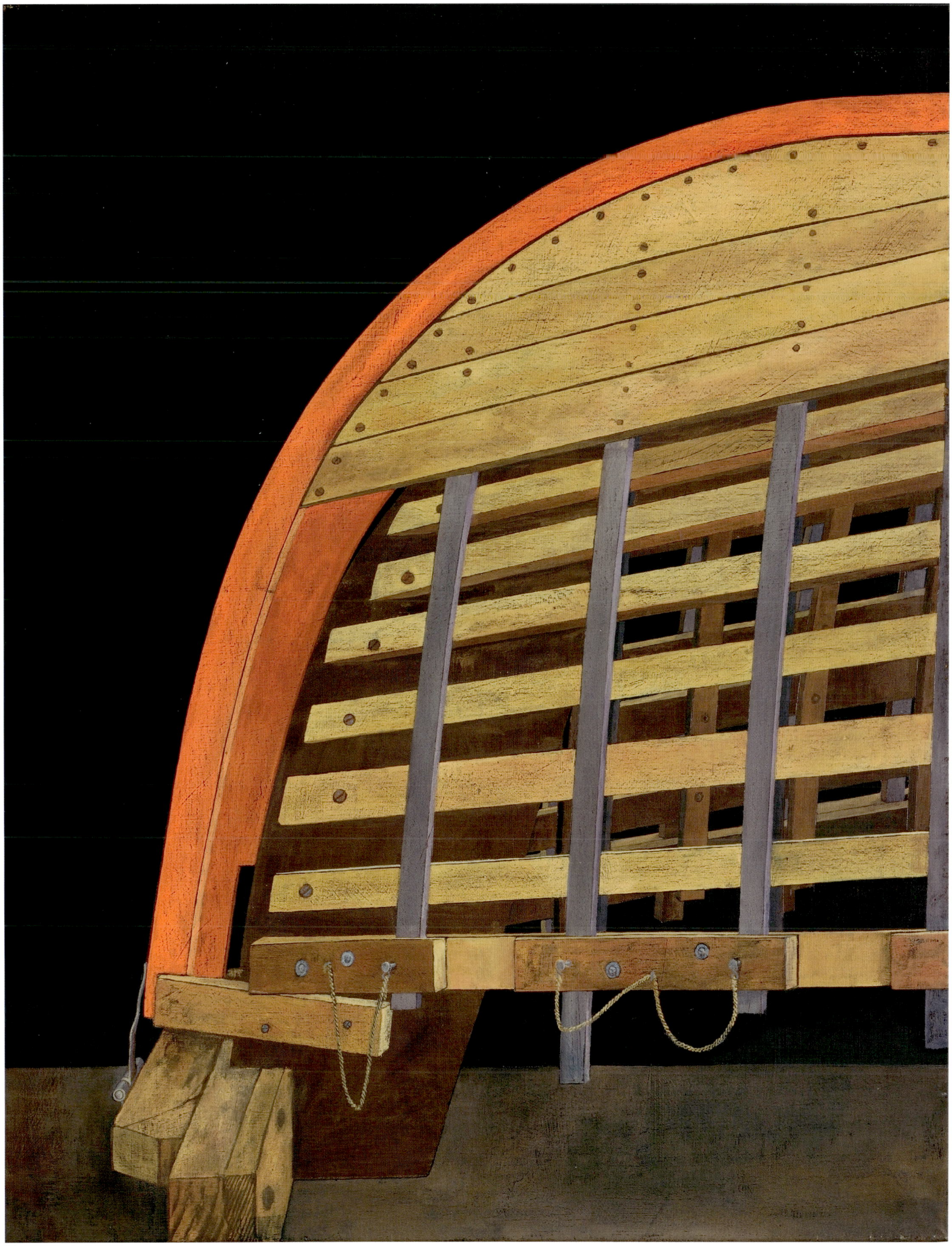

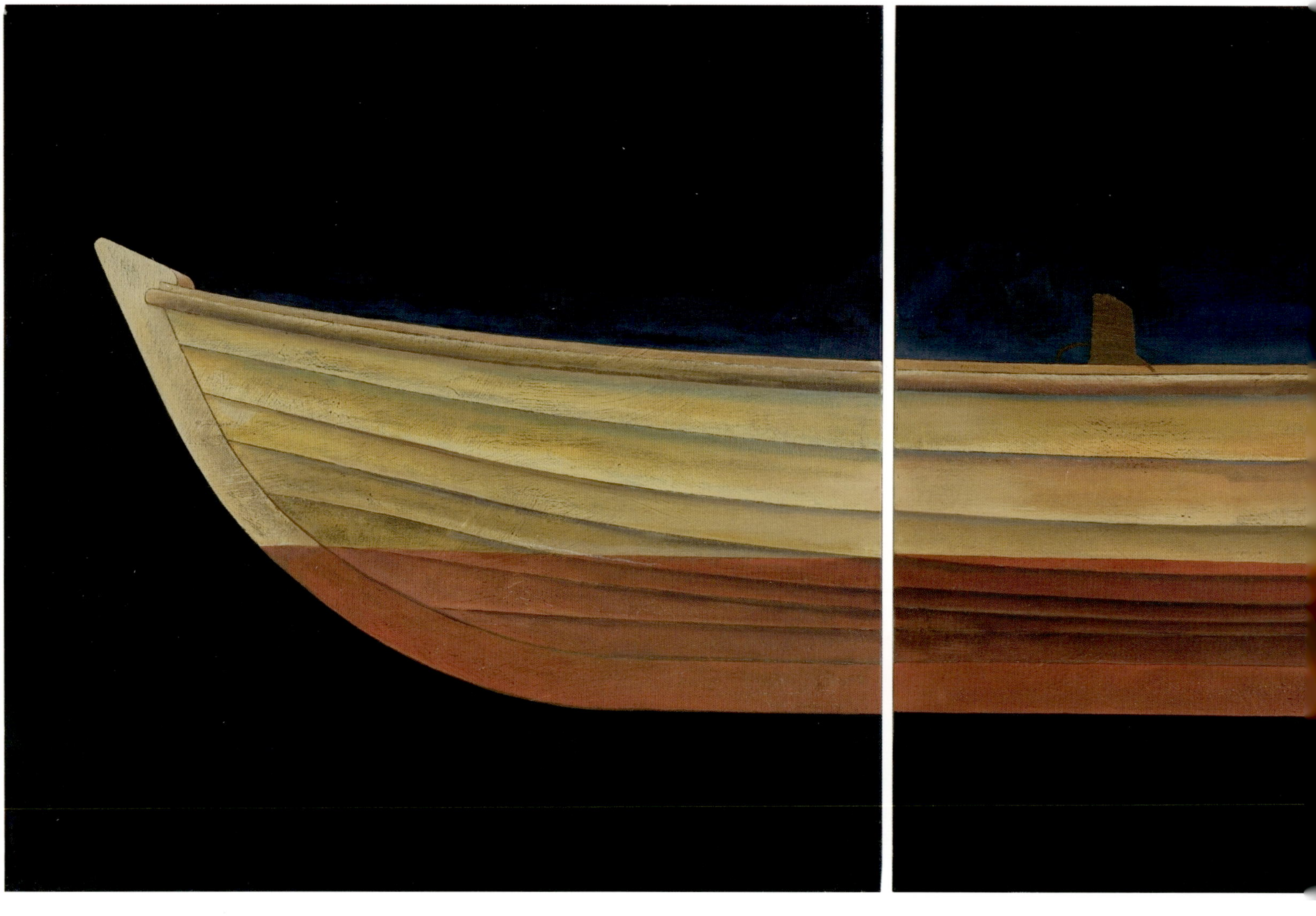

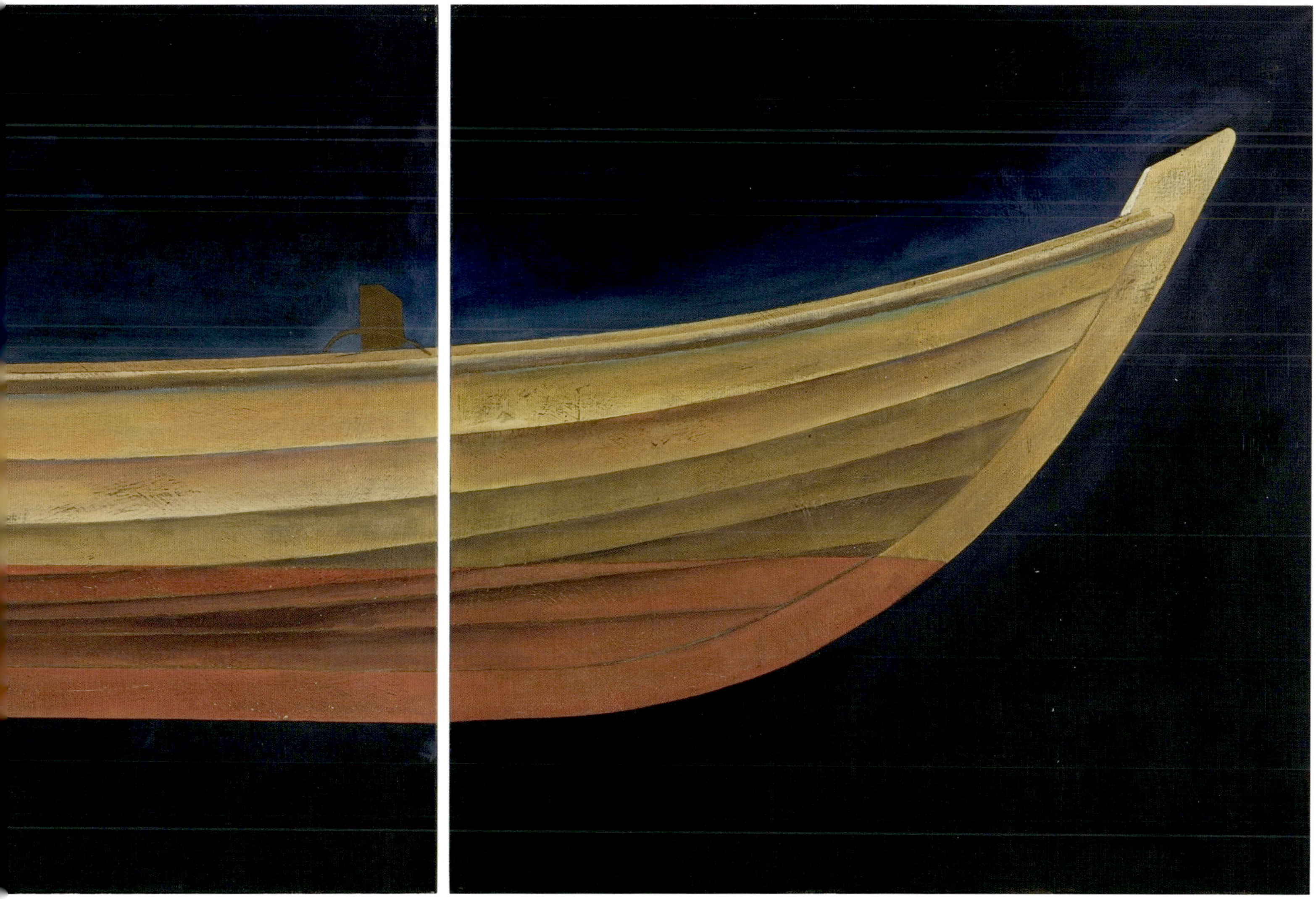

46. Shetland Fourern (Triptych)
oil on linen
91 x 274 cms 36 x 107⅞ ins

Biography

1957 Born in Brightlingsea
1972 Mate on Baltic Trader, Solvig
Apprentice Shipwright, Walter Cook & Son, Maldon (until 1976)
1973 Shipbuilding Industry Training Board, Southampton (until 1974)
1976 Colchester School of Art (Foundation)
1977 Chelsea School of Art (until 1980)
1981 Royal College of Art (until 1984) (won Anstruther Award 1983)
1984 Started Jardine Press, Stoke-by-Nayland
2007 Received Doctorate from the University of Essex

Selected Group Exhibitions

1991 Summer Show, Royal Academy of Arts
1993 "Six Artists", Wetzlar, Germany
1994 John Callahan Gallery, Boston, USA
1995 "4 from Wivenhoe", Courcoux & Courcoux, Stockbridge
"Ultra Marine", Liverpool Maritime Museum
"Forth, Tyne, Dogger", Brewery Arts, Cirencester
1996 Peter Scott Gallery, Lancaster University
"The Sea", Black Swan Arts, Frome
1997 City Art Gallery, Leeds
"An English Perspective", Union of Artists, St Petersburg, Russia
"Marine Artists", Mall Galleries, London
1998 Summer Show, Royal Academy of Arts
1999 Eastern Open, (Best in Show) King's Lynn Arts Centre, Norfolk
Mystic Seaport; New York Ship Terminal, USA
Summer Show, Royal Academy of Arts
2000 Hunting Art Prizes, Royal College of Art
Summer Show, Royal Academy of Arts
"Alphabet Soup", Printworks, Sudbury
2001 Messum's, Cork Street, London
2003 Messum's, Cork Street, London
2006 Messum's, Cork Street, London
2007 Messum's, Cork Street, London
2008 "East Coast Influences", Messum's, Cork Street, London
Geedon Gallery, Fingringhoe, Colchester
"Salthouse 08: SEAhouse, LIGHThouse, SPIRIThouse", Salthouse, Essex
The Nottage Maritime Institute, Wivenhoe, Essex
2009 Messum's, Cork Street, London
2010 "Atelier, Artists & Artists' Estates", Messum's, Cork Street, London
"East Coast Influences", Messum's, Cork Street, London
2011 "New English Art Club and Others", Geedon Gallery, Fingringhoe, Colchester
2013 "Masterpieces, Art and East Anglia" Sainsbury Centre, UEA, Norwich.
2014 "Easterlies" , Abbey Walk Gallery, Grimsby.
2014 Messum's, Cork Street, London

Shipshape Tour

2001 Firstsite at The Minories Art Gallery, Colchester
2002 Whitstable & Herne Bay Museums & Art Galleries, Kent
Black Swan Arts, Frome, Somerset
Quay Arts, Newport, Isle of Wight
Bowes Museum, Barnard Castle, Co. Durham
2003 National Maritime Museum Cornwall, Falmouth
2003–4 National Maritime Museum, Greenwich
2004 Messum's Fine Art, Cork Street, London

Shipshape & The Year of the Sea

2005 Time & Tide, Great Yarmouth
Buckenham Gallery, Southwold
Hartlepool Art Gallery, Hartlepool
Thurso & Wick, Scotland
Fermoy Gallery, King's Lynn Arts Centre (with Guy Taplin)
Hayletts Gallery, Maldon
Chappel Galleries, Chappel

Selected Solo Exhibitions

1983 "Icarus", The Minories, Colcester
1984 "Peter Grimes", at the 37th Aldeburgh Festival
1985 Ship of Fools", Hatton Gallery, Newcastle Upon Tyne
The Quay Theatre Gallery, Sudbury
1986 "Fish, Flesh or Fowl", Christchurch Mansion, Ipswich
(with Bridget Heriz-Smith and Jane Truzzi-Franconi)
1989 Printworks, Colchester (and in 1990, 1995 and 1997)
Bircham Contemporary Arts, Norfolk (and in 1992, 1995 and 1999)
1990 "The Shipwright's Trade", at the 43rd Aldeburgh Festival
Chappel Galleries, Chappel, Essex (and in 1994)
St John Street Gallery, Bury St Edmunds, Suffolk
1991 "From the Glasshouse", Heffers Gallery, Cambridge
1992 Sue Rankin Gallery, London (two man show with John Bratby RA)
"Peter Grimes", Christchurch Mansion, Ipswich
1995 "Wild Man", at the 48th Aldeburgh Festival
Simbouras Gallery, Athens, Greece
1998 "On The Beach", at the 51st Aldeburgh Festival
"Waterworks", Printworks, Sudbury
"Boatshow", North House Gallery, Manningtree
2000 "Full Circle", at the 53rd Aldeburgh Festival
2001 North House Gallery, Manningtree (two man show with John Reay)
"Blue Boat", University of Essex Gallery
"Shipshape" Tour
Firstsite at The Minories Art Gallery, Colchester
2002 Whitstable & Herne Bay Museums & Art Galleries, Kent
Black Swan Arts, Frome, Somerset
Quay Arts, Newport, Isle of Wight
Bowes Museum, Barnard Castle, Co. Durham
2003 National Maritime Museum Cornwall, Falmouth
2003–4 National Maritime Museum, Greenwich
2004 Messum's Fine Art, Cork Street, London
"Shipshape" & "The Time of the Sea" Tours
2005 Time & Tide, Great Yarmouth
Buckenham Gallery, Southwold
Hartlepool Art Gallery, Hartlepool
Thurso and Wick, Scotland
Fermoy Gallery, King's Lynn Arts Centre (with Guy Taplin)
Hayletts Gallery, Maldon
"Lifeboat", Chappel Galleries, Chappel, Essex
2006 Messum's, Cork Street, London
2007 "Fore and Aft", University of Essex Gallery
Messum's, Cork Street, London
2008 "Vessels of the East Coast", St Barbe Museum & Art Gallery, Lymington, Hampshire
"Mainly Linocuts", Hayletts Gallery, Maldon, Essex
2009 "American Boats", Messum's Fine Art, Cork Street, London
"25 Years of Jardine Press", Messum's Fine Art, Cork Street, London
Bircham Gallery, Holt, Norfolk (two man show with Stephen Hendersen)
2010 "James Dodds and the Jardine Press", Lewis Elton Gallery, University of Surrey.
Dowling Walsh, Rockland, Maine, USA
2011 Church Street Gallery, Saffron Walden, Essex
Messum's, Cork Street, London.
2012 Dowling Walsh, Rockland, Maine, USA
Drang Gallery, Padstow.
Hayletts Gallery, Maldon, Essex.
2013 Messum's, Cork Street, London
2013 Bircham Contemporary Arts, Holt, Norfolk

Collections

Britten-Pears Library, Aldeburgh; Victoria and Albert Museum; Clacton & Rochford Hospitals; Chelmsford and Essex Museums; Ipswich Borough Council, Museums and Galleries; Colchester Borough Council; Horniman Museum, London; National Maritime Museum, Greenwich; UCS East Contemporary Art Collection, Ipswich; MMoFA, Madison, Georgia, USA; The Sainsbury Centre, UEA Norwich; and many private collectors